Suzy Gershman's
born to shop
paris

The ultimate guide
for people who love to shop

12th Edition

WILEY

Wiley Publishing, Inc.

For Pascale-Agnes Renaud Sahler, who has taught me Paris for over 25 years and saved my almost French derriere many times.

Published by:

Wiley Publishing, Inc.
111 River St.
Hoboken, NJ 07030-5774

ISBN 978-0-470-38230-1

Editor: Stephen Bassman
Production Editor: Heather Wilcox
Cartographer: Guy Ruggiero
Photo Editor: Richard Fox
Production by Wiley Indianapolis Composition Services

For information on our other products and services or to obtain technical support, please contact our Customer Care Department within the U.S. at 800/762-2974, outside the U.S. at 317/572-3993 or fax 317/572-4002.

Wiley also publishes its books in a variety of electronic formats. Some content that appears in print may not be available in electronic formats.

Manufactured in the United States of America

5   4   3   2   1

Contents

Map List

About the Authors

Suzy Gershman is a journalist, author, and global-shopping goddess who has worked in the fashion and fiber industries for more than 25 years. Her essays on retailing have been used by the Harvard School of Business; her reportage on travel and retail has appeared in *Travel + Leisure, Travel Holiday, Travel Weekly,* and most of the major women's magazines. The *Born to Shop* series, now over 25 years old, is translated into eight languages.

Gershman is also the author of *C'est La Vie* (Penguin Paperback), the story of her first year as a widow living in Paris. She recently sold her flat in Paris and now divides her time between San Diego; a small house in Provence; and the airport. Her newest book is *Where to Buy the Best of Everything,* a Frommer's book. She gives shopping tours twice a year; go to www.suzygershman.com for more information.

Sarah Lahey is Editorial Director of the *Born to Shop* series. She also shows and sells English smalls at several Northern California antiques fairs. She lives with her husband and dogs, Bentley and Bex, outside of San Francisco and wears the same size as Suzy (so they can share clothes)..

To Start With

When my Grandma Jessie used to speak Yiddish, she would then cover her mouth with her hand and say, "Oh! Pardon my French!"

So when I quote her and say *"Oy vey,"* you know I'm referring to the exchange rate between the U.S. dollar and the euro and the news that some shopping ops in France have become less attractive, at least price-wise. But never mind all that. (Stop the presses: As we go to print, the euro is at $1.25, down from the $1.50 rate we used for this book. See www.xe.com for the latest numbers.)

Paris is always gonna be Paris, and it's very much worth a visit. I lived here for five years; now I come back regularly to update this book and have worked very hard to give you an insider's look at deals and goings-on, at different kinds of hotels (and apartment rentals) and at all sorts of best buys.

If you want to save a little bit of money, cut down your time in Paris and get out to the countryside where prices are basically 20% less. This book has a new chapter specifically geared to that end.

You will also do well to be a little more French in every way. Yes, do lower your voice. Also save big name chefs for special events. Don't stay in palace hotels. Don't drink soft drinks. Consider *le sandwich* for lunch (this a new French twist). Remember that tap water is totally safe in France; drink it. Don't buy a lot of clothes or own a lot of clothes and, for heaven's sake, don't travel with a lot of luggage or schlep everything you own with you. Consider *Systeme D*, which means be frugal and smart and even cagey.

Hopefully this edition will point you in the right directions for all of these measures, except maybe the modulation of your voice. As always, I thank Pascale-Agnes for her help (who else would teach me about *Systeme D?*) and Sarah Lahey for her efforts and good company . . . and the macaroons from Laduree.

Chapter 1

Best of Paris

J'adore Paris

I hope you are reading this as you plan a trip to Paris. While the dollar-euro ratio isn't great, and the inflated euro is so powerful that even locals are in pain (I don't mean bread), there's still a good time to be had.

In these pages are shopping lists that will help get your *jus* flowing. Paris is filled with great things to look at and buy. If you shop wisely, you may even save money. More realistically, you'll find something you can't find back home and at a reasonable enough price to feel pride.

With that in mind, the selections in this chapter have been chosen for people in an incredible hurry, who have no time for leisurely strolling and shopping. If you have more time, you owe yourself the luxury of checking out the finds described elsewhere in this book. However, if you must hit and run, I hope these choices will be rewarding.

BEST SPECIALTY PERFUME SHOP
Salons Shiseido
142 galerie de Valois, Jardin du Palais Royal, 1er (Métro: Palais-Royal).

The Best of Paris

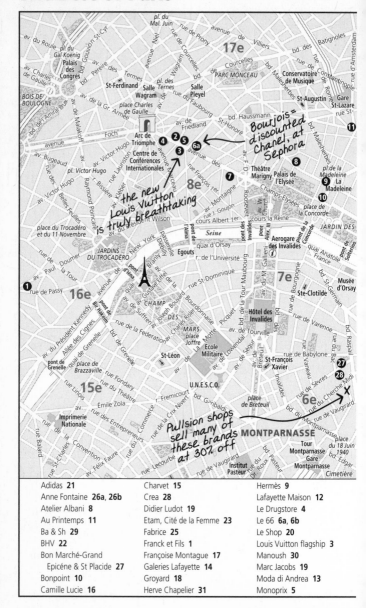

Boujois = discounted Chanel, at Sephora

the new Louis Vuitton is truly breathtaking

Pulsion shops sell many of these brands at 30% off

Adidas **21**	Charvet **15**	Hermès **9**
Anne Fontaine **26a, 26b**	Crea **28**	Lafayette Maison **12**
Atelier Albani **8**	Didier Ludot **19**	Le Drugstore **4**
Au Printemps **11**	Etam, Cité de la Femme **23**	Le 66 **6a, 6b**
Ba & Sh **29**	Fabrice **25**	Le Shop **20**
BHV **22**	Françoise Montague **17**	Louis Vuitton flagship **3**
Bon Marché-Grand	Franck et Fils **1**	Manoush **30**
Epicène & St Placide **27**	Françoise Montague **17**	Marc Jacobs **19**
Bonpoint **10**	Galeries Lafayette **14**	Moda di Andrea **13**
Camille Lucie **16**	Groyard **18**	Monoprix **5**
	Herve Chapelier **31**	

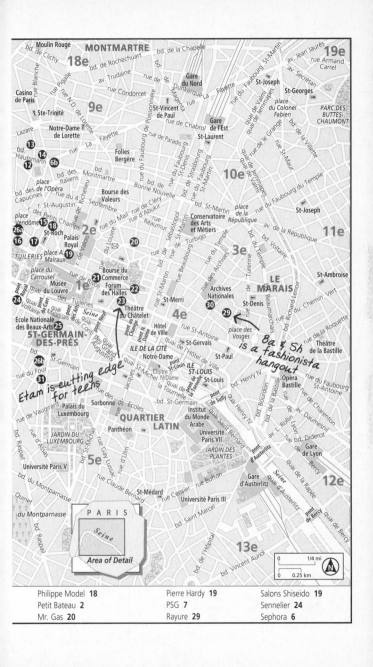

bd. de Clichy · **Moulin Rouge** · **MONTMARTRE** · **bd. de la Chapelle** · **av. Jean Jaurès** · **19e**

rue Armand Carrel

18e · bd. de Rochechouart · av. Secrétan

rue Pigalle · **av. Trudaine** · **rue de Maubeuge** · **St-Joseph** · **St-Georges**

rue Condorcet · **Gare du Nord** · rue du Faubourg St-Martin · place du Colonel Fabien

Casino de Paris · rue Blanche · rue N.D. de Lorette · **9e** · **St-Vincent de Paul** · **PARC DES BUTTES-CHAUMONT**

Ste-Trinité · rue de Chabrol · **Gare de l'Est** · quai de Valmy · quai de Jemmapes

Notre-Dame de Lorette · rue La Fayette · rue de Paradis · **St-Laurent** · bd. de la Villette

Lazare · **13** · **14** · bd. Haussmann · **12** · **6b** · **10e** · rue du Faubourg St-Maur

place · bd. des Italiens · bd. Montmartre · **Folies Bergère** · rue du Faubourg du Temple

Capucines · bd. des · de l'Opéra · r. du 4 Septembre · **Bourse des Valeurs** · bd. de Bonne Nouvelle · **St-Joseph**

r. St-Augustin · rue de Richelieu · rue du Mail · rue de Cléry · **Conservatoire des Arts et Métiers** · **11e**

place Vendôme · **15** · **18** · rue des Petits Champs · rue d'Abukir · Réaumur · place de la République · av. de la République

26a · **St-Roch** · **2e** · rue du Louvre · **20** · rue de Sébastopol · bd. St-Martin · av. Voltaire

16 · **17** · **Palais Royal** · rue de Turbigo · **3e** · rue de Turenne · **St-Ambroise**

TUILERIES · place A. Malraux · **19** · **Bourse du Commerce** · rue St-Martin · rue Beaubourg · **Archives Nationales** · rue des Archives · **LE MARAIS** · **St-Denis**

place du Carrousel · **21** · **Forum des Halles** · **St-Merri** · **30** · **29** · ***Ba & Sh is a fashionista hangout*** ←

pont Royal · **Musée** · **22** · **4e** · rue St-Antoine · place des Vosges · rue de la Roquette

24 · quai du Louvre · des Tuileries · **23** · **Théâtre du Châtelet** · **Hôtel de Ville** · **St-Paul** · **Théâtre de la Bastille**

quai Malaquais · Seine · pont Neuf · **Notre-Dame** · **St-Gervais** · **Opéra Bastille** · rue du Faubourg St-Antoine

Ecole Nationale des Beaux-Arts · **25** · pont au Change · quai de l'Hôtel de Ville · bd. Bourdon · rue de la Bastille

ST-GERMAIN-DES-PRÉS · quai de Conti · **ILE DE LA CITÉ** · **Notre-Dame** · bd. Henry IV · rue de Charenton

26b · St-Germain · quai des Grands Augustins · **Cloître N.Dame** · **ILE ST-LOUIS** · rue de Lyon · av. Daumesnil

rue du Four · ***Etam is cutting edge for teens*** · **31** · quai St-Michel · **St-Louis** · Quai d'Anjou · rue de Lyon · bd. Diderot

rue de Vaugirard · **Palais du Luxembourg** · **Sorbonne** · rue des Ecoles · **Institut du Monde Arabe** · pont de Sully · **Gare de Lyon**

JARDIN DU LUXEMBOURG · **Panthéon** · **QUARTIER LATIN** · **Université Paris VII** · quai Saint Bernard · **12e**

rue d'Assas · bd. St-Michel · **5e** · rue Gay-Lussac · rue d'Ulm · **JARDIN DES PLANTES** · quai de la Rapée

Université Paris V · **St-Médard** · rue Claude Bernard · rue Censier · rue Buffon · **Gare d'Austerlitz** · quai de Bercy

bd. du Montparnasse · **Université Paris III** · pont de Bercy

Quinet · du Montparnasse · bd. Saint Marcel · **13e**

bd. Raspail · bd. Saint Marcel · bd. Vincent Auriol · bd. de l'Hôpital

PARIS · *Seine* · **Area of Detail**

| 0 | | 1/4 mi |
| 0 | 0.25 km | |

Philippe Model **18**	Pierre Hardy **19**	Salons Shiseido **19**
Petit Bateau **2**	PSG **7**	Sennelier **24**
Mr. Gas **20**	Rayure **29**	Sephora **6**

This tiny shop, with high ceilings and royal purple decor, is the showcase of makeup genius Serge Lutens. He used to create makeup for Christian Dior and has now been with Shiseido for decades. His perfumes are also divine; even if you buy nothing, just look around and breathe deeply. The Jardin du Palais Royal is another terrific shopping experience, so check it out while you're here. Plan to spend several hours in this little piece of hidden Paris, a shopping heaven.

RUNNER-UP
Frederic Malle
140 av. Victor Hugo, 16e (Métro: Victor-Hugo).

Come here for the specialty scents, a smelling booth, and do-it-yourself or custom-made fragrance.

BEST MASS-MARKET PERFUME SHOP
Sephora
70 av. des Champs-Elysées, 8e (Métro: Franklin D. Roosevelt).

I don't care if you have Sephora at your local mall. The French stores are different, partly because Sephora is a large French chain and the flagship is right smack on the Champs-Elysées. This branch is even open on Sunday.

Everything in the large shop is color-coordinated. Fragrances have their own section, with scads of testers and lots of scent strips. There's far more than perfume; in fact, you're better off not buying perfume here, since you'll get a better price from a discounter or duty-free shop. Sephora is good for bath and beauty products (an enormous selection, including its own line of shampoos and body lotions, makeup, and hair accessories).

This is a great place for girls, preteens, and women of all ages. The inexpensive sample-size products make fabulous gifts. You'll also find books, a *parapharmacie*, a mix-your-own perfume counter, and a computer to teach you everything you need (or want) to know. There's also a good détaxe rebate here (14%).

BEST STATUS GIFTS UNDER $25

- **Hermès** soap, sold in the Saddle Shop.
- **Lanvin chocolates,** available in any grocery store.
- **Amorino** *bonbons,* flavored bits of sugar you add to your coffee. Gorgeous on the table; melt in your mouth.
- **Champagne.** In addition to the ones you've heard of, there are several good champagnes that aren't as well known in the U.S.—I swear by *nv* (nonvintage) Alain Thiénot, found at Nicolas or Monoprix. See chapter 10 for buying champagne in Champagne.

BEST GIFTS FOR $15 OR LESS

- **Amorino** bonbons: priced by the number of flavors in the box, so you can start at 5€ ($7.50).
- Anything from **Sephora,** preferably the house brand of bath goodies. The big fat eye pencils in the house brand are hot.
- **Le String** is the French version of the thong—it has been banned in French high schools since local girls were doing a Monica Lewinsky with theirs. *Sacré tush!* Sloggi is a popular brand (it's Italian), although I buy the Sloggi wannabe, Scandy, because they make *elasticité extrême* (extreme stretch) in a microfiber string that is a dream for comfort and travel—it dries in hours. From Monoprix.
- **Hot-chocolate mix** (5€/$7.50) **from Angelina,** 226 rue de Rivoli, 1er (Métro: Tuileries), the most famous tea shop in Paris.
- A box of **Mère Poulard cookies** (1.40€/$2.10). These indescribably good butter cookies are imported from Mont St-Michel. Available in any grocery store.
- A bag of real French **coffee** (2.20€/$3.30). I buy **Carte Noire.** Available in any grocery store.
- A jar of hard-to-find or exotically **flavored mustard** (2.20€/$3.30). I buy Maille brand, either cassis and red

fruits or one named Provençale. Most fun when bought at Maille's own store, place de la Madeleine, 1er (Métro: Madeleine). Most grocery stores or gourmet markets have a large selection of unusual mustard tastes—even blueberry.

- A box or bag of **tea** . . . but nothing British or easily found in the U.S. We're talking about the famous mix of red fruits, or French herbs or flavors not known to the American palate. Grocery stores carry **Elephant** brand; **Mariage Frères** is a luxury brand with its own tearooms and distribution in department stores. My favorite is the Monoprix brand of *fruits rouge*.
- A bar of milled **soap,** from a made-in-France brand *(bien sûr),* teamed with *gant de toilette,* a French-style **washcloth.** The two pieces together don't have to cost more than 10€ ($15). I like Roger & Gallet soaps, especially the more unusual scents, such as the cherry-and-tomato combination.

BEST GIFTS FOR KIDS

- **Monoprix,** a chain of "popular stores," is packed with items, ranging from a selection of books (Disney translations are nice) to LEGOS®. I also buy kids' clothes here.
- **Sephora** carries little animal-shaped bath-gel thingamabobs for .50€ (75¢) each. Each animal shape is a different scent, and there must be 20 of them in all.

BEST STORE FOR TEENAGE GIRLS
Etam, Cite de la Femme
73 rue de Rivoli, 1er (Métro: Pont Neuf).

An entire department store of style: fashion, beauty, even home touches and a cafe. It occupies a makeover of one of La Samaritaine's landmark buildings. Low prices.

RUNNERS-UP FOR TEENS & TWEENS
H&M
54 bd Haussmann, 9e (Métro: Havre-Caumartin).

The Swedish phenomenon has copies of the latest looks for men, women, and children at affordable prices. This is the flagship; there are other, smaller branches around town.

New Look
Forum Les Halles, 1er (Métro: Les Halles).

British import that competes with H&M.

BEST KITSCH
It's not hard to find kitsch in Paris—just stroll the tourist traps along the rue de Rivoli or up and down the slopes near Sacré-Coeur.

> **Buyer Beware**
>
> Although you may be attracted to the winking and blinking Eiffel Tower lamps in various TTs (tourist traps), or even the more upmarket version at Maison Lafayette (about 200€/$300), take my word for it—the best Eiffel Tower lamp you can buy is sold for $30 in Target stores all over the U.S.

BEST WHIMSY
Mr. Gas
44 av. Etienne Marcel, 1er (Métro: Etienne Marcel).

Gas has been around for years: It's a teeny-tiny jewelry shop that sells colorful, creative whimsies. Now, "Mr. Gas" has added a clothing store next door. Funky, exotic, and hip. I was told there'd be glitz.

RUNNERS-UP
Fabulous jeweled canvas handbags and totes can be had for 83€ ($125) at **Vidna** (p. 203) and **Rene Derhy** (p. 117)—these are among the best buys of my last trip.

BEST INSPIRATION
There are several stores in Paris that fashion editors and style mavens return to over and over, mostly for ideas. I find that

these stores are not so helpful for women over 50 who pray to squeeze into a size 14, not a size 4, but if you just want to be inspired . . .

Manoush

75 rue Vieille du Temple, 3e (Métro: St-Paul) and 217 rue St-Honoré, 8e (Métro: Concorde); also in Cannes and Toulouse.

I've never seen more hype for a store—except maybe **Colette** (p. 13). I find it the best of a group of newish stores that are getting a lot of buzz.

They have accessories and designer clothes and claim to be midprice range (about 200€/$300 for a dress). Everything is flashy, sexy, and creative; let's call it the "BoHo Hotstuff" look—you know, short skirts, handbags with funny slogans, rabbit-fur car coats. I'd dare say the look is more important in the south of France than in Paris, but that's just my two centimes worth. By the way, these accessories are carried in the U.S. at Bloomies and Kitson (in LA).

MOST FUN IN A MONOPRIX

Normally I buy clothes in a Monoprix, but having way too many of those in my closets around the world, I decided to spend my $100 budget on makeup. What a blast! I bought just about everything I could from the Jean-Claude Biguine line, and some fat eye crayons from Mavala; I got Liquid Clubbing from Bourjois (liquid eye liner), mascara from the Biguine line (including one called Mocha—very unusual), and my beloved Lierace foundation, called Aqua-D (sable is my color), which is sort of a tan in a tube. My final splurge was Teint Ultra Prodigieux from Nuxe, which has promised me a healthy glow to my skin without self-tan.

BIGGEST SPLURGE

I can't believe I did this, but I paid over 67€ ($100) for a 1.4-ounce tube of makeup from **Sisley.** The 23€ ($35) I paid for a

Dior lipstick is equally upsetting, unsettling, and exhilarating. Are these products worth it? I doubt it. Am I? Absolutely.

BEST FASHION ICON: TRADITIONAL

Blame it on Pablo Picasso or Coco Chanel, but the traditional striped fisherman's T-shirt has become an iconic fashion statement.

This time, the colors are not so traditional (although you'll have no trouble finding navy-and-white or red-and-white stripes). The wacky colors are usually sold in specialty stores. Brands to check out include **Le Phare de la Baleine,** passage l'Havre, 9e (Métro: St-Lazare), part of a small chain that specializes in marine looks from Brittany; **Amour Lux,** a line sold all over France (I buy mine at Galeries Lafayette) that makes the shirts in wild colors; and **St-James,** 13 rue de Rennes, 6e (Métro: St-Germain-des-Prés), which has freestanding stores and perhaps the best colors, but the highest prices. You may be shocked by the prices—often 40€ ($60) or more—but in this case, you're paying for quality (they wear forever) rather than *la mode.*

BEST FASHION ICON: NEW AGE
Herve Chapelier

390 rue St-Honoré, 8e (Métro: Concorde); 1 rue du Vieux-Colombier, 6e (Métro: St-Germain-des-Prés); 3 rue Gustave Courbet, 16e (Métro: Victor-Hugo); 53 bd de Courcelles, 8e (Métro: Courcelles).

Hervé Chapelier makes brightly colored nylon tote bags. As handbags, these are totally passé, but as totes, market baskets, and weekend gear totes, they are sublime. The major department stores stock a lousy selection, so head to the freestanding stores. The best location is the flagship, not far from the rue Royale in the heart of the best shopping in town. I use the large tote bag for my dog. Check out the new line of bags in supple leather.

BEST ONE-TRICK PONY

The trick is the very French look of black and white teamed together for casual or dress-up. Both of these brands sell only white or black shirts, blouses, and tops.

Anne Fontaine

64 rue des Sts-Pères, 6e (Métro: Sèvres-Babylone); 50 rue Etienne Marcel, 2e (Métro: Etienne Marcel); 12 rue Francs-Bourgeois, 3e (Métro: St-Paul); and many others.

Ms. Anne has shops all over town and boutiques in the major department stores. She sells only two things: white blouses and black blouses. She also has shops in select U.S. cities and an outlet store at La Vallée. And, yes, now she has a spa too. We came for the classic white shirts.

Rayure

8 rue Francs-Bourgeois, 3e (Métro: St-Paul).

Rayure is not as expensive as Anne Fontaine, and doesn't have as many stores (though the line is also sold in department stores). It carries more white shirts than black, but is competitive with Anne Fontaine in terms of styling.

BLOCK TO WATCH

Check out the two parallel streets rue St-Roch and rue du 29 Juillet in the 1er (Métro: Tuileries)—they are filling up with adorable tiny shops. To get my drift, pop into **Dominique Denaive**, 7 rue du 29 Juillet, 1er (© **01-42-61-78-22;** www. denaive.com), for resin jewelry and accessories.

BEST NEW SHOPPING AREA

Well, this is an old area that's always been hot but is now getting, uh, hotter. I'm speaking of the Marais, but not the touristy haunts—instead, the little side parts that tourists have yet to discover. Head to the new **Blanc d'Ivoire** flagship to get my drift, 25 rue Saintonge, 3e (© **01-42-77-09-35**). Also find the rue Ferdinand Duval, which is getting to be a beauty street. Start at the **Different Company,** no. 10 (℘ **01-42-78-19-34**).

If you're strong, you can keep moving east, bypass the Bastille, and take the rue du faubourg St-Antoine into more new little stores off side streets.

BEST MARKETING FOR TRAVELERS

We shoppers are the winners here—despite the temporary loss of CDG airport terminal 2E and its fabulous shopping, there are many other new stores in Paris train stations, including a Monoprix in the **Gare du Nord** (for Eurostar shopping) and a brand-new Sephora in the **Gare de Lyon** (for trains heading to Provence and Côte d'Azur). These stores offer great last-minute gift shopping and browsing opportunities while you're waiting to depart.

BEST MARKETING FOR GUYS

Paris has gone bonkers for skin care for men. Department stores, Sephora stores, and even pharmacies have lots of shelf space devoted to the notion. The first such concept store is **Comptoir de l'Homme,** 5–7 rue de Tournon, 6e. All guy skin care, all the time. ℘ **01-46-34-04-18.**

BEST ETHNIC FASHION STORE
Mia Zia
4 rue Caumartin, 9e (Métro: Havre-Caumartin).

Lest you forget that many parts of the U.S. were once French colonies, note that numerous stores throughout Paris reflect French roots in other parts of the world. Mia Zia sells clothes and home style with a touch of North Africa, which makes them great for resort wear without being costume-y. ℘ **01-44-51-94-45.** www.miazia.com.

RUNNER-UP
R by 45RPM
4 rue du Marché St-Honoré, 1er (Métro: Tuileries).

For an interesting runner-up, but with clothing from Japan (which, of course, was never under French protection), look inside this small shop. Here, jeans and clothes are made from block-printed Japanese fabrics and bandannas. © 01-47-03-45-45. www.45rpm.fr.

BEST FRENCH BRANDS FOR LARGE AMERICAN BODIES

While I do not consider myself immense, let's face it, if you are larger than a size 6, you do not have a French body. Most French clothes are made up to size 44 (American size 12) and some go to size 46 (size 14); but they are cut small and, even if purportedly large enough, many don't fit. Do not panic. Here's my secret list of brands that have their own size system or go up to size 52—these are all available in the major department stores: **Lilith, Weill, Weinberg,** and **Yohji Yamamoto.**

For casual clothing, I often visit the men's department. *Warning:* A French men's XL in mass-market clothing may still be too small.

MOST INTERESTING FASHIONISTA HEADS UP

Watch this space for a full report—but just as Paris is a city of music and a city for science, a new city for fashion (**Cite de la Mode et du Design**) is being built in the 13e. The center will host a fashion institute and exhibition spaces (and runways, *bien sûr*) and is part of the city's attempt to liven up the area between the Gare du Austerlitz and the Biblioteque National, along the Seine's Left Bank.

MOST HYPED OLD STORE IN PARIS
Groyard
233 rue St-Honoré, 1er (Métro: Tuileries).

I used to list this store along with Louis Vuitton, which was a coincidence because they're alike yet totally different. Older than Vuitton, Groyard has long been the insider's preferred brand of luggage, steamer trunks, and travel gear. It, too, has a specific logo, but unlike Vuitton, it has remained a hidden source. Few people even knew of its store right behind the Hôtel Meurice and near the famed boutique Colette. Although Groyard was first known for its luggage, the company now suddenly makes the must-have handbag or tote bag of the decade.

The venerable firm was bought in 1998 and old traditions were maintained while a new design team moved in. Suddenly, a small gimmick has been added and the skies turn bright, the sun shines, the band plays, and the waiting list is 6 months long. All that Groyard has done is to offer its regular pattern in bright colors, along with the additional service of monogramming its canvas in contrasting hues. You can also get a crown emblazoned. The result is so hot that not only do you have to fork over a movie star's ransom, but you also must wait a long time. But, honey, *ooh-la-la*.

Insider's tip: Buy your bag in France, but have the monogram or printing done in the U.S., where the waiting line is only 3 months long. The line is sold at Bergdorf's and Neiman Marcus; free-standing stores are opening in the U.S., including a new one just opened on Union Square in San Francisco. Expect to pay 1,133€ ($1,700) for the tote bag and another 333€ ($500) for the monogram. There's a new bowwow store across the street.

MOST HYPED FRENCH STORE IN THE WORLD
Colette
213 rue St-Honoré, 1er (Métro: Tuileries).

If you've never done it, then do it now. And don't ask Karl Lagerfeld for his autograph—he just hangs around trying to get new ideas. The store is a gallery on the ground floor, with trendy merchandise as objets d'art; there's a cafe with water bar in the basement. Upstairs there's designer fashion, most of which is put away. You sit and the saleswoman brings. ℭ 01-55-35-33-90.

BEST SILLY IDEA I'VE EVER HAD, PART 1

I bought one of those touristy Eiffel towers to put on top of my Christmas tree. They sell them all over town at news kiosks and TTs; I bought the 15€ ($23) size. See p. 7.

BEST SILLY IDEA I'VE EVER HAD, PART 2

This idea belongs to my friend Muffy, not me—she buys the smaller size Eiffel Tower and then glues jewels and charms all over it. Expensive item in terms of time and craft products and vintage jewels and buttons, but it's a fabulous gift.

Chapter 2

Paris Details & Money Matters

A Paris Story

I was sitting at lunch in the courtyard of the Hotel de Costes in Paris with my friends Leonard and Kristin. I spied her over Len's shoulder and nudged Kristin—take a look over there: blue dress in flounces, champagne blonde hair in a ponytail, one small diamond stud in the far ear and a diamond and enamel–jeweled flower sprouting through her other earlobe, balanced in outer space with its bud toward her perfectly made-up face.

The dress was neither navy nor royal blue, but something summer chic in between those shades. Her gray platform heels were the highest *talons* allowed by law. Her handbag was one of those newfangled Louis Vuitton bags, the kind that is actually enviable and not tacky.

In short, she was everything I came to Paris to see.

This is a shopping story, a sociology story, and a history lesson. This is what makes it all worthwhile.

Take back your Eiffel Tower, your Champs-Elysées, your world-class museums, and the Tour d'Argent. Give me a coach seat to Paris, 4 nights and 3 full days in a three-star gem, and just enough euros for lunch at Costes. Or maybe Jules Verne.

The prices may be obscene, but there's still no place like it.

Bienvenue à Paree

Hold onto your beret, Jack—there's a lot that's new in Paris. Get this: They now sell macaroons, and other French pastries, at the McDonald's McCafe on the Champs-Elysées.

I won't say that's all you can afford in Paris, because I have found many affordable treasures and deals, but things have changed dramatically in Paris. And, yes, I can (and will) steer you to hotel rooms and/or apartments for less than 133€ ($200) per night. So cheer up—you can afford to go to Paris!

If you miss out on the fashionistas at the Hotel Costes, there's still plenty more to ooooh and aaaaah over. And get this news flash: Rules on Sunday retail are easing up. A major movement to open wide up did not pass the Senate, but more and more stores will open on Sundays. However, here's the one that was ratified: The big stores now have permission to stay open until 8pm in the area known as Les Grands Boulevards.

This refers to avenue Haussmann in the 9e where Zara, C&A, H&M, Printemps, and Galeries Lafayette are all located. H&M is actually trying to stay open until 8:30pm and the Monoprix on Caumartin (behind Printemps) until 10pm. There will be a hot time in the old town *ce soir.*

There are also lots of new stores, and many American touches (**Starbucks** everywhere!), so French retail shopping is easier than ever to cope with. (That means you can sometimes return things!) But this is still France and that's why you came. The latest marketing trick from a major supplier of olive oils (**O&Co.**) is vintage olive oil. **Goyard,** which has become the must-have It bag status item in totes and luggage, has just opened a new store across the street from their 100-plus-year-old store. The new one caters to dogs.

All of the grande dame hotels have renovated or are in the process of doing so—many have hired Philippe Starck and his daughter Asa. In fact, Philippe Starck has become the new king of France.

The luxury brand names have renovated as well, and many have added on selling space—such as the newly enlarged flagship **Hermès** shop.

Also note that the capital of luxe and deluxe has really cracked down on counterfeits. You can be arrested or fined if you so much as tote a fake brand-name handbag. I'm not talking about getting a ticket for jaywalking. The fine goes up to 300,000€ ($450,000) and you can get prison time if you attempt to sell counterfeits.

And what is truly the hottest look to come from Paris and head over to the U.S. and the rest of the world? *C'est l'Afrique*—Africa.

Let me just say that when I lived in northern Montmartre, a few blocks from an area called Little Africa, no one thought it was very chic. Now the textiles have taken over all the fashion houses and the home style is becoming *le dernier cri* (the latest thing). For lots of style and not many bucks, buy the waxed batik fabrics and bring them home for a DIY project for home or body—head to Little Africa (it's safe in the day) or to the fabric markets of St-Pierre (p. 100).

The biggest news is major renovations—many boutiques or stores were closed and reconceptualized, even **Les Quatre-Temps,** the mall out at La Defense, which is handy to know about if you are doing business out there or staying with a spouse who has booked into one of those hotels out there. The **Royal Monceau,** a tony hotel with quite a past, just had an auction to sell off its interiors and is now closed . . . awaiting a "relooking" (this is a real French word!) by, *bien sûr,* M. Starck himself. **Sephora** has opened up across the street from Galeries Lafayette; everyone's doing the fox trot.

Real estate prices were very high until recently; this means that alternative neighborhoods are getting hotter. The big movie houses are moving off the Champs-Elysées because the rents are too high. The little streets between the rue de Rivoli and the rue St-Honoré in the 1er are filled with cutie-pie little shops. New stores no longer choose to open in the 6e—it's too expensive. For less-central locations, the 10e and 11e are still blossoming. See chapter 4 for the lowdown on all the neighborhoods.

Warning: As French retail expands and redefines itself, the stores are pursing the same war of the brands that stores in the U.S. have been enacting for several years now. The problem in France, however, is that the novelty brands tend to be American—especially in beauty. Don't buy in Europe what you can buy for less in the U.S. Also, note that LA (as in Los Angeles) is considered a design kingdom of its own in Europe these days—stores are touting merchandise from LA-based designers as if they had invented freedom fries.

On the other hand, there's still lots to see and be inspired by, there are different selections in those same old designer stores, and there are some items that are typically French or simply well priced . . . so you need not go home without a souvenir or two.

Paris is, of course, one of the world's premier shopping cities. Even people who hate shopping enjoy it in Paris. What's not to like? The couture-influenced ready-to-wear? The street markets? The most extravagant kids' shops in the world? Jewelers nestled together in shimmering elegance? Fruits and vegetables piled in bins like more jewels? Antiques and collectibles that are literally the envy of kings? It's not hard to go wild with glee at your good luck and good sense for having chosen such a place to visit. If the prices are higher, well, you'll just have to be a little smarter.

Alyse in Wonderland

Before you shrug and say you can't afford to shop with the low dollar or there's nothing in Paris that you can't find in the U.S., I want to remind you of a few items I've found that will surely make you smile. Whether or not you buy them doesn't matter. The point is this: No place has the *ooh-la-la* factor like Paris.

I arrived in Paris by train (took a promotional deal from San Francisco to London to save money), thus saving on taxi fare from the airport. I dropped my luggage at the apartment we had rented, a rental also to save some scratch. I walked from there to one of my favorite shopping strolls—from boulevard St-Germain on the rue du Bac to the rue de Sevres and into Bon Marché and then on to the rue du St-Placide. This is actually a straight stroll, but the streets change names.

Along the way, I bought a dress for my son's wedding for 67€ ($100), a SIM card for my telephone with local activation and 3 hours of talk time for 33€ ($50), a bottle of Guerlain perfume I have been searching for over a period of 6 years for 133€ ($200), some gifts and souvenirs (each under 6.65€/$10), and dinner for four for 40€ ($60). That's not a bad few hours of hunting and gathering. And, boy, did I have fun.

Just remember what they said in Casablanca: "We'll always have Paris." And you need not pay the earth for it. Honest.

Know Before You Go

The French Government Tourist Office in the U.S. is an excellent source for visitor information and trip-planning advice. Go online to www.franceguide.com.

If you prefer, you can call one of the U.S. offices, in New York (© 212/315-0888), Chicago (© 312/337-6301), Dallas (© 214/720-4010), or Los Angeles (© 310/271-6665).

The number of websites to check is mind-boggling. I rely on www.bonjourparis.com (p. 46) and www.hungryforparis. com (p. 57) but also a host of travel, hotel, and airfare discounters. Any search engine will provide you with a bevy of choices. One of my common tricks is to look at hotels on www.expedia.com and see what hotels I know are offered at what rates; then I go to that hotel's site or even call the hotel directly to negotiate. Let the Internet point you toward savings for your own dates of travel.

More Information, Please

For *in situ* info, a few local publications can be very helpful. The main one is *Paris par Arrondissement*, a book of intricate maps. Mine fits in the palm of my hand and is so complete that I can look up an address in the front of the book, and then check a chart for the nearest Métro stop of that destination. The book comes in large format, too. For some reason, these babies are not available in the U.S., so buy yours at any bookstore in Paris; it's also sold at some street newspaper kiosks.

I also like *Paris par Autobus,* a map guide with bus routes listed by numbers. Bus travel is slower than the Métro, but I prefer it because you get to see more. Now then, in these days when every euro counts, it's my job to tell you that there are various editions of the bus book—some cost 11€ ($17) while others cost 6€ ($9)—so shop around a bit and see which format you prefer. There are at least three styles of these books; be sure you can read the tiny print!

If you want to know about immediate events once you get here, try *Where,* a freebie magazine given out in most hotels.

Le Figaro publishes a weekly insert, *Figaroscope,* about everything that's going on in the city, including special flea markets and shopping events. It appears in the newspaper every Wednesday.

If you're staying in an apartment and your landlord has not left a television guide, you will need to buy one. TV guides are different from events guides and are always published 7 to 10 days in advance, making it difficult to find one for the current week. There is a free TV insert in each newspaper, either the Friday edition of *Le Parisien* or the weekend edition of *Le Figaro* or *Le Monde.*

ELECTRONICALLY YOURS

The Internet is a fabulous source for researching your trip to France. Hotels, airlines, and travel agents all have their own

Cookbooks for Sweet Tooths

There's a handful of Americans who live in Paris and have recently published some books about their experiences and their secret sources. **Alexander Lobrano,** an editor of *Gourmet Magazine*, offers us *Hungry for Paris* with reviews of 102 restaurants, most of which are affordable for mere mortals. **Jamie Cahill** writes about *The Patisseries of Paris,* while **Dorie Greenspan** has the all-time-best cookbook, *Paris Sweets: Great Desserts from the City's Best Pastry Shops.* All of these books can be ordered on Amazon.com.

I bought *Le Calendrier du Chineur* in Paris—it's dated by the year and published by Flammarion. This large-format paperback gives the dates of all the big flea markets and special fairs for the entire year for venues all over France.

If you are just interested in antiques dealers in Paris, the magazine *Marie Claire* publishes its own guide with 1,200 addresses. It is in French.

websites. Most major brands also have websites, as do the French *grands magasins*—the big department stores. As we go to press, none of them offers international e-commerce, but it's on the way . . . and you can get discount coupons online.

Getting online before you arrive and during your stay can help you with daily life—especially if there's a strike or you need something such as a train schedule (log on to www.sncf.fr). You can even order train tickets and print them out at home, if your French is good enough. (Any website that ends with ".fr" is likely to be in French.)

So many businesses have websites that it's impossible to give you a list. For everything you need in a one-stop site, I think the best English-language option is **Bonjour Paris** (www.bonjourparis.com). If you come to France often, you might want a subscription. For a quick look at what's happening in town, try **Time Out** (www.timeout.com), which has listings for many international cities.

🐭 ELECTRONICALLY YOURS, PART 2

- **Wi-Fi** (wireless fidelity) is in vogue; just pronounce it the French way: Wee-*Fee*. You can now connect from just about anywhere in Paris. For more on Wi-Fi, see below.
- New or renovated hotels have in-room dataports; these may facilitate connections. On the other hand, most hotels are Wi-Fi enabled, so all this other stuff is outdated non-sense to most. Many fancy hotels offer free connections; many nonfancy hotels offer free connections. On the other hand, I just paid 25€ ($38) for 1 hour of connect time at the Hôtel Meurice; 1 day (24 hr.) at the Hilton was the same price. Usually there is a weekly rate which is the equivalent of the cost of 4 days—see, now you can stay longer!
- There are **Internet cafes** and centers around town (p. 123). Hotels often have business centers or a cute little invention that enables you to buy a card and go online in the hotel lobby. Prices vary, but are less expensive than those in hotel business centers—but more than those in Internet cafes. *Warning:* If you do use an Internet cafe, remember that the French use an AZERTY keyboard, not QWERTY, so your fingers will be messed up, as will your A's and Q's.

About the Phones

If you have a tri-band phone, it will work in Europe. Usually, you have to manually switch the band and then you're set. The phone will change to a local carrier. This means it costs you a fortune to receive calls, but you can make local calls at a decent rate. Expect to pay $2 a minute to use your Blackberry.

Should your phone work on a system compatible with a SIM card, you can get a French SIM card and have a local number and pay as you go. This isn't inexpensive, but can be the most practical solution. You will pay an activation charge and then for the time, which is sold in a package. You can add more minutes online.

Born to Shop Editorial Director Sarah Lahey just lucked into a promotion at SFR, one of the French phone systems, that gave her the phone and activation and 10 minutes of start-up time for 33€ ($50)—this is a great deal.

As for local phones, here's the system: All phone numbers in France have codes built into them. All cellphones begin with 06. Toll-free numbers are usually 08 or 0800 or something similar to those in the U.S.; they may also be called "green lines." If someone has a "free phone" at home (operates on VoIP system), it begins with 09—these are getting more common. The call is free to the holder of the line, not to you!

Local phones in Paris and the greater Paris metro area begin with 01. All the phone numbers given in this book have the local numbers. The digits 02 to 05 depict other regions of France, so automatically I know that a phone number beginning with 04 is in the south of France. Since this is a Paris guide, there are no other regional codes in these pages.

Every now and then, you'll pick up a business card with an old-fashioned French phone number printed on it: It won't have eight digits. To adapt this number to the current code, within Paris, add 014.

Getting There

FLYING FROM THE U.S.

While getting to Paris may seem easy enough—after all, most of the major carriers fly there—you can sometimes find a deal. You'll also have to be creative as more airlines are cutting back on flights and more brands are consolidating. There are also fuel surcharges being added to mileage awards.

The least expensive airfares are always in winter. Furthermore, winter airfares often coincide with promotional gimmicks, such as buy one ticket, get one at half-price; buy one ticket, bring along a companion for a discounted price; or kids fly free. Also during winter, airlines may reduce the number of frequent-flier miles you need to reach a particular destination. This seldom applies to Paris, but Brussels often goes "on sale."

Winter always brings airfare price wars; when Air France announced a $299 weekend fare to Paris last winter, I think half of New York tilted into the Atlantic in a mad rush for tickets. Friends from Houston (who had the exact same rate) called me immediately. For this winter, with fuel as pricey as it is, in the heat of summer I can still book a $429 round-trip. *Pas mal.*

Don't forget online sales and online purchases—two different subjects. Most airlines allow you to register for e-mail announcements of bargains on your favorite routes. Promotionally speaking, there's a more or less standing deal that if you buy a full-fare business-class ticket with your Platinum American Express card, you get a companion ticket free. That might not be the least expensive way to get to Paris, but it's still a bargain.

Between the airlines' online specials, discounters' online fares, and airfare wars usually announced in the newspapers, you should be able to find a number of good deals.

Airfare war trick: If you buy a ticket, and a price war then makes the same ticket available at a lower price, don't just sit there and stew. The airlines will rewrite your ticket, subject to a service charge. The charge is usually $100 to $150, but you may save money overall.

Another strategy: Buy a cheapie ticket, then pay the fee to change to different dates, which may not have been included during the price war.

Also, check out consolidators, which unload unsold tickets on scheduled flights at discount prices (which vary with the season, like regular prices). You might not earn frequent-flier miles, but these tickets are great for last-minute travelers who do not qualify for 21-day advance-purchase prices. You need only about 4 business days' notice.

Don't forget the big-time tour operators. Rates are lower if you book through French tour operators or wholesalers like **Nouvelles Frontières** (www.nouvelles-frontieres.fr), a major chain of French travel agents, which calls itself New Frontiers in the U.S. For the past 20 years, I have used a travel agent broker from Alameda, California, whom I have never met but who reigns mythic in my travel and business life. When I need a complicated ticket, I write to Lilian at **Pacific Place** (pacplace@att.net), who gets my Asian and European tix. *Note:* She is best for good fares on multileg trips; a simple round-trip during a fare war can be done online without her skills.

Another note: Sometimes you will do better if you fly into a well-trafficked or promoted hub such as Amsterdam, London, or Frankfurt. The "Brussels Trick" is explained below.

Insider's tip: If you like to fly business class (who doesn't?) but can't afford the high prices, check with Air France. It often has a promotion whereby if you purchase your ticket 2 or 3 months in advance and accept it as nonrefundable, you'll get a business-class fare of about $2,200.

L'Avion is also doing a big business—this is a French carrier with lower than average business-class fares (© 866/692-6759; http://us.lavion.com). Their service began in January 2007; they fly 757s that are configured at 90 seats in a 2×2 pattern and fly only New York–Orly for their U.S. service. Service to the Middle East is expected soon.

FLYING THROUGH THE U.K.

To research this edition, I flew in and out of London on a special promotional deal from United. There was enough wiggle room on the savings that even with the price of the ongoing tickets via Eurostar, I still saved money. The savings were based on the fact that I grabbed a San Diego–Heathrow promotional fare on United ($699), and as a member of their Premiere flyers, I was automatically upgraded to Economy Plus, an extra 5 inches of room that makes a huge difference on a long haul. The train ticket (round-trip) was another $200.

If you need one-way transportation between London and Paris, but are keen on flying, an advance round-trip ticket that includes a Saturday-night stay will be less expensive than a one-way ticket. Just throw away the unused portion. *C'est la vie.* Also check out the various low-cost airlines that operate from the London area, often using alternative airports in both London and Paris. (*Beware:* Beauvais is far away!)

Also remember that London isn't the only city in the U.K. Fly from the U.S. to Manchester and then hop on a $100 round-trip to Paris from a low-cost carrier—provided you've bought that ticket far in advance.

FLYING THROUGH BRUSSELS

Don't look at me like that! This is my famous "Brussels Trick." Brussels is less than 1½ hours from Paris, thanks to speedy **Thalys** train lines. You can easily fly into Brussels and out of Paris (or vice versa), or even go to Paris for the weekend from Belgium. Sometimes, when there are airfare deals and promotions, all seats in and out of Paris are sold—so try Brussels for one leg and see if you can beat the system by being a little bit clever.

FLYING THROUGH AMSTERDAM

With the recent financial merger of **Air France** and **KLM,** you may find some great deals to Paris simply by changing planes in Amsterdam.

FLYING THROUGH FRANKFURT

Although it doesn't make good geographic sense to overfly France and then cut backward, it can make cents in a savings fashion if you hook into a deal. **Lufthansa** very often has great prices—even in high season—if you're willing to backtrack.

FLYING VIA NICE/LYON

Many people like to combine the south of France with Paris, especially because the Delta nonstop flight from New York makes it so easy. But getting to Paris can be complicated if you don't work it all out beforehand.

If you're flying **Delta** on the triangular route, so to speak, you will need a train, a car, or a plane ticket to get you to Paris. Or you can book with Air France. Since Air France has no direct flights from the U.S. to Nice, it offers an alternative that should be priced competitively when it includes Nice—you just want a layover between legs. Note that because Delta and Air France have merged many of their flights and services, you may be able to book a mixed ticket at a good price. By the same token, there is currently U.S. service to Lyon via **Delta.** Lyon is the gateway to Provence (see chapter 9).

Getting There by Train

There are many, many train fares for travel to and from Paris. Several **BritRail USA** packages allow you to choose which method you'd like to use for getting from the U.K. to the Continent; the Continental Capitals Circuit connects London with Paris, Brussels, and Amsterdam.

Rail Europe (✆ **888/382-7245** in the U.S.) sells passes for travel in specific countries (such as the France pass) that enable you to save money on train fares. The price of some products includes an automatic discount (about 30%!) off a Eurostar (Chunnel train) ticket. Note that the Eurostar ticket is not part of any pass currently available; it must be bought as an add-on. Rail Europe also offers multiple-country train passes, as well as other train-drive promotions and products. It's a one-stop agency that can arrange everything, and you'll have the train pass in hand when you land in Europe. Note that if you travel on the fast TGV trains in France with a train pass, you will need an additional reservation. The price of a train reservation varies, but within France is usually 3€ ($4.50).

Rail Europe not only has tons of train passes, but also books transatlantic flights, hotels, car rentals—the works. One of the greatest things about its system is that there are different prices based on age (youth passes, seniors, and so forth), as well as on the number of people traveling together. Not just "the more the merrier"—the more the cheaper.

If you can get by in the French language and have a French address, you can go directly online and order your tickets from SNCF—Societé National Chemin de Fer, the French rail system; log on to www.sncf.fr.

Arriving in Paris

If you're arriving from the U.S., you'll fly into either **Charles de Gaulle International Airport** (**CDG;** © 01-48-62-22-80 for English-language info on transport; www.ratp.fr) or **Orly International Airport.** Orly has not been operating international service to U.S. gateways in recent years, so this is new. CDG is a larger airport, located to the north of Paris; Orly is to the south (less expensive taxi fare to town).

A taxi to the 1er from CDG costs about 50€ ($75), including tip and the traditional surcharge for luggage. Most French taxis are small; if you have a lot of luggage, hold out for a Mercedes taxi or a van. If you have a lot of passengers plus a lot of luggage, expect to take two taxis. (Or book a van through **Paris Millénium** [p. 31].)

To transfer into Paris from Orly and/or CDG, you can use bus service to and from Etoile (take a taxi to your hotel from there), and several other midcity drop-off points.

You can also take Roissy Rail, which lets you off in town at the Gare du Nord or Châtelet, although these are better for those who have easy-to-handle luggage.

For private car service, see p. 31.

Now back to Beauvais again. Low-cost carriers often use this airport, which is well over an hour outside of Paris. If you use public transportation to get there, you must allow 3 to 4 hours before your flight departure to meet at the *rallye* point in Paris for the transfer.

Getting Around Paris

Paris is laid out in a system of zones called arrondissements, which spiral around from inside to outside. When France adopted postal codes, Parisians incorporated the arrondissement numbers into their codes as the last two digits. Codes for addresses in the city of Paris begin with 75; the last two digits match the arrondissement. For example, a code of 75016 means the address is in the 16th arrondissement (16e). The first arrondissement is written *1er;* for others, the number followed by a small "e" (2e, 3e, and so forth) signifies the arrondissement.

Knowing the proper arrondissement is essential to getting around easily in Paris. For many people, indicating the arrondissement is also a shorthand way of summing up everything a place can or may become, although the new emphasis on alternative retail is putting that myth to sleep.

Tourists are usually urged to ride the Métro, but buses can also be a treat—you can see where you're going and get a free tour along the way. *Paris par Arrondissement* usually includes bus routes, as well as a Métro map. Métro maps are available free at hotels; keep one in your wallet at all times.

BY MÉTRO

There are many Métro ticket plans. If you can speak a little French and visit Paris often enough to take the time to do this, buy a **Carte Orange.** It is exactly what it sounds like: a small orange card, with a passport-type photo. (Bring a photo, or use the photo booth in the station.) The orange ID card is inserted into a plastic carrying case with a slot for a *coupon.* The coupon is good for 1 week and is good for the bus, RER (that's *Réseau Express Regional*) within Paris, and Métro.

This option is not for everyone, as it covers an entire week, *from Monday to Monday.* (It is not for sale after Wed.) But the Carte Orange is only about half the price of the weekly tourist ticket, called **Sesame.** Bargain shopping begins at the

Métro station, *mes amis*. However, the Carte Orange doesn't pay for itself if you don't use it a lot.

Everything I've just told you is basic. Here's the new twist: Your Carte Orange can come in an electronic version called a **Navigo** card. Rather than feeding your coupon into the turnstile, you simply lay the *carte* packet on top of the turnstile, where it will be read electronically.

If you want individual tickets, you can buy a ***carnet*** at any station. The 10-ticket carnet costs 11.35€ ($17) and is good on both the Métro and the bus. An individual Métro ticket costs 1.50€ ($2.25), but with the carnet, the price drops to 1€ ($1.50). That's a pretty good savings. At some point in the near future, the carnet will be replaced with a chip-based card as well.

The **Paris Visite** transportation pass provides travel for 1, 2, 3, or 5 days; it even can include rides to the airport, outlying suburbs, and Versailles. It's an awfully good deal if you plan to use it. The pass comes in a black case in which you insert something that looks like the coupon used in a Carte Orange.

Passes are for sale at RATP stations (big Métro stations or RER stations—I look at the acronym and think "rapid transit"), SNCF (French national train) stations, and ADP (Aéroports de Paris) booths at both airports.

BY RER

If you take RER trains within the city of Paris, you can use a regular Métro ticket; some Paris Visite coupons are valid on RER out of town, even as far as Versailles. Do not be afraid of the RER, but do study it carefully as it is not as easy to use.

BY BUS

Buses are much slower than the underground, but you get to see the sights. Paris buses accept the same coupons as the Métro, cash, and (soon) bank cards. The fare, if you are paying in cash, is currently 1.50€ ($2.25). If you use a ticket from your carnet, you save almost 30%. If you have a coupon or an electronic pass, show it when you board the bus, but do not put it in the validating machine.

BY TAXI

The taxi meter drops at 2.20€ ($3.30) and goes up, up, and away—extras for luggage, for extra people, for dogs. Taxi drivers may also take you on a scenic route in order to bring the fare up, blaming traffic. Sit back and enjoy it. Tip by rounding up, not by percentage.

BY CAR

If you plan to visit the countryside or Disneyland Paris, you may want to rent a car. As long as you avoid driving around the place de la Concorde, you'll be fine. As an added convenience, most major car-rental agencies will allow you to drop the car at a hotel, saving you the time and trouble of returning it yourself.

If you intend to drive around Paris (silly you), be sure you know the parking regulations and how to work the meters, which provide a ticket that proves you've paid. (Display it prominently in your windshield.) Just because you don't see a meter like we have in the U.S. doesn't mean that parking is free. (Look for payant marked somewhere.) Also, you may need a newfangled parking *carte* from a news kiosk to get the ticket; few machines actually take cash.

If you prefer a car and driver, contact **Paris Millénium** (© **01-30-71-93-03;** fax 01-30-71-97-91); ask for Mathieu, who speaks perfect English. There are special Born to Shop rates for airport transfers (120€/$180) and shopping tours. When I am staying in an apartment, I always put the savings on rent toward using **Millénium** because their drivers will schlep the luggage for me . . . with a smile.

About That Money

Just about everyone who contemplates a visit to Paris is concerned about the dollar-euro ratio and the high cost of travel. What I want to stress is that there are two separate financial problems going on, only one of which is specific to Americans or those shopping with U.S. dollars.

If you get into a serious conversation about costs, money, and the euro with a Frenchman, you will hear the lament that things in France now cost in euros what they used to cost in francs. The most common example given is a cup of coffee, which was traditionally 5 francs. Now it costs 5 euros (or more in Cannes or at a fancy hotel in Paris; less in a corner bar and slightly less at Starbucks). French friends tell me they can barely survive the cost of living as inflation has taken over their lives. One friend even admitted that she can no longer afford a rotisserie chicken. (Cost of chicken: 10€–20€/$15–$30, depending on a variety of factors.)

The low exchange rate for the USD is a totally different issue. (It continues to fluctuate wildly; for this edition we went with 1€ = $1.50, but as we go to print the rate is back down to $1.25. Check www.xe.com for updates.)

While I can fix neither of these situations, I will pass on my own survival tip. I ask myself if the value of a meal or an item I am contemplating is worth it to me if the euro and the USD were at parity. In short, I don't like 6€ Cokes or 27€ tapas entrees or 20€ organic chickens . . . never mind that they really cost *me* $9, $40, and $30, respectively. You will be happier if you face prices as they are in euros rather than always converting them to USD.

Currency Exchange

CASH

The French post office will change U.S. dollars into euros but will not take any bills larger than $50. Fewer banks are willing to change dollars these days; there are many *cambios* that will do so—they are in tourist areas. Your hotel will also change dollars. Check out Amex and other money-changers on rue Scribe for the best rates in town.

ATMS

You can use your ATM card from the U.S. to withdraw euros from French ATMs, which can be found everywhere, including at the airport (so you can have euros for your taxi into town). Just look for the Cirrus, PLUS, or NYCE logo (some bank cash machines are only for local bank cards).

There are some U.S. bank cards that do not charge a fee for international withdrawals. Find out about yours; consider changing bank cards. Mine charges $5 a pop!

AMEX & VISA

Card members can draw on their American Express cards for cash advances or to cash personal checks. (Never travel without your checkbook.)

It's relatively simple: You write a personal check at a special desk and show your card, have it approved, and then go to another desk to get the money in the currency you request. Allow about a half-hour for the whole process, unless there are long lines. The same desk usually handles cash advances.

Some Visa cards allow you to take cash loans from your bank while you are in a foreign destination. With some types of cards, you can write a check in dollars at a hotel and get back euros.

Note that all bank cards now charge an additional conversion rate when you charge abroad.

TRAVELER'S CHECKS

You can buy traveler's checks in euros, which will be good for later trips to other destinations—but this does lock in the rate, which can be good news or bad news.

I still think they're great, and I *love* having "free money" for my next trip if I didn't use all the checks I bought. I used to get mine through AAA, so I didn't have to pay a fee. On the other hand, there are some downsides.

In recent years, I've had more and more trouble cashing traveler's checks.

Debit Cards

U.S. and French debit cards work on different formats. You will probably use your U.S. debit card more like a credit card for your end of the transaction in France; you will probably have to sign a transaction slip. *Note:* I got a notice from my U.S. bank saying that my U.S. debit card could be used internationally only six times. Check your bank's policy.

If you drive, your U.S. card may not work in a French gas pump.

Tips on Tipping

For tipping, forget your old trick of handing out U.S. dollars. These days, no one wants them. What they really want is a 2€ ($3) coin or a 5€ ($7.50) bill.

Tipping in Paris can also be confusing because all restaurant and hotel bills include a service charge and many guidebooks tell you not to add an additional tip. While you do not have to add a tip to a restaurant check, it's often done—simply round up the bill or plunk down an extra euro or two or five. It's all the waiter will see of your real tip; think 5€ on a meal, less for drinks.

Détaxe Details

Détaxe is the refund you get on TVA, the 19.6% value-added tax on all goods sold in France (except goods needed for home repairs, which carry a 5.5% tax). TVA is similar to sales tax in the U.S. The French pay it automatically. Tourists can get a refund on it.

There are more and more ways of getting that refund. The basic détaxe system—the process of getting a refund on this tax—works pretty much like this:

You are shopping in a store with prices marked on the merchandise. This is the true price that any tourist or any national must pay. If you are a French national, you pay the price without thinking twice. If you are a tourist who plans to leave the country within 6 months, you may qualify for a détaxe refund. Currently, the minimum by French law for a détaxe refund is 175€ ($263) for a person spending this amount (or more) in one store on a single day. You may no longer save up receipts over a period of time. To qualify for a tax refund, you must spend the money in the same store on the same day. For this reason, planning one big haul at one of the department stores is your best bet.

If you go for the détaxe refund, budget your time to allow for the paperwork. It takes about 15 minutes to fill out each store's forms, and may take 20 to 60 minutes for you to receive the forms back, because the store must process them. But you never know—I've zipped through the line in less than 5 minutes. Allow more time than you need, just in case.

Tip: Return to the department store the moment it opens, and head directly to the détaxe desk.

You will need your passport number (but not necessarily the passport itself) to fill out the paperwork. The space that asks for your address is asking for the name of your hotel. You do not need to provide its address. After the papers are filled out, they will be given back to you with an envelope, usually addressed to the store. Sometimes the envelope has a stamp on it; sometimes it is blank (if the latter, you must affix a stamp to it before you leave the country). At other times, it has a special government frank that serves as a stamp. If you don't understand what's on your envelope, ask.

At the airport, go to the Customs official who processes the détaxe papers. Do this before you clear regular Customs or part with your luggage. There are two ways to do this: (1) Check your luggage, but keep your purchases separate and carry them onboard with you, or (2) wheel your packed luggage to the Customs office and be prepared to unpack the items.

The Customs officer has the right to ask you to show the merchandise you bought and are taking out of the country. Whether the officer sees your purchases or not, he or she will stamp the papers, keeping a set (which will be processed) and giving you another set. Place this set in the envelope and mail it to the shop where you made your purchases. (Sometimes the Customs officer keeps the specially franked envelopes. Don't worry; they'll be mailed.)

Note: Since unification in 1993, you claim your détaxe when you leave your final E.U. destination to return to the U.S. For example, if you are going on to Belgium from France, you claim everything as you exit Belgium and process your paperwork there. You'll get the French laws and the French discounts, but the paperwork itself is done at Belgian Customs. Ditto for Britain, Italy, and elsewhere in the E.U.

When the papers get back to the shop and the government has notified the shop that its set of papers has been registered, the store will grant you the discount through a refund. This can be done on your credit card (the shop will have made a dual pressing) or through a personal check, which will come in the mail (see below).

So that's how the system works.

Now, here are the fine points: *The way in which you get your discount is somewhat negotiable!* At the time of purchase, discuss your options for the refund with the retailer. Depending on how much you have bought, how big a store it is, or how cute you are, you may get a more favorable situation. This has become more complicated in the past year or two since Global Refund is taking over most of the refund business and insists you take a cash refund from them at the airport. Whenever possible, you want your refund applied to a bank card.

Here are the two most popular ways to get your refund, in order of preference to the tourist:

• The retailer sells you the merchandise at the cheapest price possible, including the tax refund, and takes a loss on the income until the government reimburses him or her. He explains that he will not get the rest of his money unless you process the papers properly. Being as honorable as you are, of course you process the papers. This is "instant détaxe," and is the practice in some name-brand stores and most parfumeries.

- You pay for the purchase, at the regular retail price, with a major credit card. The clerk makes a second imprint of your card for a refund slip, marked for the amount of the détaxe. You sign both slips. When the papers come back to the retailer, the shop puts through the credit slip. The credit may appear on the same monthly statement as the original bill, or on a subsequent bill. Just remember to check that the credit goes through.

The very best way to take the refund is on your credit card. Although cash seems like an easy and flashy choice, you will lose money on this choice.

DÉTAXE ON TRAINS, BOATS & FERRIES

If you leave Paris by train (such as the overnight train to Istanbul), you may be in a panic about your détaxe refund. Not to worry. As mentioned above, you now apply for the refund as you leave the E.U. If your train is taking you to another E.U. country, you do not even have to think about filing for your détaxe refund in France.

If your train (or ferry) is taking you to a non-E.U. country, such as Turkey, you will need to do the paperwork on board.

Shortly after you board the international train, the conductor for your car will poke his head into your cabin, introduce himself (he speaks many languages), ask for your passport, and give you the Customs papers for crossing international borders. If you are on the sleeper, he handles the paperwork in the middle of the night while you snooze.

If you are catching the *QM2* in France, transiting to Southampton (U.K.) before a transatlantic crossing, you do the détaxe at the port when you leave France. At check-in for the ship (which is on land, not on board), ask where the Customs agents are so you can have your paperwork stamped.

U.S. Customs & Duties

To make your reentry into the U.S. as smooth as possible, follow these tips:

- Know the rules and stick to them.
- Don't try to smuggle anything.
- Be polite and cooperative (up until the point when they ask you to strip, anyway).

Also, remember the following:

- You are allowed to bring in $800 worth of merchandise per person, duty-free. (Books, which are duty-free, are not included.) Each member of the family, including infants, is entitled to the deduction.
- Currently, you pay a flat 10% duty on the next $1,000 worth of merchandise.
- Duties thereafter are based on the type of product and vary tremendously.
- The "head of the family" can make a joint declaration for all family members. Whoever is the head of the family should take responsibility for answering Customs officers' questions. Answer honestly, firmly, and politely. Have receipts ready, and make sure they match the information on the landing card. Don't be forced into a story that won't wash under questioning. If you tell a little lie, you'll be labeled a fibber, and they'll tear your luggage apart.
- Have the Customs registration slips for your personal goods in your wallet or otherwise easily accessible. If you wear a Cartier watch, be able to produce the registration slip. If you cannot prove that you took a foreign-made item out of the U.S. with you, you may be forced to pay duty on it. If you own such items but have no registration or sales slips, take photos of the goods and have them notarized in the U.S. before you depart. The notary seal and date will prove you had the goods in the U.S. before you left the country.

- The unsolicited gifts you mailed from abroad do not count in the per-person rate. If the value of the gift is more than $50, you pay duty when the package comes into the country. Remember, it's only one unsolicited gift per person. Don't mail to yourself.
- Do not attempt to bring in any illegal food items—dairy products, meats, fruits, or vegetables. Generally speaking, if it's alive, it's forbidden. Coffee is okay. Any creamy French cheese is illegal, but a hard or cured cheese is legal as long as it has aged 60 days.
- Elephant ivory is illegal to import. Antique ivory pieces may be brought into the country if you have papers stating their provenance.
- Antiques must be 100 years old to be duty-free. Provenance papers will help, as will permission to export the antiquity, since it could be an item of national cultural significance. Any bona fide work of art is duty-free, whether it was painted 50 years ago or yesterday; the artist need not be famous.

Airline Parity

There is no such thing as airline parity—it is a horrible trick that is going to cost you big bucks. Whether you are paying for a pet ticket or extra baggage, note that carriers set their fees from the French end in euros at parity. Soooo if the website tells you an extra piece of luggage costs $110, if you send that extra piece from France, it costs 110€ ($165). Ouch!

Shopping Details

HOURS

Shopping hours in Paris are extremely irregular and independent. (Welcome to France.) Thankfully, they are big-city hours, so you needn't worry about a lot of downtime, as in

Italy or the French provinces. There are plenty of shopping opportunities, even on Sunday and Monday, along with some late-night shopping ops here and there.

Generally speaking, *stores are open Monday, or part of Monday.* Stores that are closed on Monday morning—usually small establishments—open anytime from noon on, or sometimes from 1, 2, or even 3pm. Department stores and branches of the major chains are open on Monday morning, and so are about 50% of the stores in the prime shopping areas on the Left Bank.

During the rest of the week, most stores consider 10am to 7pm standard hours, but there are many exceptions to this rule, such as it is. Some stores open at 10am, except 1 day of the week, when they open at 9:30am. Some stores are open until 10pm on Thursday only. A few stores are open until 8 or 9pm every weekday, especially in high-traffic areas.

There is a new movement toward 11am openings in smaller shops, especially in funky (alternative) neighborhoods.

In summer, many stores close for lunch on Saturday, but stay open later in the evening. Some stores are open for lunch during the week, but close for lunch on Saturday.

France has about 15 bank holidays a year; stores may close on these holidays. Beware the month of May! Not only does May have about 10 holidays in it, but it's also hard to know when stores will be open. May 1 is a huge holiday, when everything is closed. May 8 is a less important holiday, and stores may or may not be open—check ads in *Le Figaro.* Your hotel concierge may not know. Also note that openings may be related to the part of town. On May 8, I was shut out in the 16th arrondissement, but found stores in most other neighborhoods open. Go figure.

Bastille Day, July 14, is a holiday, and stores are closed—but some small retailers open, if only for a few hours, to take advantage of the crowds in the streets.

The entire month of August may be unusual. Most of France closes down on August 15 for the Feast of the Assumption, but some stores close for the entire month, or just from August 14 to August 31.

SUNDAY SHOPPING

Although traditional Parisian retail stores close on Sunday, there is still an enormous amount of shopping on offer. Aside from the flea-market business, nowadays entire neighborhoods are jumping. Also keep your eye on the news as Sunday shopping is expected to take hold within the next decade.

Meanwhile, check out these:

- The **Louvre,** with the adjoining mall Carrousel du Louvre, the Antiquaires des Louvre, and all the touristy shops on rue de Rivoli.
- The **Marais,** including the retail street rue Francs-Bourgeois, where most stores are open.
- The **Champs-Elysées,** where most stores open on Sunday at noon (except Monoprix, which does not open on Sun). Champs-Elysées stores are open into the night in summer; this includes Monoprix.
- The **Ile St-Louis.**

Many stores that open on Sunday are closed on Monday.

Antiquing on Sunday is a national hobby; don't forget to check the newspapers, or ask your concierge about special weekend shows or events. From February to May, the weekends are dense with special events, many of which highlight shows for antiques, *brocante* (used items, not necessarily antiques), or both.

EXCEPTIONAL OPENINGS

The French government allows retailers five exceptional Sunday openings during the year. These are most often taken around Christmas, but there's usually one in September or October for back-to-school shopping and often one the first Sunday during the summer sales. Often, openings on holidays in May are also known as exceptional. Exceptional openings are usually advertised in newspapers like *Le Figaro*.

SALE PERIODS

Officially, the French government sets the dates of the sales, and there are only two sales periods: one in winter (Jan) and one in summer (late June to July). However, many retailers, strapped for cash, offer assorted promotions and discounts these days. A few, like Hermès, have special events held outside the stores. These events are advertised and listed in papers; check *Le Figaro* for the page called Le Carnet du Jour for sale ads.

The big department stores turn their sale promotions into megadeals, with banners all over the storefronts and enticing titles. You don't need to speak French to get the picture.

The thing that I find most frightening about these French promotional sales is that they last a set time and are then over. The sale merchandise does not stay marked down. I once fell in love with a tablecloth at a department store and decided to think about it. When I went back, the 3-day promotional sale was over and the price was up 25%.

Personal Needs

Pharmacies are marked with a green neon cross; at least one in each neighborhood must be open on Sunday. When a pharmacy is closed, a sign in the window indicates the nearest open pharmacy. If the neon is illuminated, the store is open.

Machines in all Métro stations and pharmacies sell condoms, often male and female versions in machines that are coded blue or pink. Honest.

Monoprix on the Champs-Elysées is open until 10pm in winter and midnight in summer—it stocks any personal needs you can imagine, except books in English.

If you need a book in English, try **W. H. Smith,** 248 rue de Rivoli (Métro: Concorde), which sells American and British books and periodicals. Most luxury hotels sell daily or Sunday London newspapers. Or head to Left Bank bookstores/

expat hangouts **Village Voice,** 6 rue Princesse (Métro: Mabillon), or **Tea & Tattered Pages,** 24 rue Mayet (Métro: Duroc). For the most part, books in English are outrageously expensive, so try the stores that sell used editions.

Airport Shopping

Both Orly and CDG have more than their share of shopping opportunities—in fact, the shopping is so brisk that the airports have their own shopping bags. Stores at CDG are fancier than those at Orly, but you will have no trouble dropping a few, or a few hundred, euros at either.

Those in search of cosmetics and fragrance bargains should already have bought them in Paris at the duty-free shops that offer 20% to 40% savings. You will save only 13% at the duty-free stores at the airport. The selection at the airport may be better than the selection on your plane, but the airline's prices can be better.

It pays to take the duty-free price list from the plane when you arrive and save it for comparison when shopping at the airport at the end of your trip. You'd be surprised how often an airport price can be the same as a department-store price.

Legally speaking, you may not buy duty-free goods if you're leaving for another E.U. destination. To be precise, you can buy them, but you will pay the full retail price.

If you are departing the E.U., you may buy at the duty-free price (13%–14% less than regular retail).

To learn what stores are represented at the airport, check out www.aeroportsdeparis.fr. Note that these shops are interspersed among several different terminals, so you must know which terminal you're using to accurately assess your future shopping adventures. Yes, there are sales during national sales periods.

Chapter 3

Eating & Sleeping in Paris

Are You Sleeping?

When pricing hotels, especially during promotions, be sure to read the fine print. Some hotels require a minimum stay of 2 nights for you to qualify for a bargain price. Some "deals" are good only on weekends. Bear in mind that prices may be per person or per room. Cancellations must usually be made 48 hours in advance; watch out! July and August are high season for airfare, but low season in terms of hotel rooms in Paris. Some of the best deals of the year can be made then.

The rack rate, or official room rate, at a midrange hotel in Paris is 400€ ($600) and up. For multistar luxury in the lowest category, you are generally asked to pay about 800€ ($1,200). It can go up (easily). Avoid Paris when it's most fully booked (and, therefore, most expensive), in May, June, September, and October.

- **Think winter.** December. Think January, February, March.
- **Think tragedy.** It's terrible, but it's true. In times of war and sorrow, when no one is traveling, there are airfare and hotel deals galore.
- **Think opening day . . . or reopening day.** New and newly renovated hotels introduce themselves and woo back regular clients with amazing deals and perks. When InterContinental

reopened the Grand after 2 years of serious renovations, there were many good deals to lure back lost customers. Perhaps the best deal in Paris was the Discovery Package offered by the new Hilton Arc de Triomphe. *Note:* Specifically ask your travel agent about new openings.

- **Go down a notch (or more) in hotel choice.** Yes, we'd all like to stay at the Four Seasons, but other hotels abound. Best of all, there are hotels you've never heard of that you will enjoy. It's okay if you don't stay in a palace.
- **Try a less chic neighborhood.** There are wonderful hotels in Montmartre (18e) or Bastille (12e) that you will really like (I promise), and they cost less because they are not in the Marais or the 6e, the 1er, the 8e, or the 16e. Branch out a little.
- **Use associations and memberships to your advantage.** AAA, AARP, and American Express card members get deals on prices, upgrades, or even gifts.
- **Look at creative promotions.** Some hotels reduce their rates if you book way in advance. Some will do a euro-to-dollar parity exchange. Every 2 weeks in advance you book at **Novotel,** you get a further reduction in rate.
- **Work with hotel associations and chains.** Most hotels are members of associations or chains that have blanket promotions. Leading Hotels of the World offers a fabulous corporate rate. Most hotels have rates frozen in U.S. dollars for at least a portion of the year, especially when they are in a promotional period, but often in summer. These invariably have to be booked in the United States, but usually offer incredible value. Some hotels offer special rates for certain months; others offer these rates year-round!
- **Never assume that all hotels in a chain are equal.** Even if you're talking about big American chains, such as Hilton or Sheraton, you will find hotels in every category of style and price within the same chain.
- **Learn the French chains.** Americans may know the **Sofitel** brand, but they possibly have not heard of **Libertel**—a great chain of three- and four-star hotels. You may know **Best Western** from the U.S., but the France Best Western

group has different ownership and better hotels. Not all French chains are equal, but whenever I hear of someone staying in a Libertel, I am impressed by that person's travel savvy; ditto for Best Western.

- **Compare apples to apples.** Get the best price you can from one or two luxury or palace hotels, and use that as your base line so that you can figure out what you are really getting with other hotel offers.

- **Think package tours.** Airlines and tour operators often offer you the same trip you could plan for yourself with the kinds of hotels you really want to stay at, but for less money. Check them out. Beware, however: On a package tour, you may not get as good a room as you would on your own, and your chances of being upgraded are lower.

- **Think competition.** When the George V closed to transform itself into the Four Seasons, two neighboring hotels—the deluxe Prince de Galles and the Queen Elizabeth—enjoyed increased business. With the Four Seasons now open, try these hotels, which may try to lure you with price cuts.

- **Don't forget online deals.** The hotels themselves as well as hotel discounters and specialty websites often offer great deals online. Spend time on this research, as websites can offer a variety of deals, often at the same hotel. I like Hotels.com. Remember, some discounters' websites charge for booking and do not let you cancel. When I find an attractive deal through a hotel broker, I call the reservations desk and ask them to match it on a personal basis.

- **Consider the grab-and-run technique.** I have a friend who came to Paris with a reservation for 3 nights at one hotel, but a plane ticket for a 10-day stay. She went online and checked hotel deals from a cybercafe in Paris and moved every few days, chasing the best deals and testing different hotels and neighborhoods.

- **Check out www.bonjourparis.com.** This site has tons of info on Paris (and all of France), as well as hotel deals. When booking with any online source, if you're considering a hotel you do not know, check out not only photos but also

My Two Favorite Apartment Rentals

Having lived in Paris, I often prefer to stay in an apartment, which enables me to relive my fantasies . . . and save. I have two apartments that I use regularly and I reluctantly share them with you. Book as far in advance as possible. Both are on the Left Bank and have excellent public transportation nearby.

A budget studio: This flat in the former loft or grange is charm personified, if you can handle the stairs and the lack of doorman or concierge. You walk through the building, through the courtyard, and into the rear building, where you go up two flights of stairs. There you find the studio of your dreams with exposed beams and even a sleeping loft, although you must be a gazelle to make it up to the loft. Open kitchen; sofa bed sleeps two (besides the bed in the loft); large bathtub; usual amenities like TV and Wi-Fi. The rate is 650€ ($975) per week but drops to a flat fee of 1,000€ ($1,500) for 2 weeks or 2,000€ ($3,000) for 4 weeks. Contact Simon by writing simonjhsn@gol.com.

A luxury two-bedroom: Also on the Left Bank, in a large bourgeois building near the top of the Luxembourg Gardens, this flat can sleep five and comes with maid service as well as a phone that offers unlimited free calls to the U.S. Two bedrooms, two bathrooms, Wi-Fi, TV, designer chic at 2,700€ (about $4,050) per week. You are also expected to tip the housekeeper another 50€ ($75). Contact KVF@gmail.com.

your own map. A hotel with buzzwords such as Tour Eiffel or Arc de Triomphe may not be very close to these landmarks, no matter what the name implies.

- **Rent an apartment.** If there are more than two in your group, you can get more of the feel of living in Paris—while saving money to boot—by renting an apartment. Go to www.VBRO.com, FindRentals.com, or any of a zillion other sites. An apartment might give you a lot more space (and flexibility) for the same rate as a hotel room. You also have the option to cook or eat a few meals in the apartment.

Comparing Palace Hotels

Palace hotels usually cost over 667€ ($1,000) a night. I have listed them in this edition because the shopper who is interested may want to compare, just to see what you're going to get for that kind of scratch. If you are more of a $500-a-night person, read on. And don't sweat it; I've got plenty at $200 a night below that.

Fouqets Barriere
av. George V, 8e (Métro: George V).

If there wasn't so much going on in Paris hotels, I'd say this was the most exciting thing to hit town. Certainly all my friends in town came over to gawk with delight.

   The hotel is a new-build adjoining the famous Fouquet's bistro on the Champs-Elysées. For the uninitiated, Fouquet's is a major showbiz hangout and the place where the celebs go after award ceremonies to see and be seen. Locals call this the bling-bling hotel because it is truly jaw-dropping in its chic and decor and technological advances. The TV in our room was invisible in a mirror until you turned it on. And get this: Everything in the minibar was free! This is the hotel created to put every other palace hotel onto its derrière.

RATES Rooms start at about 600€ ($900) per night.

CELEBRITIES It's the Cannes-do scene.

BEAUTY Jacques Garcia does it again.

EATS Fouquets is right downstairs; there's also a gourmet restaurant in a courtyard.

PACKAGES The Barriere hotel chain has among the best promotional deals in France.

FOR RESERVATIONS Call ℡ 800/745-8883 in the U.S. or 01-40-69-60-00 in France. Log on to www.lhw.com/FouquetsBarriere.

Four Seasons George V
31 av. George V, 8e (Métro: George V).

If you want to know why people pay the big bucks to stay here, it's not just the flowers, the decor, or the location. I must say, I've never, ever been pampered like this. Everyone in the hotel knew my name. (I am certain they have photo drills each night.) While the Internet service in the room was priced at 23€ ($35) per 24-hour period, guests are granted a half-hour a day of free Internet access in the business center. The price of local phone calls was obscene; the price of room service was moderate. There is a phone *cabine* in the lobby so that you can easily retreat there to use your phone card.

RATES You cannot get a room for under $667€ ($1,000) per night.

CELEBRITIES Movie-star heaven. No names, please.

BEAUTY The pool is gorgeous, as is the entire spa area. There's a wide variety of treatments, including one with chocolate. Bulgari bathroom amenities are freely stocked. The flowers, by Jeff Leatham, make the hotel one of the highlights of Paris.

EATS The three-star Le Cinq is famous, but La Galerie is a good place to eat and just stare at the flowers and the crowd. You'll pay 33€ ($50) for a burger lunch, but it's worth it considering the theater involved.

PACKAGES This hotel has various promotions that include a lot—such as a free spa treatment or dinner in the three-star restaurant.

For reservations from the U.S., call ℂ **800/819-5053,** or 01-49-52-70-00 locally; or log on to www.fourseasons.com.

Hôtel Meurice
228 rue de Rivoli, 1er (Métro: Concorde or Tuileries).

Oh my heavens, that's all I can say! Philippe Starck and his daughter have done over much of the public space, and your eyes will simply pop out of your head. Then there's the laven-der-flavored macaroons. If you can't stay here, at least come to tea to see what happens when Starck meets Dalí.

RATES   Officially begin at 800€ ($1,200).

CELEBRITIES   More European in its celebrity net, the hotel attracts a lot of fashion and publishing people, and royalty.

BEAUTY   The contrast of the Starck touches with the grande-dame nature of the palace is mesmerizing—the hotel is simply stunning and staggering in its drama.

EATS   The chef, Yannick Alléno, has three stars and offers up a creative *carte*; one of the best deals in town is the lunch. The dining room is as gorgeous as the food.

PACKAGES   The variety of packages can make the high prices more attractive; for example, the "Just Between Us" package provides shopping addresses, a private shopping tour, and various perks at luxury stores. Reservations for this package must be made at least 3 weeks before arrival (to line up your tour) and are based on double or triple occupancy—perfect if a bunch of girls want to go together on a Paris shopping spree and can share a room.

   For reservations from the U.S., call Leading Hotels of the World (© **800/223-6800,** or 01-44-58-10-10 locally; fax 01-44-58-10-15).

Royal Monceau
35 Av. Hoche, 8e (Métro: Etoile).

As I write this, the hotel is closed, not to reopen until 2009. Still, you need to know all about it as this is earmarked to be the next hottest thing in hotel flavors with a Philippe Starck interior (what else ?). I know the GM from Cannes and he went to the Crillon in between gigs; so we are talking big-time VIP amenities. Film at 11.

Not Quite Palaces

If you love your luxury hotel, but prefer to pay under $400 a night for a room, you'll find that the above hotels are out of your budget. In fact, it's pretty hard to find a deluxe hotel that combines amenities with price. Here are a few suggestions that get my vote; prices are in the $500-per-night range.

Hilton Arc de Triomphe
51–57 rue de Courcelles, 8e (Métro: Courcelles).

This hotel is swank beyond imagination with theatrical Art Deco everything, from lobby to rooms. The staff is fabulous and the air is far more friendly than at a more formal palace. The only downside is that the place has 512 units, so if you want small and *intime,* it isn't for you. Also note that the folks who stay here—or the ones I see in the lobby, anyway—tend to be more casually dressed than the guests at the Four Seasons or the Meurice. There seem to be a lot of groups, too. This hotel is the single-most popular destination for bookings with mileage points.

This hotel opened in May 2004 and is like no other Hilton in the world. The hotel bought the rights to the Emile-Jacques Ruhlmann estate, so the Art Deco theme more than permeates the space—it's a total movie set combining genuine signed pieces with reproductions from the original drawings. (Yes, you can buy the furniture.)

The location seems odd at first—this is essentially a residential area—but you're within walking distance of all major streets and can enjoy the hidden charms of the rue Courcelles (with one of the best resale shops in Paris). The first Carita/Decleor spa is here, called Mosaics. The no. 84 bus, right outside the front door, connects the hotel to all of Paris if you aren't walking or taking the nearby Métro.

The rate is usually around 333€ to 400€ ($500–$600); I did Expedia and found a double for $520, which, if you get a promotional deal, can include breakfast for two. Breakfast is a very comprehensive buffet. Call © **800-HILTONS** in the U.S., or 01-58-36-17-17 locally, or log on to www.hilton.com.

Tip: The "other" Hilton, called Hilton Suffern, is next to the Eiffel Tower and is somewhat shabby. However, I could have booked it for $266, half off the fancy Hilton.

Hotel de Sers

41 av. Pierre 1er de Serbie, 8e (Métro: George V or Alma-Marceau).

The atrium, which uses a projector to change the colors of light, thus affecting the mood and ambience, is a nice touch; the concierge service sent me a printout to confirm all bookings and a map with walking instructions. The attention to details was seductive. The clients were very hip—the kind of travelers who always wear black.

The hotel is smack-dab in the middle of the luxury 8e shopping district, around the corner from the Four Seasons George V. There is an Internet station in the lobby or free access in your room, if you have your computer with you.

Best yet, while my room had a price tag of 420€ ($630) inside the closet, I had booked with Yellin Hotels (www.yellinhotels.com) and was paying 223€ ($335), a rate that included continental breakfast. I'd return in a heartbeat. The local phone number is © **01-53-23-75-75**. Or log on to www.hoteldesers.com.

Hotel Pont Royal

7 rue Montalembert, 7e (Métro: Rue du Bac).

This is one of those hidden-in-plain-sight finds that you might overlook because it isn't flashy. The hotel has one of the best shopping locations in Paris, especially if you love the Left Bank—it's more or less at the corner of rue du Bac and boulevard St-Germain. There are buses and the Métro out the door and you can walk easily to the major museums. If you are a foodie, you already know that Atelier de Joel Robuchon is in the hotel and Pierre Gagnier's Gaya is across the street.

The hotel itself is a little bit British in feel, in an old, French aristocratic manner. The lobby is paneled in wood; the furnishings throughout are *moderne*. It's a homey little palace, not one that makes you nervous. The hotel is known for its place in literary circles and is also a registered landmark. Note that it is a member of a small chain, HRR (Hotel et Residence Roy)—the other hotels are hidden jewels as well, although not always at bargain prices.

The hotel website had a number of promotions and fair deals with prices beginning just under 200€ ($300). A good offer through Yellin Hotels: bed-and-breakfast with all taxes and everything included, in high season, with upgrade, for 223€ ($335). The local phone number is ✆ 01-42-84-70-00, or check www.hotel-pont-royal.com or www.yellinhotels.com.

Value Luxury Hotels

The hotels below are four-star finds, nicer, fancier, or jazzier than my "finds" above, but more expensive and often visited by groups. Since their rates can be 333€ ($500) a night, they are an alternative to luxury $1,000-a-night beds but a step above a three-star.

Hotel du Louvre
Place André Malraux, 1er (Métro: Palais-Royal).

This hotel hosts some of the fashion shows during the spring and fall collections. It is directly across the street from the Louvre and Palais Royale. Local phone ✆ 01-44-58-38-38.

Hotel St-Lazare
108 rue St-Lazare, 8e (Métro: St-Lazare).

Rooms here are uneven; don't be shy if you don't like your room—ask to see others. The hotel itself is a landmark

Reasonable Rates:
From Expedia, with Love

Right before this book went to the editors, I went online and checked out summer rates at Expedia—they were flat rates covering July and August and were listed in USD. I found a very nice selection of what I have to call "in-between hotels." This means they are slightly over $200 (in most cases) but stay just under $500.

I am listing only hotels that I have stayed in or at least know well, and it's hard to make value judgments—since there's about a $100 difference between the Lotti and the Ambassador Opera, I'd probably take the Ambassador. *But*, the Lotti is a very nice hotel, and to many people the location alone could be worth the extra $100 a night. Frankly, I think you have to know Paris very well in order to make wise choices here, but I just want to give you some spread.

I would stay in any of these hotels and have, in fact, stayed in most of them.

Base-line information: The **Marriott Champs-Elysées** was listed at $832 per night.

- **Ambassador Opera** (east of Galeries Lafayette): $239
- **Le Faubourg Sofitel** (across from Crillon): $372
- **Lotti** (across from the Meurice): $338
- **Lutétia** (only grande dame on Left Bank, at Sevres Babylone near Bon Marché): $282
- **Westin** (across from the Meurice): $462
- **InterContinental Le Grand** (overlooking Garnier Opera): $443
- **Hotel Montaigne** (boutique hotel on av. Montaigne, the luxury shopping street): $330
- **Normandy** (slightly shabby, fab, old grande dame near Louvre): $177

building and has the wonderful location of being next to the St-Lazare train station and a block from major department stores. I just found this at a summer rate—for high and low season—for $239 on Expedia. I lived in this hotel once and can recommend it if you don't mind tour groups. Local phone ✆ 01-40-08-44-44.

Millennium Opera

12 bd Haussmann, 9e (Métro: Chaussée-d'Antin).

This could be the insider's find of the day. Located 2 blocks east of Galeries Lafayette (and, yes, the Garnier Opéra), the hotel is grand, chic, and seemingly unknown. Therefore, it offers incredible rates. I found it on Expedia for under $200 a night; my friends used the hotel site and got an even better rate—and for high season! The location takes a little bit of getting used to, but at these prices you're going to love it. Upgrade yourself to a club floor and get many perks. Call ✆ 01-49-49-16-00 locally, or log on to www.millenniumhotels.com.

Suzy's Secret 3-Star Finds

There are a few chains that invariably come in with rates around 133€ ($200) with good locations in Paris. I like **Golden Tulip** as well as **Best Western.** I'm not wild for Citadines, which offers apartment hotels that are too spare for my tastes. There's a large **Holiday Inn** at République that was listed for $168 a night, which is a perfectly respectable eastern Paris area for those folks who like real-people Paris. I'm also not shy about suggesting you look into **La Defense,** a business park outside Paris with good transportation (5 min. to Champs-Elysées) and large, modern, chain hotels as well as an excellent shopping mall.

Hotel de l'Elysee

12 rue Saussaies, 8e (Métro: Champs-Elysées Clemenceau or Miromesnil).

If I had a hotel like this in every city, I'd be a happy traveler. This is a small three-star, 1 block from the rue du Faubourg

St-Honoré. It's charming and well priced—expect to pay about 167€ ($250) a night. Some rooms are a tad dark; ask for a front-of-the-house room if you care. Continental breakfast is $15 more. Rooms are not huge, but the decor is comfy. Some bathrooms have tubs; some do not. TVs do have CNN; there is an Internet station in the lobby. The local phone number is © 01-42-65-29-25. You can sometimes book through Orbitz at © 800/733-5916.

Hotel Ferrandi
92 rue du Cherchemidi, 6e (Métro: Vanneau).

Rooms in this gem go for 133€ to 200€ ($200–$300) per night and offer everything you want in terms of intimate small hotel, cozy decor and a photo-worthy main salon in this 30-room wonder. Each room is different but is filled with antiques. The hotel is part of a small chain of three-stars; check out www.hotels-paris-rive-gauche.com for the other properties, which tend to be a little farther east, all on the Left Bank. In August, even the best rooms are under $200 per night. © 01-42-22-97-40. www.leferrandi.com.

Dining with Care

On my last flight back to the U.S. from Paris, I sat next to a 15-year-old guy who was on a school trip to Spain and France. I asked him about the highlights of his trip ("futbol") and the food. The food, he explained, had not been very good except for his last night. He was bumped from his return flight and given a free overnight voucher for hotel and dinner at an airport hotel. There he had the best meal of his young life . . . and finally discovered what all the fuss is about.

Since even your most basic (and average) meals are going to be expensive, choose them with care.

DINING $MARTS

In the land of the 5.35€ ($8) Coca-Cola, you need to be careful. First tip: Don't drink Coca-Cola.

Other thoughts:

- Avoid "organic" foods at fresh food markets. They are called *bio* in French and are 30% more expensive than regular.
- Consider food shopping at gas stations that have minimarts. The Shell station on the rue de Rennes near St-Germain-des-Prés has the least expensive rôti chickens in town.
- Picnic more often. Buy foods in grocery stores or at street markets.
- Test neighborhood *traiteurs* who provide already-cooked foodstuffs and meals.
- Consider le fast fooding.
- Visit the famous chefs for lunch, not dinner. You get the same food at substantially lower prices. Ducasse offers an 80€ ($120) menu at **Jules Verne** (inside the Eiffel Tower) that will knock your socks off.
- Use Alexander Lobrano's book *Hungry for Paris* (www.hungryforparis.com), which recommends many eateries with fixed-price meals at 33€ to 50€ per person. While that's still 33€ to 50€ ($50–$75) per head, for Paris that's not bad. His list is not a roundup of the usual suspects, so be flexible and try something new.

Chapter 4

Shopping Quartiers in Paris

The Bastille Is Up

Paris is a city of neighborhoods. The word *arrondissement* is not synonymous with *neighborhood*—each arrondissement contains many neighborhoods, or quartiers. Some quartiers straddle portions of two arrondissements.

As a tourist, you'll probably stick to a dozen or so must-see neighborhoods to which you'll want to return someday. Some areas you visit only for shopping, but for the most part, you wander to take in everything—sights, shopping, dining, and more. Certain streets will fulfill all your fantasies of what Paris should be. While the city limits sprawl all the way to the highway loop Périphérique (and beyond), my parts of town are compact and easy to manage.

Left Bank Shopping Quartiers

When it comes to shopping in Paris, you must decide if you are just looking or if you actually want to buy something. Do you want a fantasy experience or a real-people experience? Do you mind crowds of tourists, or would you prefer to be surrounded by the people whose home you have invaded? Is your time so limited that you just want the one address that will give you the most value? Please answer these questions for yourself as you read up on my favorite shopping districts and browsing treats. *Allons-y.*

The St-Germain-des-Prés Métro stop works for all the main touristy and tony shopping areas on the Left Bank, except for the far-flung ones, which by definition aren't the touristy ones.

If you have no particular plan, but want to browse the best of the Left Bank, just look at a map, pinpoint convenient Métro stops, and decide where you want to be around noon. I often arrange my patterns of exploration so that I end up leaving the Left Bank through the Sèvres-Babylone or the Rue du Bac Métro stop (because then I don't have to change trains). At the end of a hard day's shopping, especially if you are laden with packages, you might want to forgo a long, complicated journey on the Métro. Look at bus route maps to adjust to your own digs.

If you prefer a taxi, flagging one can be difficult in this area. Go to the Lutétia or to the taxi rank in front of Café Lipp near Emporio Armani on boulevard St-Germain.

ST-GERMAIN-DES-PRÉS, 6E

MÉTRO St-Germain-des-Prés.

SHOPPING SCENE Does anyone here speak French? Young, hip, and busy, but very touristy.

PROFILE To many visitors, this is the core of their Paris. They don't even care that more and more designer stores are moving in. They just want to sit at a cafe and feel like they're part of this world.

St-Germain-des-Prés is the main drag of the Left Bank and the center of the universe. Take the Métro or have a taxi drop you at the church, and you'll be at the center of the action, ready to hunt down the stores and the shoppers.

The Left Bank

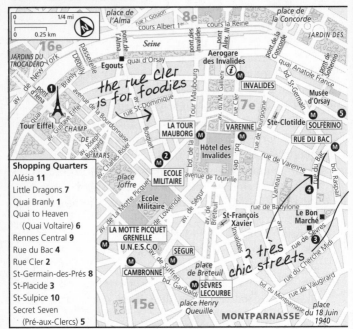

Shopping Quarters

Alésia **11**
Little Dragons **7**
Quai Branly **1**
Quai to Heaven
  (Quai Voltaire) **6**
Rennes Central **9**
Rue du Bac **4**
Rue Cler **2**
St-Germain-des-Prés **8**
St-Placide **3**
St-Sulpice **10**
Secret Seven
  (Pré-aux-Clercs) **5**

You can begin the day with breakfast (coffee and crois-sants) at any number of famous cafes, like **Les Deux Magots** or **Café de Flore.** Sure, a cup of espresso costs 4€ ($6) and fancy coffee or hot chocolate costs up to 6€ ($9), but this is the greatest show on earth. You can sit for hours and watch the passing parade. By the way, Café de Flore has the best hot chocolate in Paris.

Stores that can afford the rent on the boulevard cluster around here. In addition to **Etro, Emporio Armani,** and other big names, there's **Sonia Rykiel,** at no. 175, and **Shu Uemura,** a fabulous Japanese cosmetics firm, at no. 176.

Note: On the surface, this area is very touristy, but as you get closer to the Seine and into the design showrooms and fancy antiques shops, the air changes—as does the attitude. These stores and dealers are very closed; they prefer their own company or rich French speakers who know their stuff. There

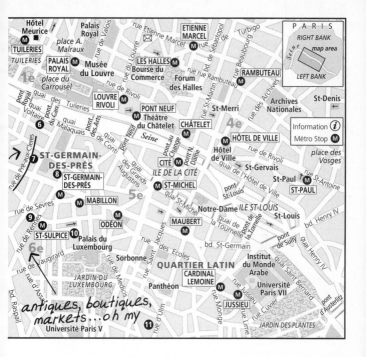

are plenty of snobby and status-y places back here that tourists never visit or find.

RENNES CENTRAL, 6E & 14E

MÉTRO St-Germain-des-Prés or St-Sulpice.

SHOPPING SCENE Real-people Montparnasse (14e) leads to touristy Left Bank.

PROFILE At one of the major intersections of the Left Bank, two streets converge in a V—the rue de Rennes and the rue Bonaparte. Bonaparte runs behind the church as well; Rennes does not.

Rue de Rennes is the central drag of this trading area. It's a pretty big street with a lot of retail stores; the farther it goes from St-Germain, the less fancy the stores become. Rue de Rennes has a big-city feel, so it isn't exactly the charming Left Bank scene you may have expected.

Closer to boulevard St-Germain, rue de Rennes holds many big-name designer shops, from **Celine** to **Habitat,** as well as **Gap, Stefanel, Kenzo,** and **Burberry.** Also here are a number of hotshot boutiques, such as **Loft,** and trendsetters like **Estéban** (home scents).

LITTLE DRAGONS, 6E
MÉTRO Sèvres-Babylone or St-Germain-des-Prés.

SHOPPING SCENE Shoe freaks.

PROFILE West of Rennes Central (see previous listing) are several very small, narrow streets crammed with good things to eat and to wear. They are epitomized by the **rue du Dragon,** which is why I call this neighborhood Little Dragons. The bus stop calls it Croix Rouge.

You'll want to check out rue de Grenelle and rue des Sts-Pères and this part of the rue du Cherche-Midi. Just wander—get lost, get found. This whole warren of streets abounds with great shops, many belonging to designers of fame.

The area is sandwiched between the Sèvres-Babylone Métro stop and the neighborhood I call Rennes Central. To one side is **Le Bon Marché,** one of Paris's biggest and most famous department stores. You can also easily walk to St-Placide from here (see below).

ST-SULPICE, 6E
MÉTRO Mabillon, St-Sulpice, or St-Germain-des-Prés.

SHOPPING SCENE Chic, in the know.

PROFILE The core of this area lies between rue Bonaparte and place St-Sulpice. It comes complete with a gorgeous church, a park, several designer shops (**Castelbajac, YSL**), and the new **Shanghai Tang** (inside Maison de la Chine). Also here is the jewel-box pastry shop of Paris's most famous pastry chef, **Pierre Hermé,** 72 rue Bonaparte.

This area stretches behind the park and *place,* over to the rue Tournon and the rue de Seine, and includes the American-style mall **Marché St-Germain.** The side streets are full of small designer shops, exciting to discover.

RUE CLER, 7E

MÉTRO Ecole Militaire or Motte-Picquet.

SHOPPING SCENE Foodies.

PROFILE The Sunday-morning market on the rue Cler, in the 7e adjoining the 15e, is one of my favorite Sunday treats. Some consider it just another Paris food market. I consider it a religious experience. There is a market every day except Monday. Sunday is simply the most fun.

RUE DU BAC, 7E

MÉTRO Sèvres-Babylone or Rue du Bac.

SHOPPING SCENE Left Bank snobbish.

PROFILE As a residential neighborhood, you can't beat the 7e—not even in the 16e. As a shopping neighborhood, you can't beat the **rue du Bac,** especially if you like looking at the lifestyles of the rich and Parisienne.

You can get here by the easy method or the longer, more complicated, but more fun method. For the former, take the Métro to the Rue du Bac stop and walk away from the river on rue du Bac. For the latter, begin on the Right Bank, cross the bridge at the Louvre (see that bright golden statue of Jeanne d'Arc?), and hit the quai at rue du Bac. Walk toward the Rue du Bac Métro stop and away from the river. You get 3 or 4 more blocks of shopping this way. While it's not the best part of the rue du Bac, it's great fun. The street twists a bit, but just wander, following the street signs. You will quit rue du Bac only when you get to **Le Bon Marché.**

SECRET SEVEN: PRÉ-AUX-CLERCS, 7E

MÉTRO Rue du Bac.

SHOPPING SCENE Privately chic. You came with the car and driver, didn't you?

PROFILE This is just a 2-block stroll in another world, a world inhabited by very rich and chic women. This walk takes you along the rue du Pré-aux-Clercs, which lies between boulevard St-Germain and the river.

Left Bank Discount Neighborhoods

ALÉSIA, 14E
MÉTRO Alésia.

SHOPPING SCENE Discount heaven.

PROFILE This is one of the city's major discount districts. Prices in some places may not be the lowest, but there are a good half-dozen shops to choose from. Not every store in this area is a discount house, so ask if you are confused. Don't make any assumptions!

Most of the discount houses have the word *stock* in their name, which means they sell overruns. Some shops bear a designer's name plus the word *stock;* others have store names, without alluding to what is inside. **Stock 2,** a spacious space at 92 rue d'Alésia, sells men's, women's, and kids' designer clothes at discount prices. Most of it is from **Daniel Hechter,** but there are other brands as well.

Don't miss **Cacharel Stock** (no. 114), with fabulous baby and kids' clothes. It carries some men's and women's things, but I've never found anything worthwhile here that wasn't for children.

The stock shop of **Diapositive,** a big, hip line, is at no. 74. But the highlight of the block is undoubtedly **SR** (no. 64), which stands for—shout it out, folks—**Sonia Rykiel.** The clothes here are old, but they are true-blue Sonia.

When you shop this area, keep store hours in mind. Stores generally don't open until 2pm on Monday; many close for the entire month of August. And, again, remember that not all of the stores are discount; they just want you to think they are.

ST-PLACIDE, 7E

MÉTRO St-Placide or Sèvres-Babylone.

SHOPPING SCENE St-Placide abuts the chichi department store Bon Marché and feeds into fancy rue du Bac, but its style is a million miles away. This is a street of discounters and jobbers—tons of fun, if you like down-market shopping.

PROFILE This area is not particularly near Alésia (although you can walk from one to the other), but mentally the two are sisters—homes of the discount shop, the stock shop, the great bargain.

There are maybe 10 stock shops in this 2-block stretch. They are not inviting from the outside—you must be the kind of person who likes to rifle through racks and bins. The most exciting shops are **Vidya,** the Nitya outlet; **Crea,** an arts-and-crafts store that has nothing to do with discounts; and the local branch of **Le Mouton à Cinq Pattes.** St-Placide feels a bit seedy and isn't as attractive as Alésia—but there's nothing wrong with the neighborhood, and it is safe. Not every store offers discounts, but many do.

Right Bank Shopping Quartiers

The neighborhoods below are listed in roughly geographical order, starting in the west with the 16e and working to the east.

PASSY, 16E

MÉTRO Passy or La Muette.

SHOPPING SCENE Rich casual, with a black-velvet headband and pearls.

PROFILE Passy is the main commercial street in one of the nicest districts in one of the nicest arrondissements. It has a little of everything and is convenient to other neighborhoods. You can visit Passy on your way to the Eiffel Tower, Trocadéro, or the resale shops of the 16e, or you can catch the Métro and be anywhere else in minutes. If possible, visit Passy on a Saturday morning—then you will really be French.

The Right Bank

The street has been booming ever since the opening of **Passy Plaza,** an American-style mall with that number-one American tenant, Gap. Go to Passy Plaza for a lesson in French yuppie sociology. Shop the supermarket in the lower level, the various branches of American and British big names, and the French candy store.

Franck et Fils, a small department store formerly for blue-haired old ladies with apricot poodles, has been redone. Now, somewhat in the style of a smaller Bon Marché, it is very chic.

Shopping Adventure

Actually, I'm sending you to a street market here—it stretches from Lena to Alma-Marceau and is held on Wednesdays and Saturdays. The market is mostly food but has some spices, soaps, and dry goods and a delightful look at the rich as they shop.

VICTOR HUGO, 16E

MÉTRO Victor-Hugo.

SHOPPING SCENE Chic, French, and rich . . . with well-groomed dogs.

PROFILE This uptown residential neighborhood is still where the big money shops. Victor Hugo is one of the fanciest shopping streets in Paris. Years ago, many big-name international designers had shops here. Most of them have moved, giving the neighborhood a more intimate feel. Today, most shoppers appear to be regulars who live nearby. This isn't the kind of street tourists normally visit to actually shop; you come here to get a feel for a certain part of Paris, to experience a lifestyle that is totally unknown in America, and to pretend you're a French aristocrat.

GEORGE V, 8E

MÉTRO George V or Alma-Marceau.

SHOPPING SCENE Between two Métro stops, this area is hidden in plain sight; it's a "secret" district of small boutiques where the staffs know shoppers—and their dogs—by name. There are some name-brand stores, but most are either in the cult league (**Creed** perfumes) or tiny branches (**Hermès**).

PROFILE This nugget centers on avenue Pierre 1er de Serbie, between Alma-Marceau (and av. Montaigne) and the Champs-Elysées. The Four Seasons George V is at the heart of this area and its surrounding shops.

CHAMPS-ELYSÉES, 8E

MÉTRO Franklin D. Roosevelt.

SHOPPING SCENE Outdoor mall.

PROFILE The tourist mobs and shopping-cinema-cafe ratio make this one of the most crowded parts of Paris. The stores go from the ridiculous to the sublime. In a single block, there's Virgin Megastore, the Disney Store, and Monoprix. At the far end, closer to the Arc de Triomphe, is the newly reopened Le Drugstore; across the street is a brand-new branch of Cartier. Someone thinks the neighborhood is on the way up.

Along the way, you'll see numerous car showrooms, parfumeries, drugstores, movie theaters, airline offices, cafes, and change booths. A few big-name designers have stores here. The **Galerie du Claridge** minimall has two levels (go downstairs, too) and the best selection of the kinds of shops you want to see; most of them are big names. **Starbucks** has joined up too, but is a tad hard to find.

If time is precious, you might want to make sure you've paid homage at **Monoprix,** 109 rue de la Boétie, and popped into **Paris St-Germain,** where you can have football shirts imprinted with the name of your choice. Go to the cinema in English and eat at a car showroom—check out the cafe in the **Renault** showroom for a snack, lunch, or dinner.

In the past few years, the Champs-Elysées has changed a lot, and some of it has been changing for a long time: The **Disney Store, Virgin Megastore,** and flagship **Sephora** brought new life to the most famous street in Paris. Then came the tearoom **Ladurée, Louis Vuitton** (where Japanese visitors may beg you to stand in line for them), and the **Gap** flagship. There are also branches of French chains like **Lacoste, Petit Bateau,** and the French equivalent of Gap, **Celio,** as well as a spurt of luxury brands at the top end, such as **Cartier** and **Montblanc.**

AVENUE MONTAIGNE, 8E

MÉTRO Franklin D. Roosevelt or Alma-Marceau.

SHOPPING SCENE The internationally rich, chic, and bored.

PROFILE Landmark shoppers. The avenue Montaigne has become a monument to itself. **Dior** and **Ricci** have always been here. For years, the **Chanel** boutique was a secret jealously guarded by those in the know. Then, Montaigne became the mega-address it is now. Of course, the Italians also came: **Krizia, Ferragamo, Max Mara,** and **Dolce & Gabbana.**

One stroll down the short street's 2 blocks of retail stores will give you a look at those famous names, as well as **Loewe, Thierry Mugler, Ungaro, Porthault, Celine, Christian Lacroix,** and **Valentino.**

Some of the other places are old-fashioned French shops that deserve a visit just to soak up the atmosphere. Try **Au Duc de Praslin** (for candy and nuts) and **Parfums Caron,** with its giant glass bottles filled with scents not carried in department stores in Paris, let alone America.

RUE DU FAUBOURG ST-HONORÉ, 8E

MÉTRO Concorde.

SHOPPING SCENE Rich regulars from out of town.

PROFILE This used to be the fanciest retail therapy in town. Now there are some multiples (chain stores) and some wannabe big names. **Façonnable** has moved in, but so have **La Perla** (jazzy lingerie and bathing suits), **Tod's,** and even **Lolita Lempicka.** Old standbys range from **Hermès** (check out the expanded flagship) to **Sonia Rykiel,** with international big names (**Bottega Veneta, Ferragamo**) thrown in.

MADELEINE, 8E

MÉTRO Madeleine.

SHOPPING SCENE Upscale international, plus foodie heaven.

PROFILE Scads of food specialty shops cluster here. The heart of the area is a string of famous food shops almost in a row— **Hédiard, Fauchon, Nicolas** (the wine shop), **Maison de la Truffe,** and more. Fauchon has all but gutted itself and started over, and now has an extremely interesting tea department.

Stretching away from the church on rue Royale, there's **Polo/Ralph Lauren** and the glass-and-porcelain showrooms that give way to the name-brand shopping on **Faubourg St-Honoré.**

Now, what I call the New Madeleine is a single block on the Baccarat (west) side of the Madeleine church. Boulevard Malesherbes has long been home to Baccarat and Burberry. Now there are three new stores in a row: **Sia, Shiseido,** and **Résonances.**

HIDDEN MADELEINE, 8E

MÉTRO Madeleine or Concorde.

SHOPPING SCENE Real people who know what they are doing and where they are going.

PROFILE I've nicknamed **rue Vignon** "Honey Street" because it's the home of the **Maison de Miel,** one of the leading specialists in French honey. This street runs on the other side of **Fauchon** (just as the rue Boissy d'Anglas runs behind Hédiard). Vignon holds a few smaller clothing shops, as well as other places I like to explore. It's chic without being touristy. This is one of my favorite streets in Paris, and I often use it as my route for cutting over to *les grands magasins*. There are now a number of soap stores, and since the French invented the process that created triple-milled soap, this is a good place to get souvenirs.

DEPARTMENT-STORE HEAVEN, 9E

MÉTRO Havre-Caumartin or Chaussée d'Antin.

SHOPPING SCENE In summer, a zoo. At other times, middle- to upper-middle-class French suburbanites and out-of-towners mix with an international crowd.

PROFILE This 3-block-long, 2-block-deep jumble of merchandise, pushcarts, strollers, and shoppers is a central trading area. You need to see it now because of the brand-new Lafayette Maison store. Go early (9:30am), when you're feeling strong and the crowds aren't in full swing. Winter is far less zoolike than summer.

The two major department stores are reinventing themselves in front of our very eyes. Both **Au Printemps** and **Galeries Lafayette** have redone their various buildings. Furthermore, Galeries has opened another store called **Lafayette Maison,** for home style; it will knock your socks off. Also check out **Lafayette Gourmet,** the grocery store—it's fabulous, with a new wine library and much more to make you dizzy with delight.

You can enter the new area from the rue de Provence. Speaking of rue de Provence, this is a great street (although it's more like an alley) to know about. Printemps has three buildings in a cluster here and has also opened **Citadium,** an architectural wonder of a French version of the Nike store.

Where the rue de Provence crosses the pedestrian rue de Caumartin, you can pop into **Monoprix** (downstairs, below the Citadium) or walk north to **Passage le Havre,** half a block away. This is an American-style mall, with **FNAC, Sephora,** and many branches of popular midlevel French clothing chains.

On the far side of Galeries Lafayette, toward the rue Lafayette, there's **Bouchara** for affordable home style and a brand-new, giant-size **Sephora** across the street.

RUE DE RIVOLI, PART ONE, 1ER

MÉTRO Concorde or Tuileries.

SHOPPING SCENE International tourists on their way somewhere.

PROFILE The rue de Rivoli is the main drag that runs along the back side of the Louvre. The Louvre was once a fortress, which is why it seems to go on forever. They just don't build 'em like that anymore. Exit the Métro at Concorde and face away from the Eiffel Tower. Now you're ready to walk.

I call this part of the street "Part One" because it is the main tourist area (see p. 76 for the scoop on Part Two). The rue de Rivoli continues after the Louvre, but has an entirely different character. Part One has a few chic shops toward the Hôtel de Crillon end, but soon becomes a good street for bookstores, such as **W. H. Smith.** As you get closer to the Louvre, the stores get more touristy. Here you'll find tons of tourist traps, all in a row.

OPÉRA, 1ER

MÉTRO Opéra.

SHOPPING SCENE Touristy.

PROFILE Transition City. The avenue de l'Opéra, running between the Garnier Opéra and the Palais Royal, has always been a big commercial street with little of interest except for a lot of airline offices. Now things are looking up: The first **Starbucks** in Paris opened in the middle of the block (Métro: Pyramides), and more and more nice stores are coming onboard.

Old standbys include **Brentano's** bookstore and **Monoprix.** Along with the reopening of the InterContinental Grand and the redone **Café de la Paix,** there's also a **Benetton** store in the next block and a newly redone **Lancel** across the street. The well-known duty-free cosmetics firms **Michel Swiss** and **Raoul et Curly** are both on avenue de l'Opéra.

PLACE VENDÔME, 1ER

MÉTRO Tuileries or Opéra.

SHOPPING SCENE Hidden, quiet, discreet.

PROFILE Ritzy. The far side of the place Vendôme is the rue de la Paix, which dead-ends 2 blocks later into place de l'Opéra. There are more jewelers here (including **Tiffany & Co.**) than on West 47th Street in New York. Well, sort of. It seems Paris is living through the War of the Couture Jewelers. It's not enough that every fancy jewelry shop has always been represented here—**Chanel** decided to move in with its own real-jewelry store (none of that costume stuff, please). To up the ante, **Dior** opened a real-jewelry store nearby. Is it hot here, or what? Maybe these diamonds just make me sweaty.

Don't confuse **Charvet** (a men's store) with **Chaumet,** a jeweler. There are several men's haberdashers on this street—everyone from **Alain** (Figaret) to **Zegna,** with lots of storefronts now taken over by **Alfred Dunhill.** Figaret is not quite as famous as others in the neighborhood, but is a local hero for shirt making for both men and women. There's also a range of **Armani,** from the high-end store on your left (with Opéra to your rear) to **Emporio** on your right.

RUE ST-HONORÉ, 1ER

MÉTRO Concorde, Tuileries, Madeleine, or Opéra.

SHOPPING SCENE In the know.

PROFILE This is a district I think of as "Behind the Meurice." It includes not only the rue St-Honoré, which begins at the rue Royale, but lots of side streets and hidden shopping venues, such as the Marché St-Honoré. The district also includes the rue Castiglione. Packed with designer shops of known and unknown reputations (**Jacqueline Peres, Annick Goutal, Guerlain, Payot, Hans Stern**), rue Castiglione is the connecting street from the Tuileries to the place Vendôme and rue de la Paix.

Okay, so here's the inside scoop: The Faubourg St-Honoré got the reputation, but in truth, the big-name designer shops do not end where the Faubourg St-Honoré changes names and becomes plain-old rue St-Honoré, which happens once you cross the rue Royale.

On the plain-old rue St-Honoré, there are branches or flagship stores of everyone from **Joseph** (British stylemeister, with cafe) to **Grès** (as in Madame), including names we would follow anywhere, like **Longchamp, Hervé Chapelier,** and **Nitya.** As you move uptown toward the Palais Royal, you find **Goyard,** a luggage brand that is older than Louis Vuitton; **Colette** the infamous; and the teeny-weeny **Astier de Villatte.**

PALAIS ROYAL, VICTOIRES & BEYOND, 1ER & 2E

MÉTRO Palais-Royal.

SHOPPING SCENE Trendsetters.

PROFILE If you want your shopping experience very French, upscale, and special, this is it. The **Jardin du Palais Royal** is my single-best Paris shopping experience. (It's good for non-shopping husbands who can appreciate the park, the history, and much style.) The Jardin du Palais Royal and the area around Victoires have seen a good bit of turnover. The don't-miss-it retailer is the gardening shop **Le Prince Jardinier,** which is next door to **Shiseido**'s perfume shop—an older must-do if there ever was one. Note that the brand has launched a dozen new scents. Across the way is the new **Marc Jacobs** boutique, which leaves me cold. Give me **Didier Ludot** and his resale wonders any day.

You'll find the place des Victoires nestled behind the Jardin du Palais Royal, where the 1er and the 2e connect. Facing it is a circle of hotels; the ground floor of each holds retail space. Wonderful shops fill the streets that radiate from the *place*.

The main drag is the **rue Etienne Marcel,** which has long housed some of the big *créateurs* (designers). You can save this area for last, and depart the neighborhood by browsing this street before heading toward the Forum des Halles or the

Beaubourg. Or you can start your stroll from the Etienne Marcel Métro stop and work backward.

The rue Etienne Marcel is important in the lexicon of high style because so many cutting-edge designers, many of them Japanese, are here. There has also been an influx of stores for women who wear very tight jeans, such as **Diesel Style Lab** (35 rue Etienne Marcel), **Miss Sixty** (49 rue Etienne Marcel), and **Replay** (36 rue Etienne Marcel). Peep into **Kokon To Zai** (48 rue Tiquetonne), which also has a branch in London.

If you care, note that one side of Etienne Marcel is in the 1er and the other is in the 2e. The extension, **rue Tiquetonne** (which has a ton of good stores), is also in the 2e. Don't forget to check your trusty map before you leave Victoires—you can continue in any number of directions. You can easily walk to the Forum des Halles or Opéra, or to the boulevard Haussmann and the big department stores, or to the rue de Rivoli and the Louvre. The world starts at Victoires, and it's a magnificent world.

MONTORGUEIL, 1ER & 2E
MÉTRO Les Halles

SHOPPING SCENE If it's good enough for Queen Elizabeth II, then it might interest you, too.

PROFILE This is a small pedestrian area, tucked next to Les Halles and famous for its food markets and vendors. It's especially bustling on a weekend and offers up that real-Paris feel that will make you want to move in. There are several restaurants and many historic storefronts—some shops have no numbers and possibly no names. Just take it all in, hungrily.

LES HALLES, 1ER/MIDTOWN-BEAUBOURG, 3E
MÉTRO Les Halles or Rambuteau.

SHOPPING SCENE Funky; teen- and tourist-oriented.

PROFILE Two landmarks dominate this area: the American-style mall at **Les Halles** (which replaced the famed food halls) and the **Centre Georges Pompidou,** the art museum.

Surrounding them are all sorts of shopping styles, from museum stores to vintage-clothing shops to those that sell videos and posters and books and faience. (Don't ask me why the **Quimper** people opened a store in this district, at 15 rue St-Martin.) While a mall may not be your idea of how you want to shop in Paris, if it's raining, remember that Les Halles is large and filled with branches of all the big names in international retail. It's mobbed on Saturdays.

RUE DE RIVOLI, PART TWO, 1ER & 4E

MÉTRO Pont Neuf or Hôtel de Ville.

SHOPPING SCENE Real, with some emphasis on teens, tweens, and real-people budgets.

PROFILE The rue de Rivoli changes names to become the rue St-Antoine, leading directly to the Bastille. Along the way are some junk shops and discounters, as well as the path to the place des Vosges and the Village St-Paul.

I like this part of the rue de Rivoli—a zoo on Saturday, by the way—because it packs in a lot, and the stores are not too expensive. It's changed a lot and now has a lot of well-priced shops. They might not offer couture, but they have stuff to look at and things real people can afford to buy.

Etam, Cité de la Femme, has made a huge impact by opening an enormous department store, not like the dinky Etam branches all over Europe. I like **C&A,** the Dutch department store that is not known for upscale shoppers or chic fashions. It carries copies of fashion looks, big sizes (by French standards), and washable clothes (who can afford dry cleaning?), and nothing costs more than 50€ ($75).

MARAIS/PLACE DES VOSGES, 3E & 4E

MÉTRO St-Paul.

SHOPPING SCENE Fabulous, funky fun; Sunday-afternoon "in" scene.

PROFILE The rebirth of the Marais is no longer news, but new shops continue to open, making it a pleasurable area to explore every time you visit Paris. From the Métro, follow the signs toward place des Vosges. Or take a taxi to the **Musée Picasso** and wander until you end up at the place des Vosges. (This is difficult wandering; you will need a map if you start at the Picasso Museum.)

The area between the church of St-Paul and the Seine holds the **Village St-Paul** (for antiques). The Marais lies across rue St-Antoine and is hidden from view as you emerge from the Métro. You may be disoriented; I've gotten lost a number of times. That's why taking a taxi here is a good idea. There's also no hint of charm until you reach the Marais.

While the heart of the neighborhood is the place des Vosges, this is a pretty big neighborhood with lots of tiny, meandering streets to wander. Take in the arcade that surrounds the *place*. The side streets are dense with opportunities, from the chic charm of **Romeo Gigli** to the American country looks of **Chevignon.**

The main shopping drag is **rue Francs-Bourgeois;** look for it on a map when you're at the Picasso Museum, as the medieval streets tend to get you turned around. This street has a few cafes, a few stores that sell used family silverware by weight, and many branches of high-style stores, such as **Ventilo** for ethnic gloss and the newest branch of scent-master **Estéban.**

Between the well-known areas, a bunch of little streets house funky shops that sell everything from high-end hats to vintage clothing. Check out antiques at **Les Deux Orphelines,** 21 place des Vosges, and contemporary housewares and style at **Villa Marais,** 40 rue Francs-Bourgeois. Adjacent to all this is the Jewish ghetto, with stores that sell Judaica; check out the rue des Rosiers. There is talk about turning the rue des Rosiers into a pedestrian area, but shopkeepers are currently in revolt, not wanting construction work to slow down their business.

Because most stores are open on Sunday afternoon, the entire area is dead on Monday.

If you are sick of this area or find it too touristy, move over slightly within the upper 3e and check out **rue Charlot,** which is becoming the "in" destination for cutting-edge shops and fashion editors who look for the next word. The store **Food** has gotten a lot of the press in this area, but the whole street is filled with shops and eats.

THE ISLANDS, 4E

MÉTRO Pont Neuf or Cité; RER C: St-Michel.

SHOPPING SCENE Touristy, but charming—the tourists who think they know something or have found the real Paris.

PROFILE There are two islands out there in the Seine, joined by a little footbridge in the rear of Nôtre-Dame. Ile St-Louis is the more famous; Nôtre-Dame is on the Ile de la Cité. There's tourist shopping near Nôtre-Dame, and a flower and bird market near the police station, but the real fun is on the Ile St-Louis. The rue St-Louis en l'Ile has many cute shops, cafes, and ice-cream stands, all of which are open on Sunday.

CANAL ST-MARTIN, 10E

MÉTRO République.

SHOPPING SCENE You're wearing black, right? Or a baggy vintage something or another over a pair of leggings with cowboy boots? Skateboard at the ready?

PROFILE Don't look now, but the heretofore déclassé 10e is becoming chic, led by the area surrounding the Canal St-Martin. Overlooking a canal of the Seine, it has plenty of cafes, lots of in-line skating on weekends, and quite a few funky stores, with more along the side streets. The main action is on the **quai Valmy** and the **quai de Jemmapes** on the other side— all Paris quais change names every few blocks and on both sides of the water.

When you exit the Métro, use a map to guide you to the canal. Or take a taxi to the **Hôtel du Nord,** 102 quai de Jemmapes, and explore from there. The hottest store is **Antoine et Lilli,** 95 quai de Valmy, which sells fashion and kitsch. There's a cafe, so you can sip and soak up the area while staring at the patrons. Other with-it cafes: **Chez Prune** and **Café Purple.**

OBERKAMPF/CHARRONE, 11E & 12E

MÉTRO Ledru Rollin.

SHOPPING SCENE Don't trust anyone over 20.

PROFILE If the district were so cute that it would break your heart to see it change, I'd be the first to say so. Instead, it's mostly multiples on the rue St-Antoine and small stores to the side streets. Yes, there's a Starbucks on rue St-Antoine.

To explore, move away from avenue Ledru-Rollin and onto Charrone; you will transverse the 11e and 12e. While you're here, segue over to Métro Faidherbe-Chaligny, a corner of the 11e with more funky shops. But wait: Back on the rue St-Antoine, where you started, is the tiny rue St-Nicolas, home to **Caravanne 19** at no. 19. This store gets tons of press. It's actually two stores, and so-so to me, but considered everything the hood should or could be.

BASTILLE, 4E & 12E

MÉTRO St-Paul or Bastille.

SHOPPING SCENE Hip, moving to mass-market.

PROFILE Bastille is benefiting from the rebirth of the nearby Marais, one arrondissement over, and the ugly but renowned new opera house. The artists have moved in; so have the Americans (to live, not to set up shop). Long known for its home-furnishings stores, the district is gaining some galleries and interior-design shops of note. Branch stores of the big names in French retail are here, as is Gap (and Starbucks; see above).

Yet moving away from Bastille, there's the funky **Marché Aligre,** where I recently took a group of American journalists who all hated it. If you have no ethnic funk in your soul, stick to the **rue St-Antoine** and maybe the **Viaduc des Arts.**

The contrasts in the neighborhood are part of the fun. Jean Paul Gaultier's flagship shop, **Galerie Gaultier,** is at 30 rue St-Antoine. Lead yourself away from mass market and into the adjoining district (see above).

MONTMARTRE, 18E

MÉTRO Les Abbesses or Anvers.

SHOPPING SCENE Uphill, it's touristy as you get into Montmartre and near Sacré-Coeur. Down by the Métro Anvers, it's discount heaven, but very déclassé.

PROFILE Tourists mix with locals in search of a bargain at the fabric and discount sources nestled into one side of the hill. The most famous discount icon in Paris, **Tati,** is in this area. You've got to be strong, but this is fun for some.

WARNING *Mon Dieu,* what a schlep! I investigated the famous place du Tertre in Montmartre, where the artists supposedly hang out, and was royally ripped off—and breathless from the walk up the hill. I'm not certain which facet of the adventure came closer to giving me a heart attack—the number of stairs I climbed to get to the church, or the fact that the portrait artists run price scams.

Bypass the tourists (and the merry-go-round) and head directly to where serious shoppers hang: The fabric markets are great fun and there are some junk stores that sell overstock from bins. If you can stand the jumble, you might love it here. Start with **Reine,** the high-class fabric market, then move from all the littles at the remnants store to **Marche Dreyfus** to all the trimmings sold from adjacent shops.

EDGE OF TOWN 18E & ST-OUEN

MÉTRO Porte de Clignancourt.

SHOPPING SCENE Largest flea market in Paris.

PROFILE Before we get into what's going on in this part of Paris, let me offer a few warnings and explanations so you don't get lost or confused.

TRANSPORTATION If you're going to the flea market, you want the Métro stop Porte de Clignancourt, although the market is in the town of St-Ouen. Ignore other addresses, Métros, or bus stops with St-Ouen in their names.

SHOPPING From the Métro (or bus) stop, you'll walk through a junky flea market that sells new items and wonder what is going on. No, this is not the famous flea market. You must get to the other side of all this junk.

LUNCH Since you will undoubtedly have a meal out here, note that the market contains several fast-food stalls (crepes, frites, and the like), as well as bistros and restaurants. The real talk of the town, however, is a restaurant a block from the market, **Le Soleil,** 109 av. Michelet (© **01-40-10-08-08**). It's a terrific bistro, the owner speaks English (and eight other languages), and the crowd has mostly been sent by Patricia Wells, who has written extensively about the place. Make a reservation, especially for weekend lunch.

Now for the market itself. It actually consists of many small markets, each with its own personality. For a full description and a map, see p. 219.

Chapter 5

Paris Resources
A to Z

Accessories

. . . .

Paris department stores have very good accessories departments, and buying from them makes good use of your tourist discount card (10% off the top)—and goes toward your 175€ ($263) spending requirement for a détaxe refund that gives another 12% discount.

Bon Marché does not have a discount card and they do have among the best accessories departments in Paris. I was just there and spied a headband of such magnificence and whimsy that I considered paying the 133€ ($200) on the tag because I knew I would be transported into another realm whenever I wore it. Instead, I examined it—and others like it—very carefully, then bought the needed ingredients for about $10 and made my own. This is what Paris is for.

The category of goods called accessories is wide, so see also the sections in this chapter on costume jewelry, shoes, and handbags. And, yes, the French have fabulous handbags for less than $1,000—which is not the case in many other countries. See p. 118 for more on handbags.

Camille Lucie

232 and 206 rue de Rivol, 1er (Métro: Tuileries).

I hate to start off the chapter with a bargain listing or with big personal confessions, but here we are. I was not looking for this store originally. It is simply next door to the Hôtel Meurice, and it bit me in the behind. When I got addicted, I found another branch up the street, and I have also seen others popping up all over town. The shops look somewhat like TTs (tourist traps) and may not be your kind of thing. I do understand, but let me confess and then you can decide how you feel.

The store sells copies of the most expensive jewelry; wedding rings are its specialty, although there are also cocktail rings and some other accessories. The price is two rings for 50€ ($75). Because the rings are not real gold and because I wash my hands frequently and do not remove my rings, I buy two of the same ring. They will last longer if you take better care.

There are almost 250 stores in this popular chain—all over France—and the big-name French jewelers are hopping mad.

BEST BETS Check out the multi-ring unit in gold and diamonds that slips and slides onto your finger and sparkles like the Eiffel Tower on fire. ✆ **01-42-96-41-90**. www.camille-lucie.com.

Fabrice

33 and 54 rue Bonaparte, 6e (Métro: St-Germain-des-Prés).

Vintage or made with vintage parts, here's jewelry that is ethnic and faux ethnic, chunky and funky, and more, more, more. Fabrice has two stores separated by some other buildings; the prices are pricey, but you get the feeling the stuff is collectible. Every now and then, there's real gold in there with the fun stuff. I was staggered that the object of my obsession was an 18-carat necklace with a price tag of 8,000€ ($12,000). More often, you're looking at items in the 200€ to 400€ ($300–$600) range. There are some clothes and other accessories (handbags) now too. ✆ **01-43-26-57-95** or 01-43-26-09-49. www.bijouxfabrice.com.

Françoise Montague

231 rue St-Honoré, 1er (Métro: Tuileries).

Located inside a courtyard off the rue St-Honoré, this hidden resource provides retail and wholesale jewelry with a few different looks. Lots of items are made with tons of jewels, including wire collars that you just want to heap around your neck as if you belonged in a Modigliani painting—they're about 110€ ($165) each. There's also resin, mostly fashioned into flower brooches, for about 55€ ($83). Don't miss this one. ✆ 01-42-60-80-16.

Petrusse

46 bd Raspail, 6e (Métro: Sèvres-Babylone).

Shawls and wraps ranging from paisley with beads to angel wings on air. Prices begin around 50€ ($75) and go over 200€ ($300). Most items actually seem worth the price, especially if you are accessorizing an evening ensemble.

BEST BETS I fell for an ordinary enough Indian pashmina in pale shades of pink and lavender swirls that was hand-beaded in crystal and magic—worth every sou (about 167€/$250).

Philippe Model

33 place du Marché St-Honoré, 1er (Métro: Tuileries).

Although he has just written a book on home style, Philippe Model is most famous as a hat maker. Besides the usual fluff (or unusual fluff, as the case may be) for the racetrack, there's everything from art to wearable.

Shade

63 rue des Sts-Pères, 6e (Métro: Sèvres-Babylone).

Ali Baba and the young *créateurs* of France have teamed up—Shade has everything from kitsch to fantasia. This store is on a printout given to fashion editors visiting Paris who are looking for the latest. ✆ 01-45-49-30-37.

SHOP TALK This is a very good street for browsing.

Activewear

Adidas

148 rue de Rivoli, 1er (Métro: Tuileries).

They offer the German brand for shoes and active wear and the Stella McCartney line of gear that is selling out all over the world. ✆ **01-58-62-51-60.**

PSG (Paris Saint Germain)

27 av. des Champs-Elysées, 8e (Métro: Franklin D. Roosevelt).

This store selling sports souvenirs and active wear represents the local football team Paris Saint Germain (often written PSG), as well as other Europe Cup teams. It's a two-story affair with clothes and accessories, but best of all is the fact that you can buy any shirt and for another 8€ ($12) have your name—or anyone's name—put on the back, while you wait. ✆ **01-56-69-22-22.**

Art Supplies

The big department stores carry both crafts and art supplies; **BHV** (p. 94) has the best selection. For stores that sell art supplies only, I suggest one legend: Sennelier. The other listings are more arts-and-crafts shops that sell everything. U.S. crafts shops tend to have a larger selection at a better price, but you never know what novelty you'll find.

Crea

55 rue St-Placide, 6e (Métro: St-Placide).

Smack-dab in the middle of 2 blocks of discount stores and just a shout from the department store Bon Marché, this shop is so exciting that my palms itch and my mouth gets dry as I approach. It's got all sorts of supplies and crafts and do-it-yourself notions. The store is part of a chain with branches all over France; the other Paris branches are mostly in residential areas that a tourist is unlikely to visit. They do have classes, demonstrations, and many promotions.

WEB TIPS 🖱 You can sign up for the classes and demos online. The website is in French (as are the classes) but it's easy to figure out . . . and the classes are, *bien sûr*, demos, so you can get the gist. Workshops often cost 40€ ($60). 𝄞 01-53-63-14-90. www.crea.tm.fr.

Loisirs & Creation

Carrousel du Louvre (Métro: Louvre) and others.

This is a major French chain and not the most sophisticated (think crafts for the kids); but this location is easy and if you have kids along, it's going to be a successful visit after the Louvre. There are about 20 stores dotted around France; this is the one you want. Open Sundays.

Sennelier

3 quai Voltaire, 7e (Métro: Assemblée Nationale).

Located right on the Seine (and not too near any Métro stops), this is the most famous atelier of supplies in Paris—and, yes, all the big names have shopped here. I find the prices outrageous; most tourists who buy here just want to say they have done so.

WEB TIPS 🖱 Excellent website; click on the British flag to get it in English. 𝄞 01-42-60-72-15. www.sennelier.fr.

Children's Clothing

If you're the kind of mom—or grandma—who likes to drop a bundle on a single outfit for your little darling, Paris welcomes you and your moola. You'll have no trouble finding expensive shops where you can swoon from the high fashion and high prices.

Note: French clothes don't fit like U.S. clothes—they're smaller and closer to the body. French kids' clothes are usually marked by the age in years, just like American clothes: 8A means 8 years *(8 ans)*. For an American 8-year-old, buy size 10A. A size chart appears on the inside back cover of this book.

- Don't forget about the **department stores,** which have rather famous children's departments and much more moderate prices. **Galeries Lafayette** has a large array of designer brands for kiddies, even from American designers like DKNY.

- If you're into euro busters, dash immediately to **Monoprix.** Its kids' fashions (boys, girls, and infants) are wonderful and well priced.

- If you want bigger savings, and are strong of mind and psyche, check out the bins at **Tati** and the jobbers on the rue de Steinkerque in the 18e, like at **Sympa;** see p. 194.

- If you like a one-stop kind of destination, hit the rue St-Placide near Bon Marché (Métro: Sèvres-Babylone), which has a branch of just about every kids' clothing brand in France. These are not discounted.

- Some of the trendy boutiques also have kiddie divisions. They include **H&M,** 53 bd Haussmann (Métro: Chaussée-d'Antin or Havre-Caumartin). I find the quality is not as good as at Monoprix, but some pieces are just so adorable that you have to snap them up.

- Couture baby wear is the latest thing—not really made to measure, but from the couture houses. **Christian Dior** sells a baby bottle that is adorable—and a great gift.

- If you're looking for children's shoes, you will need a size chart (see the inside front cover) and some luck. My favorite source is a cheapie chain called **André,** with branches everywhere—they have copies of all the hot styles that usually cost about 20€ ($30) a pair.

FRENCH CHAINS FOR KIDS

Bonpoint

15 rue Royale, 8e (Métro: Madeleine); 53 rue du Tournon, 6e (Métro: Odéon); and others.

You won't do better than Bonpoint for an expression of style, chic, and quality. This is the leading status symbol for French mothers. While the line held onto classic styles for a very long time, it has since moved into fashion, so that whatever trend Mom is wearing—or the fashion magazines are featuring—can also be found in kids' sizes. Prices are not low.

There are several Bonpoint shops around town. Some specialize in kids' shoes; one has furniture only. A few sell maternity wear.

SHOP TALK If you're impressed with the clothing, but can't hack the prices, try the outlet store, where last season's collection is sold for a fraction of the uptown price. The outlet (42 rue de l'Universite; Métro: Solférino; © 01-40-20-10-55) is closed on weekends, but is convenient to your Left Bank shopping and the Gare d'Orsay.

Bonpoint has a new concept store, with museum-like showcases and a children's play area. Don't think play area as you know it; this is a French château from the turn of the 19th century. Honest. Call © 01-47-42-52-63.

Du Pareil au Meme

15 rue Mathurins, 8e (Métro: Madeleine), and others.

I consider Du Pareil au Même (written DPAM sometimes) the best of the mass-market kiddie boutiques, and I curse the fact that my niece has grown up and no longer wears kids' clothes. Most of the line is casual and in strong colors; prices are very affordable, even with the lousy exchange rate. There are stores in every shopping district in Paris. © 01-42-66-93-80. www.dupareilaumeme.fr.

Petit Bateau

116 av. des Champs-Elysées, 8e (Métro: George V or Etoile), and about a dozen other addresses.

The famed maker of T-shirts has opened a new flagship. There are now a few U.S. stores, where prices are higher than those in Paris. The line is also available in department stores. ✆ 01-40-74-02-03. www.petit-bateau.com.

Shop & Save

There are discount shops on the rue St-Placide, 7e—named **Pullsion**—that sell the brand for 30% off. Métro: St-Placide, Vanneau, or Sèvres-Babylone.

Tartine et Chocolat

105 rue du Faubourg St-Honoré, 8e (Métro: Concorde).

French-style maternity dresses and layettes, both classic and nouveau. My fave: the big pink hippo in pink-and-white stripes sitting in a playpen, just begging to be taken home to someone's child. Also in the major department stores. ✆ 01-45-62-44-04.

Tout Compte Fait

101 bis rue d'Alésia, 14e (Métro: Alésia).

After DPAM, this is my favorite of the lot—good colors, good prices, hot styles. There are about 30 branch stores in Paris, and I shop here when I go to La Défense—which may not be for everyone. ✆ 01-45-39-84-85. www.toutcomptefait.com.

Continental/International Big Names

Despite the fact that the French think French fashion is the best in the world, they have graciously allowed other designers to open in Paris. Of course, the Italians have a good number of shops, representing some of the most famous names in fashion; and a handful of the designers are British (John Galliano, Alexander McQueen, Stella McCartney).

Many of the world's biggest names come from other countries yet show their lines in Paris (Valentino, Hanae Mori, Kenzo, Yohji, and so on), and so have come to be considered French designers. In most cases, nationality doesn't matter—it's the clothes.

The list below separates the non-French brands by house, not by designer. Note that many of the following names have outlet stores at La Vallée (p. 208), outside of Paris. For French designer brands, see p. 105.

Akris
54 rue du Faubourg St-Honoré, 8e (Métro: Concorde); 49 av. Montaigne, 8e (Métro: Alma-Marceau).

Armani Collezioni
41 av. George V, 8e (Métro: George V).

Bottega Veneta
14 rue du Faubourg St-Honoré, 8e (Métro: Concorde); 12 av. Montaigne, 8e (Métro: Franklin D. Roosevelt).

Burberry
55 rue de Rennes, 6e (Métro: St-Germain-des-Prés); 8 bd Malesherbes, 8e (Métro: Madeleine).

Carlos Miele
380 rue St-Honoré, 1er (Métro: Concorde or Tuileries).

Cerruti 1881
15 place de la Madeleine, 8e (Métro: Madeleine).

D&G Superstore (Dolce & Gabbana)
244 rue de Rivoli, 1er (Métro: Concorde).

Dunhill
3 and 15 rue de la Paix, 2e (Métro: Opéra).

Emilio Pucci
36 av. Montaigne, 8e (Métro: Franklin D. Roosevelt).

Emporio Armani
25 place Vendôme, 1er (Métro: Tuileries); 149 bd St-Germain, 6e (Métro: St-Germain-des-Prés).

Ermenegildo Zegna
10 rue de la Paix, 1er (Métro: Opéra).

Escada
275 rue St-Honoré, 8e (Métro: Concorde); 53 av. Montaigne, 8e (Métro: Franklin D. Roosevelt).

Etro
66 rue du Faubourg St-Honoré, 8e (Métro: Concorde); 177 bd St-Germain, 6e (Métro: St-Germain-des-Prés).

Fendi
1 rue François-1er, 8e (Métro: Alma-Marceau).

Ferragamo
50 rue du Faubourg St-Honoré, 8e (Métro: Concorde); 68–70 rue des Sts-Pères, 6e (Métro: Sèvres-Babylone).

Giorgio Armani (Black Label)
6 place Vendôme, 1er (Métro: Tuileries).

Gucci

3 rue du Faubourg St-Honoré, 8e (Métro: Concorde); 23 rue Royale (Métro: Concorde); 350 rue St-Honoré, 1er (Métro: Tuileries); Rond-Point des Champs-Elysées, 8e (Métro: Franklin D. Roosevelt).

Helmut Lang

219 rue St-Honoré, 1er (Métro: Tuileries).

John Galliano

384 rue St-Honoré, 1er (Métro: Tuileries).

Marni

57 av. Montaigne, 8e (Métro: Alma-Marceau).

Max Mara

31 av. Montaigne, 8e (Métro: Alma-Marceau); 265 rue St-Honoré, 1er (Métro: Concorde or Tuileries); 100 av. Paul-Doumer, 16e (Métro: La Muette); 37 rue du Four, 6e (Métro: St-Germain-des-Prés).

Missoni

1 rue du Faubourg St-Honoré, 8e (Métro: Concorde).

Miu Miu

16 rue de Grenelle, 7e (Métro: St-Sulpice).

Moschino

32 rue de Grenelle, 7e (Métro: Solférino).

Mulberry

45 rue Croix des Petits Champs, 1er (Métro: Palais-Royal).

Prada

10 av. Montaigne, 8e (Métro: Alma-Marceau).

Roberto Cavalli

68 rue du Faubourg St-Honoré, 8e (Métro: Concorde);
moving to rue Cambon at some future date.

Tod's

29 rue du Faubourg St-Honoré, 8e (Métro: Concorde).

Trussardi

8 place Vendôme, 8e (Métro: Tuileries).

Valentino

19 av. Montaigne, 8e (Métro: Alma-Marceau).

Department Stores

The biggies offer a lot of bang for your time, but they can get incredibly crowded on Saturdays and in summer. If your time in Paris is limited, go to these stores early and use them to your best advantage: Check out the designer fashions and all the ready-to-wear clothing floors, and you will immediately know what's hot and what's not.

There are common-sense reasons to shop at a department store—aside from the obvious time savings. There are financial benefits, too, if you do all your shopping in 1 day at one store and earn the required amount for détaxe.

In the past year or so, the two major department stores have both outdone themselves with eye-popping results. **Lafayette Maison,** opened in early 2004, is good for home style and souvenirs. **Printemps**—in all of its base stores—is adding on new elements, brands, and dimensions faster than I can type.

REMEMBER Allow at least 15 minutes for the détaxe paperwork, which you must commence in the department store. Expect it to take longer if it's the middle of the tourist season or during sale periods.

WARNING If you go for the sales, steel yourself. There are herds and hordes of people, trash cans within the stores are overflowing, and the atmosphere is far from pleasant.

Bazar de l'Hotel de Ville (BHV)
52–56 rue de Rivoli, 1er (Métro: Hôtel de Ville).

If you think this is a funny name for a store, you can call it BHV (pronounced beh-ahsh-*veh*), or remember that the full name of the store tells you just where it is—across from the Hôtel de Ville. The store is famous for its do-it-yourself attitude and housewares. You owe it to yourself to go to the basement (SS) level: If you are at all interested in household gadgets or interior design, you will go nuts.

> ### Shop Talk
> Note that there are new additions to the store in separate buildings, located behind the main store. There are a men's store, a travel store, a pet store, and a bike store directly behind the main store.

BEST BETS The basement—called SS—has excellent hardware plus the adorable Café Brico.

Open Monday through Saturday from 9:30am to 6:30pm, and until 10pm on Wednesday. Call © **01-42-74-90-00.**

Franck et Fils
80 rue de Passy, 16e (Métro: La Muette).

Franck et Fils is a specialty store. It's elegant, easy to shop, uncrowded, and relatively undiscovered by tourists. You can find respectable, classical fashions in an atmosphere geared for madame. You'll feel very French if you browse, although you may get bored if you're expecting something hot or hip. I buy my Chanel-style camellias here: just 10€ ($15) each!

Open Monday through Saturday from 10am to 5:30pm. Call © **01-44-14-38-00.**

Galeries Lafayette

40 bd Haussmann, 9e (Métro: Chaussée-d'Antin); Centre Commercial Montparnasse, 14e (Métro: Montparnasse/ Bienvenüe).

Lafayette Gourmet

38 bd Haussmann (upstairs), 9e (Métro: Chaussée-d'Antin).

Foreign visitors get a flat 10% discount on most purchases (except food and red-dot items) with a discount card that's available free from the Welcome Desk. (Be sure to present yours before the sales clerk rings you up.) You can also receive a coupon for this 10% discount from your U.S. travel agent or hotel. The export discount is 12% after an expenditure of 175€ ($263); do not confuse the flat 10% discount with the 12% détaxe discount—you're really looking at 10% plus 12%.

When you use the discount card, don't be surprised if you're sent to a main cash register; there are several on each floor, so it's no big deal. It's just annoying if you don't know about it.

Galeries Lafayette holds a fashion show on Wednesdays throughout the year, and also on Fridays from April to October. It's free, but you need reservations (© 01-48-74-02-30). The show is in the Salon Opéra. Use the Auber entrance, then the Mogador escalator, and head to the seventh floor. The fashion show is quite jazzy and good and has no commentary, so there's no language problem; free refreshments are served. It's worth doing—it gives you a preview not only of what's available in the store but also of hot looks and trends.

The store is really a small city spread over three buildings. There's a post office, a shoe-repair kiosk, a bank (an ATM that takes U.S. cards is outside on the wall on rue de Chaussée-d'Antin), a penny-candy store, souvenir departments, an exposition space, and a separate museum with real exhibits on culture, not shopping. The expo space is on the third floor. The store has been famous for its giant expos for the past century; they may amuse you. There are salons, there's a spa, there's everything. When I'm asked to categorize this store in terms of an American point of reference, all I can say is: It's Macy's.

Open Monday through Saturday from 9:30am to 6:45pm, Thursday until 9pm. (The store is expected to be able to stay open later at night in the near future.) Also open on the Sundays prior to Christmas and a few other exceptional openings. Closed on French holidays. Call ✆ **01-42-82-30-25** or log onto www.galerieslafayette.com.

Lafayette Homme
38 bd Haussmann, 9e (Métro: Chaussée-d'Antin).

Lafayette Maison
35 bd Haussmann, 9e (Métro: Chaussée-d'Antin).

Le Bon Marché
22 rue de Sèvres, 7e (Métro: Sèvres-Babylone).

Bon Marché is the chicest of the French department stores. It is also divided into separate buildings, like many of the other stores. Building no. 2 is smaller and houses a sensational gourmet grocery store (**La Grande Epicerie**) and more fashion upstairs, as well as the very unique **Delicabar** for lunch or snacks.

Essentially, Bon Marché was re-created in the past decade to represent the needs of the upmarket French woman. This store does not offer a tourist discount card, but will give détaxe, of course. The store reminds me a lot of Barney's New York. Don't miss the basement (SS) level of the main store, which has crafts items, paper goods, children's toys, and so on.

Open Monday through Saturday from 9:30am to 6:30pm. Call ✆ **01-44-39-80-00.**

Au Printemps
64 bd Haussmann, 9e (Métro: Havre-Caumartin).

Brummell (Men's Store)
Rue Provence and rue Havre-Caumartin, behind Printemps de la Maison, 9e (Métro: Havre-Caumartin).

Printemps de la Maison
72 bd Haussmann, 9e (Métro: Havre-Caumartin).

Printemps Design
Pompidou Center museum, 4e (Métro: Rambuteau).

Printemps Italie
30 av. d'Italie, 13e (Métro: Italie).

Printemps Nation
25 cours de Vincennes, 20e (Métro: Porte-de-Vincennes).

Printemps Republique
10 place de la République, 11e (Métro: République).

Au Printemps is much smaller than Galeries Lafayette, so you really cannot compare the two. The stores think they are competitive; I do not. I'd say Printemps is Saks; Galeries is more Macy's.

Keeping with its more upmarket image, the store is always adding on brands and concepts to make you visit—the latest is that superchef Alain Ducasse has taken over the restaurant.

The main store consists of three separate stores: **Brummell,** the men's store, which is behind the main store; the home store, **Printemps de la Maison;** and the fashion store, **Printemps de la Mode.** Brummell has been renovated and is now sensational; there's a great cafe and bar organized by Paul Smith on the top.

The Maison store has more than just housewares—its newly renovated floors of beauty products are just begging you to try them all; there's also a good bookstore and paper shop. The fashion store has floors of luxury brands, as well as space for teens and tweens.

Just like Galeries Lafayette, Printemps has a coupon that entitles foreign visitors to a 10% discount. Ask for yours at the Welcome Desk on the street floor of the main fashion store, and you'll receive something resembling a credit card; you must show your passport. The 10% discount does not apply to food, books, or sale merchandise. This has nothing to do with the détaxe refund; if you qualify for détaxe, you get an additional 12% off.

WEB TIPS 🖰 You can get your discount card online, which saves the time of getting it at Customer Service in the store. The card is good for up to 2 years after issue date.

Printemps hosts a free fashion show on Tuesdays year-round, and also on Fridays from March to October. The show is at 10am on the seventh floor, under the cupola. Commentary is in English and French; the show lasts 45 minutes.

Open Monday through Saturday from 9:35am to 7pm. On Thursdays, the store is open until 10pm! Also open on the Sundays prior to Christmas and some other exceptional openings. Call ✆ **01-42-82-50-00** or log on to www.printemps.fr.

Designer & Conceptual Clothing/ Inspirations

Ba & Sh

22 rue des Francs Bourgeois, 3e (Metro: St. Paul).

One of a handful of fashionista hangouts where publishing gurus linger to spot new trends and the design kids gape at the next cool looks. Located on the main shopping area of the Marais, this store is open on Sundays. ✆ **01-42-78-55-10.**

WEB TIPS 🖰 Google will invariably read this as "bash" and tell you about all sorts of parties. Type in "ba & sh store in paris france" if you are looking for more info, or try www.ba-sh.com.

Le 66

66 av. des Champs-Elysées, 8e (Metro: George V or Franklin D. Roosevelt).

Okay, so I'm old and this makes me think of Philips 66 or the old store Light that stood here but is no longer with us. Le 66 is the anchor to a new mall on the C.E., and it specializes in designer names chosen to have a cutting edge. It's kind of a Colette (p. 13) meets Le Drugstore with Nike thrown in . . . and a DJ. ✆ 01-53-53-33-80.

l'Eclaireur

3 rue des Rosiers, 3e (Metro: St-Paul).

Another "important" store for getting the right look; also in the Marais. To make it all clear (excuse pun) this is a one-look stop where you can see multiple designers doing the Euro-Japonais look in a warehouse setting. It's a lot like Barney's in the vibe and clientele, with clothes for men and women as well as a cafe. You'll find it on the Right Bank, down the street from Hermès (p. 109).

SHOP TALK This is one of the more established of the wild-child boutiques in the newfangled Marais. Others include **Surface 2 Air** and the Russian couturier **Gaspard Yurkievich.**

Manoush

75 rue Vieille du Temple, 3e (Metro: St-Paul).

Head to the edge of the Marais for this branch (there are other stores dotted around Paris). See p. 8 for a description of this hipper-than-thou source to inspire and delight the editorial crowd. Call ✆ 01-44-54-54-59, or try www.manoush.com.

Fabrics, Notions & So On

For those who sew, Paris, the home of fancy seams, offers plenty to get creative with. While fabric may not be less

Sarah & I Do Montmartre

Sarah told me she had never been to Montmartre and especially wanted to go with me for her first time, since I had lived in that district of Paris for 3 years. I quickly explained that I lived in northern Montmartre, not the glam part, but when she insisted, I gave her a tour that turned out so great that I'll pass it on here. We took the Métro to Lamarck so Sarah could get the idea of the stairs and the northern parts of the area; this is where I used to live. Then we took a taxi up the hill, passing Sacré-Coeur (and all those tourists), and got out at the funicular at the church. This was a 5€ ($7.50) taxi and a real treat. We rode the cabel car (one Métro ticket) and got off at the bottom of the hill, near the carousel, and then turned left (if your back is to the cabel car) and went into the fabric market. We spent 3 hours in the fabric stores and could have stayed all day.

We found fabric prices fair enough and visited **Reine** (3 and 5 place St-Pierre; ✆ **01-46-06-02-31;** www.tissus reine.com) and then **Dreyfus** (2 rue Charles Nodier on the corner of place St-Pierre), then went bonkers for tassels and trim at **Moline SAS** (1 place St-Pierre; www.tissus-moline. com) before cutting into the little stores and alleys on rue d'Orsel and what I call the TTTs (tissus tourist traps). We ended up in the street of junky jobber shops like **Sympa** (rue Steinkerque) and then hopped into the Métro at Anvers. God, did we have fun. And it wasn't expensive fun.

expensive than at home, the selection is so incredible that you will be unable to think about price.

If you want a taste of the world of couture or just a silly adventure, you may want to spend a few hours in the **Marché St-Pierre** area in the 18e, a neighborhood that sells fabrics and notions almost exclusively, located on top of the hill on the far side of Montmartre. Couture ends are for sale; shopkeepers are friendly. Some working knowledge of French will be helpful, as well as lots of cash.

Bouchara Haussmann (1–3 rue Lafayette, 9e; see p. 193)—near **Galeries Lafayette**—is a more attainable source; they carry the good stuff, but this chain (there's one in every major French city) is more famous for its copycat fabrics at good prices. Note that the ground floor is devoted to home style and gives little hint that this is an excellent source for home sewing needs.

Foodstuffs

If you're looking for an inexpensive gift to bring home, consider taking small but tasty treats or even putting together your own food basket. Foodstuffs are not necessarily easy to pack or lightweight, but they can be rather inexpensive and are very much appreciated by foodies. When I asked my son what he needed as a wedding gift, without hesitation he said, *"Fleur de sel."*

My usual food gifts include the salt, or a jar of **Maille**'s Provençale mustard. You can purchase a selection of four Maille's mustards, which makes a great hostess or housewarming gift. (Note that this firm has seasonal new launches in tastes and flavors; the oddball and new flavors are most often not exported to the U.S.) I also like to give rose-petal confiture (usually **Fauchon**) and **Carte Noire** coffee. You know I really love you if I've brought you olive oil. (**Puget,** in a tin, *fruitee.*)

The easiest, and probably the cheapest, place for foodstuff shopping is **Monoprix.** There's a Monoprix on the Champs-Elysées, another behind Printemps on boulevard Haussmann, and yet another at St-Augustin; all locations are central to most hotels on the Right Bank.

If your palate or your pocketbook is advanced, Paris has no shortage of food palaces. As far as I'm concerned, **La Grande Epicerie** (at Le Bon Marché) and **Lafayette Gourmet** (on bd Haussmann) are more reasonably priced than the more famous houses, and more fun to shop. Don't forget the entire rue de Buci, with two grocery stores and many small shops, including a branch of **Oliviers & Co.,** an olive oil specialty shop.

The circle of stores surrounding the place de la Madeleine is almost entirely food specialty shops, including **Maille** and **Maison de la Truffe,** as well as some of the food palaces such as **Fauchon** and **Hédiard.** One block over on rue Vignon is the **Maison de Miel,** the honey shop. You will not starve in Paris, or lack for gifts to bring home.

You cannot bring back any fresh foods; processed hard cheeses are legal, but all others are not. Dried items (such as mushrooms) are legal; fresh fruits and vegetables are not. Foie gras is currently being boycotted as some sort of political payback. Eat yours in France.

For information on stores for wine, see p. 143. For the "Spices & Flavors" section, see p. 138.

Boulangerie St-Ouen

111 bd Haussmann, 8e (Métro: Madeleine).

Paris has plenty of good bread shops. So you're wondering what is wrong with me to send you to this slightly out-of-the-way address. Do you trust me? This shop is special because it makes bread in shapes, including the Eiffel Tower! Furthermore, you can get yours with an egg wash, which preserves it (the staff will ask if you want the bread for eating or for display).

Fauchon

26 place de la Madeleine, 8e (Métro: Madeleine).

Prices are high here, and many items are available elsewhere (have you been to a Monoprix or Inno lately?), but it's a privilege just to stare in the windows. The salespeople are extraordinarily nice. © 01-70-39-38-00.

Hédiard

21 place de la Madeleine, 8e (Métro: Madeleine).

Originally a spice merchant, this flagship is located around the bend from Fauchon and Marquise de Sévigné (chocolates),

⌐ MyBoulangerie.com

Sarah and I were shipping boxes stuffed with bags of **Carte Noire** coffee via the French post office to ourselves in the U.S. when Sarah got the bright idea to look online. She said there were so many sources for this coffee—and other French foodstuffs—that it was embarrassing to use your weight allowance or postal bucks. A friend slipped me the card for a service called **www.myboulangerie.com** that provides French breads and foodstuffs. In the U.S. call © **888/692-6852.**

Hédiard competes handily with Paris's other world-class food stores. It's been in the food biz since the mid-1800s, and there is little you cannot buy in this shop.

BEST BETS *Fruits confits*—little squares of fresh fruit shaped into nibbles and dusted with granular sugar, about 10€ ($15) for a small box of heaven. I'll take pear, *s'il te plait.*

It also delivers, but room service may not be amused. There is another branch (smaller) of Hédiard at the Four Seasons George V. © **01-43-12-88-88.**

La Grande Duchesse

13 rue de Castellane (Métro: Madeleine-Tronchet).

If you've ever been on a foodie prowl in St-Remy de Provence, you probably know that Le Petit-Duc is one of the most important places to go for antique recipes for cookies and nibbles. Now the duke has come to Paris by way of the duchess.

BEST BETS Be sure to buy something in their old-timey tins, which, even after the crumbs have flaked away, are collectible. © **01-42-66-12-57.** www.lagrandeduchesse.com.

Lenotre

10 av. des Champs-Elysées, 8e (Métro: Clemenceau); 48 av. Victor Hugo, 16e (Métro: Victor-Hugo); 5 rue du Havre, 8e (Métro: Havre-Caumartin); Hôtel Novotel Paris Tour Eiffel, 61 quai de Grenelle, 15e (Métro: Bir Hakeim).

Lenôtre will always mean chocolate and dessert to me, but the store is also a full-fledged deli where you can pick up a picnic. It's open on Sunday (quite unusual) and will gladly guide you through any pigout. For a price, Lenôtre will even deliver to your hotel. The breakfast special makes it even more fun to be French for a day. As Lenôtre grows, changes, and branches out, it continues to add new concepts, such as cooking lessons, tools, and all sorts of things to try.

BEST BETS There's a 1-day class in macaroon making and I sure don't mean those little coconut monsters served on Passover. Roll over, Pierre Hermé!

Note: The Champs-Elysées location is not directly on the Champs-Elysées and may be a tad hard to find—it's in what's called the Carré Marigny, across from the American Embassy. ✆ 01-42-65-85-10.

Oliviers & Co.

28 rue de Buci (Métro: St-Germain-des-Prés); 81 rue St-Louis en l'Isle, 4e (Métro: St-Michel, then walk across bridges); 3 rue de Levis (Métro: Villiers); and others.

This chain, begun by the people who created L'Occitane, specializes in olive products—everything from designer tapenade to olive oils from different parts of the Mediterranean. There are French, Spanish, Italian, and even Greek oils, all of which you can taste. A small can of oil costs around 18€ ($27); every now and then, one is on special—there was a big sale on Serbian olive oil last time I was here, no joke. You'll also find soaps, beauty treatments, olive-wood products, and much more—great gift items in all price ranges. O&Co. has some American branches, but prices are higher in the U.S.

BEST BETS To keep ahead of the copycats, this line has recently begun to feature vintage olive oil. Certainly this is a great gift to bring home to a foodie. Wrap in bubble wrap and plastic inside your luggage and pray.

French Designers & Big Brands

Andre Courreges

46 rue du Faubourg St-Honoré, 8e (Métro: Concorde); 40 rue François-1er, 8e (Métro: Franklin D. Roosevelt); 49 rue de Rennes, 6e (Métro: St-Germain-des-Prés); 50 av. Victor Hugo, 16e (Métro: Victor-Hugo).

Courrèges invented the miniskirt and gave us white patent leather boots. Despite his past excesses, he has a very traditional basic line, some dynamite ski wear, and little that is weird or wacky. You can still find some stuff so reminiscent of the 1970s that you don't know if it's new or old merchandise.

Azzedine Alaia

7 rue de Moussy, 4e (Métro: St-Paul).

Tunisian-born Alaïa shocked Paris fashion with his skintight, high-fashion clothes (the Band-Aid dress) and his first boutique in the up-and-coming Marais neighborhood. Now people expect the unusual from him; get a look at the architecture of this place and you'll know he'll never disappoint. The clothes are only for the young and those with figures like movie stars, but the man is on the cutting edge of fashion and retail. Like many shops in the Marais, this one opens at 11am. ℂ 01-42-72-19-19.

Balenciaga

10 av. George V, 8e (Métro: George V).

Black dresses are the house specialty, but everything is new and chic and hot, now that Nicolas Ghesquiere has taken over. Atelier has just been totally renovated for the utmost in chic. ℂ 01-47-20-21-11.

Barbara Bui

50 av. Montaigne, 8e (Métro: Alma-Marceau); 23 rue Etienne Marcel, 2e (Métro: Etienne Marcel).

Barbara Bui is not well known to Americans, but has done so well in Paris that she now has four shops. There are also outposts in New York's SoHo and in Milan. The stores are sparse in their design and chic in their simplicity; there are new boutiques in a row on avenue Etienne Marcel, as well as a cafe (no. 23). If you like Prada, test the waters. © 01-40-26-43-65 or 01-49-23-79-79.

Celine

36 av. Montaigne, 8e (Métro: Franklin D. Roosevelt); 3 av. Victor Hugo, 16e (Métro: Victor-Hugo).

Celine has pretty much lost the horsy motif and the idea of going after Hermès; now it's all sleek, sophisticated, and casual—yet rich, rich, rich. Scarves, bags, and ready-to-wear are the specialties, with an emphasis on creativity in materials, such as string knits.

BEST BETS The handbags have been the standouts in recent years. Prices are lower here than at Hermès, but they are not modest. © 01-56-89-07-91.

Chanel

31 rue Cambon, 1er (Métro: Tuileries); 42 av. Montaigne, 8e (Métro: Franklin D. Roosevelt or Alma-Marceau); 21 rue du Faubourg St-Honoré, 8e (Métro: Concorde).

What becomes a legend most? The mother house, as it's known in French, which holds both couture and a boutique at the famed rue Cambon address, tucked behind the Ritz.

There aren't a lot of bargains in this recently renovated store, but serious shoppers will undoubtedly qualify for a détaxe refund. Sale prices in the U.S. may be surprisingly competitive. There's not a total match in terms of selection, so that's the real reason to shop here. Forget savings.

A lot of the accessories—which are the only things that mortals can hope to embrace—are put away in black cases, so you have to ask to be shown the earrings and chains, which is no fun and puts a lot of pressure on you. However, the sales help in this department is usually nice, and the selection is fun. I try to treat myself to a pair of earrings whenever I'm feeling flush; they start at just over 100€ ($150). (There's also a specialty Chanel accessories store at 25 rue Royale; Métro: Madeleine.)

Expect to pay 4,000€ ($6,000) or more for a new suit. If you're game, try a used Chanel suit. A classic is a classic is a classic, no? Check with **Réciproque, Dépôts-vent de Passy,** or **Didier Ludot.** Used suits are not cheap (this is not a new trick): You'll pay around 2,200€ to 3,000€ ($3,300–$4,500). Ludot usually sells the blouse with the suit, but that raises the price of the suit; at Chanel, the blouse is another purchase. *Note:* Used Chanel is less expensive in New York and London; also try eBay.

> **Buyer Beware**
>
> If by any chance you expect to find faux Chanel in French flea markets, you can forget it. France is very strict about copyright laws; Chanel is even stricter. You want a pair of imitation earrings for 20€ ($30)? Maybe in China or on NYC's Canal Street, but not here.

Charvet
28 place Vendôme, 1er (Métro: Opéra or Tuileries).

Although Charvet sells both men's and women's clothing, it's known as one of the grandest resources for men in continental Europe. Elegant types (read Duke of Windsor) have been having their shirts tailored here for centuries. You can buy off the rack or custom-made. Off the rack comes in only one sleeve length, so big American men may need custom-made.

The look is Brooks Brothers meets the Continent: traditional yet sophisticated. The shop's mini–department store is filled with *boiserie* (wood paneling) and the look of old money. A men's shirt, like all quality men's shirts these days, costs well over 100€ ($150); there's a minimum order of three. © 01-42-60-30-70.

WEB TIPS 🖱 There is no consumer website, unfortunately. Do not go to www.charvet.fr or www.charvet.com because you will get industrial sites.

Christian Dior

30 av. Montaigne, 8e (Métro: Alma-Marceau); 25 rue Royale, 1er (Métro: Madeleine).

What would Monsieur D. (as he was called) say now that Dior is the rage of *teenage girls?* Make room for all Dior has become since its reinvention with John Galliano—and get a load of all the glitz. This large house fills many floors—you can get ready-to-wear, costume jewelry, cosmetics, scarves, menswear, baby items, and wedding gifts, as well as couture. In fact, several little shops cluster around the main "house," and you can wander around, touching everything.

There's a store for fancy jewelry (as in real gemstones) at no. 28, and very small Dior branches at 16 rue de l'Abbaye, 6e (Métro: St-Germain-des-Prés), and 35 rue Royale (Métro: Madeleine). The rue Royale address specializes in shoes and bags. ✆ 01-40-73-73-73.

Emanuel Ungaro

2 av. Montaigne, 8e (Métro: Alma-Marceau); 2 rue Gribeauval, 7e (Métro: Rue du Bac).

If you were to translate the colors of the rainbow through the eyes of a resident of Provence, you'd get the palette for which Ungaro is famous. The couture house is a series of three connecting chambers, so you can see many aspects of the line in one large space. Don't be afraid to walk in and take a look. Manu himself is retired. ✆ 01-53-57-00-22.

> **Shop Talk**
>
> There's a young Brazilian designer, rather new on the scene, named Carlos Miele, who is being touted as the new Ungaro. See p. 90.

Façonnable
9 rue du Faubourg St-Honoré, 8e (Métro: Concorde).

Façonnable has taken over the high street of every French city and moved into vacant space on the Faubourg St-Honoré. Under the auspices of Nordstrom, it has come to the U.S. with stores in major U.S. cities.

There are suits, but that's not what one buys here. The best clothes are simply preppy menswear, although there is a lot of room for color in shirts and tops. The basics are basic: navy blazers, khaki trousers, Top-Sider shoes. You get the preppy picture.

Gerard Darel
22 rue Royale, 8e (Métro: Concorde).

This midlevel designer has numerous free-standing stores and representation in department stores; he also advertises heavily in women's magazines, so you may fall for the ads first. The line is simple and tasteful; the ads are evocative of Jacqueline Kennedy Onassis and actually have more flair than the current collection. The new face of the line is Mamie Gummer, Meryl Streep's daughter. © 01-45-48-54-80.

Givenchy
8 av. George V, 8e (Métro: Alma-Marceau); 28 rue St-Honoré, 1er (Métro: Concorde).

The couture house is upstairs at 29–31 av. Victor Hugo. The men's store takes up three floors and sells everything. Women's accessories and ready-to-wear are in two separate shops. © 01-44-31-49-91. www.givenchy.fr.

Hermès
24 rue du Faubourg St-Honoré, 8e (Métro: Concorde).

Perhaps the best-known French luxury status symbol comes from Hermès. The Hermès scarf is universally known and coveted; the handbags often have waiting lists. I've gone nuts for the enamel bangle bracelets. Since they cost about the same as a scarf, you may want to reprogram your mind for a new collectible. And the tie? It's a power tie with a sense of humor; that's all I can say.

Remember, in order to get the best price at Hermès, you need to qualify for the détaxe refund. Plan to buy at least two of anything, or four ties (unless you buy a saddle, of course).

Shop Talk

Tom and Katie Cruise sent Nicole and Keith Urban a full range of gifts from the baby line when little Sunday Rose was born.

Don't forget to see if your airline sells Hermès scarves and ties in its on-plane shop; they usually cost slightly less than at Hermès (although the selection is often limited). I recently flew both Air France and Delta, and Hermès was less expensive on Air France than on Delta.

If you want used Hermès, see the "Resale & Vintage" section on p. 197; **Didier Ludot** is the most famous specialist.

WEB TIPS 🖰 Hermès sales are not held in the store but are 3-day extravaganzas usually announced in the local papers. I recently got the heads-up on dates and locations from www.chicshoppingparis.com, a website run by an ambitious (and young and beautiful) Suzy Gershman wannabe in Paris. ✆ 01-40-17-47-17. www.hermes.com.

Jean Paul Gaultier

44 av. George V, 8e (Métro: George V); 30 rue Faubourg St-Antoine, 12e (Métro: Bastille).

Junior Gaultier

7 rue du Jour, 1er (Métro: Les Halles).

This is a mini–department store and tribute to a huge talent. Despite his wackiness, Gaultier is getting a reputation for wearable style. Take in the high-tech shock appeal of Gaultier's unique mix of video tech, fashion, and architecture. The younger line (Junior) is less expensive and not appropriate for anyone over 40. Make that 30. Discount shops on rue St-Placide sometimes sell it. *Also note:* Another Gaultier store is in the Galerie Vivienne, 2e. © **01-44-43-00-44** or 01-72-75-83-12.

Kenzo

3 place des Victoires, 1er (Métro: Bourse); 16 bd Raspail, 7e (Métro: rue du Bac); 23 rue de la Madeleine, 8e (Métro: Concorde); 60–62 rue de Rennes, 6e (Métro: St-Germain-des-Prés); 1 rue du Pont Neuf, 1er (Métro: Pont Neuf).

Yes, Kenzo does have a last name: Takada. Yes, Kenzo is Japanese, but he's a French designer. Yes, Kenzo has retired, but the line lives on. The clothes are showcased in big, high-tech stores designed to knock your socks off. The line isn't inexpensive, but there are great sales. © **01-73-04-20-03.** www.kenzo.com.

Lacoste

372 rue St-Honoré, 8e (Métro: Concorde).

Lacoste is often called *le crocodile* in France, which is confusing for those of us who consider it an alligator! This is one of those tricky status symbols that you assume will be cheaper here—after all, it is a French brand—but it isn't. You can pay 75€ ($113) for a short-sleeved shirt in France; this is no bargain. Price the shirts in the U.S. before you buy them in France. © **01-44-82-69-02.**

Lanvin

15 rue du Faubourg St-Honoré, 8e (Métro: Concorde).

The House of Lanvin is one of the oldest and best-known French couturiers, due mostly to its successful American advertising campaigns for the fragrances My Sin and Arpège ("promise her anything"). In recent years, the line has been in transition as the house tries to find its place in the modern world. I have no idea how it has stayed in business. © **01-44-71-31-73.**

Leonard

36 av. Pierre 1er de Serbie, 16e (Métro: Franklin D. Roosevelt).

Léonard is a design house that makes clothes, many from knitted silk—but it's perhaps more famous for the prints on its clothes. These prints are sophisticated, often floral, and incorporated into ties and dresses. A men's tie costs about 80€ ($120), but it makes a subtle statement to those who recognize the print. A discounter named Betty at the place d'Aligre sells Léonard stock.

Louis Vuitton

101 av. des Champs-Elysées, 8e (Métro: George V); 6 place St-Germain, 6e (Métro: St-Germain-des-Prés); 57 av. Montaigne, 8e (Métro: Alma-Marceau or Franklin D. Roosevelt).

Louis Vuitton opened his first shop in 1854 and didn't become famous for his initials until 1896, when his son came out with a new line of trunks. Things haven't been the same since.

Nor will you ever be the same after you've seen what's been going on in Paris. Check out the new Champs-Elysées store, built to showcase the ready-to-wear line designed by Marc Jacobs—during construction, the store was dressed as a giant LV handbag. Now the inside of the store looks something like a spaceship and is decorated with vintage trunks and suitcases. There are floors and floors, including a museum. It's truly breathtaking.

On the Left Bank, the front door of the shop is worthy of a half-hour of silent, stunned appreciation. The store is on different levels, and you weave up, down, and around. Toward the front of the store is the house collection of restored but older LV luggage and steamer trunks; these are for sale. You may also bring in your old ones for repair or renovation. Call toll-free © 08-10-81-00-10.

Loulou de la Falaise

21 rue Cambon, 1er (Métro: Concorde).

Loulou has been famous for decades as the muse of Yves Saint Laurent. When YSL closed up shop, Loulou opened hers—a small boutique that sells some of her own things (vintage YSL), along with things she finds, likes, and displays. It's mostly accessories, with some clothes; stock varies enormously. Prices are high, but this is the real *ooh-la-la* . . . or *ooh-lou-lou*. ✆ **01-45-51-42-22** or 01-42-60-02-22.

WEB TIPS 🖑 My computer told me I could buy the domain name from the owner. Hmmmm. You can see and buy the look on various sites online. Try a search for "loulou" at www.hsn.com.

Marithe et François Girbaud
38 rue Etienne Marcel, 1er (Métro: Etienne Marcel).

Masters of the unisex look, Marithé and François are still making the only clothes that make sense on either sex with equal style. They have many lines—you may never see everything these designers can do. The main store is a must because of the architecture.

Nina Ricci
39 av. Montaigne, 8e (Métro: Alma-Marceau).

We can cut to the chase here: Nina Ricci is a couture house that has been trying to remake itself à la Gucci or other, hotter lines. The store has been redone, and sometimes the clothes are streamlined and young. In short, this is not your mother's Nina Ricci. (If you don't need a ball gown, but are looking for a gift for someone you want to impress, consider the gift department, which is small enough to consider with one big glance.) This store is closed Saturday and from 1 to 2pm daily. ✆ **01-40-88-64-51.**

Sonia Rykiel
70 rue du Faubourg St-Honoré, 8e (Métro: Concorde); 175 bd St-Germain, 6e (Métro: St-Germain-des-Prés).

Sonia Rykiel Woman

4 rue de Grenelle, 6e (Métro: Sèvres-Babylone).

Yes, they sell vibrators and sex toys. No, I won't tell you more, except to say this is at the Sonia Woman store. Sonia has just celebrated a big anniversary in business and has renovated her flagship store on boulevard St-Germain.

The main store, for men and women, has the breadth of the SR lines, still famous for knits, but also embellished with leathers, accessories, perfume, and even a 95€ ($143) lariat key chain. Visit the outlet if you're a true fan—you might get lucky. I've been there when it was great and when it was lonely; you simply never know. Sonia's things are unique—they're classics and stay in style forever. The 20- and 30-year-old sweaters have a cult following.

Ventilo

267 rue St-Honoré, 1er (Métro: Concorde); 7 bis rue du Louvre, 2e (Métro: Etienne Marcel); 13–15 bd de la Madeleine, 1er (Métro: Madeleine).

Armand Ventilo is Dries Van Noten for the average woman—a symphony of beads and ethnic chic, with slightly exotic touches that make it fashionable, yet memorable. Paris has a half-dozen Ventilo shops; I've been to most of them, and each one feels different. As a good lesson in the use of space, they reflect the customer's reaction to the clothes. Some of the stores have tearooms; some sell the home line. The Madeleine shop is the flagship. ✆ 01-44-76-82-95.

Yves Saint Laurent

Rive Gauche, 19–21 av. Victor Hugo, 16e (Métro: Victor-Hugo); 38 rue du Faubourg St-Honoré, 8e (Métro: Concorde).

Despite his death, the business carries on. The old couture space has been turned into a museum, but the casual line (Rive Gauche) is going strong and a new line (24) is being developed to woo the 20-somethings to the flock. ✆ 01-42-65-74-59.

French Multiples

This section is filled with names and brands you hopefully know little about. From a price standpoint, I've tried to cover from low-end to bridge—everything except big-name designers, which are in the next section of this chapter.

Most of these brands can be found in big department stores, but they also have their own stores with larger selections. In fact, they often have several stores in Paris, so if you find a brand that interests you, ask your concierge if there's a location closer to your hotel than what's listed.

Agnes B.
3 and 6 rue de Jour, 1er (Métro: Etienne Marcel); 6 rue du Vieux-Colombier (Métro: St-Germain-des-Prés).

This international chain of ready-to-wear shops sells casual clothes with enough of a fashion look to make them appropriate for big-city wearing. There are lifestyle stores branching out that feature art galleries, makeup, men's clothing, kiddie clothes, travel gear, and more. ℭ 01-42-33-27-34.

Apostrophe
17–19 av. Montaigne, 8e (Métro: Alma-Marceau).

This is a high-fashion line for women with money and style—but more of the former than the latter, plus a need for not too much style, lest they not be taken seriously. It's a big-time career look in France. ℭ 01-56-89-20-80.

Devernois
255 rue St-Honoré, 1er (Métro: Concorde).

This is sort of an old-lady brand that offers enough fashion to make it worth looking at. I buy from here because the clothes are comfortable and fit me (I'm large). Each season the selection is different, so it's hard to know if you will love or hate the line. The specialty is knitwear; it's similar to Rodier, but with more colors and prints.

Etam

73 rue de Rivoli, 1er (Métro: Pont Neuf).

There's a longer listing for Etam on p. 141, wherein I rant and rave about the flagship store in Paris. Every shopping district in Paris (maybe all of France) has Etam stores—some sell lingerie and others sell fashion, meaning copies of the latest looks at low, low, everyday prices.

Georges Rech

54 rue Bonaparte, 6e (Métro: St-Germain-des-Prés).

This is a bridge line that many locals consider designer or big-name. He makes great suits and work clothes for young women who want to look classy, yet stylish. There is a stock shop on rue d'Alésia, 14e (p. 202).

Isabel Marant

1 rue Jacob, 6e (Métro: St-Germain-des-Prés).

I have listed the address for the most convenient branch, but if you're into alternative neighborhoods, this designer's shop near the Bastille (16 rue de Charonne; Métro: Bastille) is one of the new storefronts in an up-and-coming area—all in keeping with her image as a hot young thing doing clothes that are a bit daring, but still wearable.

Lilith

5 rue Cambon, 1er (Métro: Concorde); 12 rue du Cherche-Midi, 6e (Métro: Sèvres-Babylone).

You must take me with a grain of salt here—I am tall and a tad heavy in the bottom, and I like clothes that are comfortable and can be worn with flats. If you like Eileen Fisher or Armani, a soft color palette, and plenty of layers, you'll go nuts for this inventive designer, who uses myriad fabrics and textures, buttons, pockets, and Euro-Japanese droop to do her own thing. My girlfriend Diane, very short, also wears the brand, so don't shrink from it.

Paul & Joe
46 rue Etienne Marcel, 2e (Métro: Etienne Marcel).

This is also a designer bridge line and, despite the sound of the name, it's French. Many fashion editors push this brand—it's considered cutting edge with women under 30.

Plein Sud
2 av. Montaigne, 8e (Métro: Alma-Marceau).

The designer (Faycal Amor) would like you to think of this as a designer brand; it's hot and colorful, chic and body-conscious, and very rock 'n' roll.

Rayure
8 rue Francs-Bourgeois, 3e (Métro: St-Paul).

Since no look is more quintessentially French than the white blouse teamed with black skirt (or black trousers), there are several firms that are famous for their tops. Among them is Rayure, which does all-white or all-black tops much like Anne Fontaine, but for less money. Sold in department stores also.

Regina Rubens
16 av. Montaigne, 8e (Métro: Alma-Marceau).

I don't have it in me to classify this as a full-fledged designer line, although business must be good enough to have this kind of address. The clothes are for working women who wear suits or classy put-togethers and don't want to look boring, but can't be too over-the-top, either. The store will take special orders if you are hard to fit; there is also a stock shop in the 14e.

Rene Derhy
7 rue de Sèvres, 6e (Métro: Sèvres-Babylone); 163 rue de Rennes, 6e (Métro: Rennes).

Bright colors, swirly prints, BoHo ethnic charm with tons of energy and pizazz. Moderate price range. Sarah and I each bought summer totes here for about 67€ ($100) apiece that were among the best values of the trip.

Stella Cadente
93 quai de Valmy, 10e (Métro: République or Jacques Bonsergent).

This Stella is not a person named Stella, as in McCartney, but the Latin word for star—and the shop is one of the stars of the now-funky/chic Canal St-Martin. The clothes are colorful and sometimes drapey, often with embroidery, beads, and feathers.

Tara Jarmon
73 av. des Champs-Elysées, 8e (Métro: Franklin D. Roosevelt).

Gucci copies that are affordable; feminine and sometimes hip clothes at moderate prices.

Zadig & Voltaire
1–3 rue du Vieux-Colombier, 6e (Métro: St-Sulpice).

Every time I go into one of these stores, I think it's Zaftig, not Zadig . . . silly *moi*. This is slim-line fashion for the 20-something crowd that works and needs clothes that are hot (style-wise), but not shocking. The stores carry both the house line and some big-time designer names. There is a spa in the branch at 18 rue François-1er, 8e (Métro: Franklin D. Roosevelt).

Handbags (Everyday)

No one does handbags like the French; *non,* not even the Italians. If you want to splurge on one thing, a handbag is a great notion—especially a brand that isn't well known in the U.S., so you can get a style that few others will have.

Most department stores have enormous handbag departments, usually on the ground floor. It makes more sense to buy a handbag at a department store if you can use the tourist discount card.

I found that there are stunning 200€ ($300) bags in Paris, which is not the case in the U.S., so look around for these and skip the thousand-dollar or thousand-euro examples.

Herve Chapelier

1 bis rue du Vieux-Colombier, 6e (Métro: St-Germain-des-Prés); 390 rue St-Honoré, 8e (Métro: Concorde).

These bags are a cult status symbol and the must-have accessory in Paris, especially in summer as a weekend tote, beach bag, or carry-on.

BEST BETS Printemps and Galeries Lafayette sell a few bags, but ignore that fact (bad selection) and go only to one of the Hervé stores, where you can see the wide range of yummy colors and combinations. For some reason, there are also cashmere sweaters, but forget them; you came for the bags. Almost all styles cost around 100€ ($150); many are half that price.

My dog travels long distance all in his Sherpa bag, but goes shopping in an Hervé tote. ✆ 01-44-07-06-50.

Jerome Dreyfuss

1 rue Jacob, 6e (Métro: Odéon).

Next time I can't find Born to Shop Editorial Director Sarah Lahey, I will know where to look: at the small atelier of Paris's new handbag king, M. Dreyfuss. If you are used to paying $1,000 for a bag, you are in luck—most here cost 333€ to 467€ ($500–$700).

BEST BETS There are a few styles done in a few different leathers or textiles that are at once slouchy, chic, casual, and dressy. I went wild for the purple. Sarah wanted the sparkly beige—yet the bargain (and most sensible of the lot) seemed to be the denim one. ✆ 01-43-54-70-93. www.jerome-dreyfuss.com.

Just Campagne

152 bd St-Germain, 6e (Métro: St-Germain-des-Prés); 342 rue St-Honoré, 1er (Métro: Tuileries).

These casual handbags are especially good for weekend or suburban use; I'm smitten with one that resembles a leather feed bag for a horse and is lined with a nylon pull-string sack inside the feed bag—unusual but fun, and very chic. With prices in the 333€ ($500) range, this is your alternative to the $1,000 bag.

Lancel

8 place de l'Opéra, 9e (Métro: Opéra); 127 av. des Champs-Elysées (Métro: Etoile); and others.

This is another French brand that many Americans don't know too well, a fact that may change now that the brand has opened a truly huge store on the Champs-Elysées. The handbags are considered a must-have upper-middle-class status symbol in France. They make excellent travel bags—some styles are not real leather, and some models have an outside flap pocket that is perfect for a plane ticket and passport. Lancel has changed a lot recently, so what was once a signature line now seems to compete with Tod's in terms of sleek designs—and, sometimes, prices. There's also luggage, and, in the men's space, clothes and accessories and even books, notebooks, and computer gear. © 01-47-42-37-29.

> **Insider's Tip**
>
> Buy your handbag at a department store so you can use the store's discount card.

Lollipops

40 rue du Dragon, 6e (Métro: St-Germain-des-Prés).

They wholesale and retail, they sell in department stores around the world, and they franchise. They are Lollipops, a line of shoes, small accessories, and bags that are creative and inexpensive, expressive and whimsical, and often great for fashionistas, teens, and tweens. ✆ **01-42-22-09-29.** www.lollipops.fr.

Longchamp
404 rue St-Honoré, 1er (Métro: Concorde).

This totally renovated and rejuvenated flagship has teamed with an English designer (shhhh! don't tell the French!), so a classic now has tons of fabulous bags, totes, and luggage. Many leather items are coated to withstand the weather. The logo is a flying greyhound, but the hardware with a piece of bamboo (usually metal, but possibly resin) is more of a status symbol. Although traditionally these bags are in solid colors, some of the new designs are prints or multitones. Available at department stores, too. ✆ **01-43-16-00-16.**

Renaud Pellegrino
8 rue de Commaille, 7e (Métro: Assemblée Nationale).

This man is a cult hero who first came to fame when it was revealed he was the genius behind Hermès handbags. He went off on his own over a decade ago, but has moved shop several times. This is the new location. You can't really get going for less than 450€ ($675), but if you want the best in unusual and special, *voilà*. It's all made by hand. There are also shoes. ✆ **01-41-65-35-52.**

Sequoia
72 bis rue Bonaparte, 6e (Métro: St-Germain-des-Prés); 6 rue Francs-Bourgeois, 3e (Métro: St-Paul).

This brand of handbag considers itself more sophisticated and expensive than a line for teens, but it's still not top-of-the-line French luxe. In the past few years, it has gotten more sophisticated and often been inspired by major looks from the big names. For the set that likes a handbag in the 175€ ($263) range; also sold in department stores.

Hardware

Okay, so maybe you don't think you came to Paris for hardware stores, but you might find them interesting, fun to shop, and affordable. Better yet, you may find supplies you can't get at home. The doors have stood at attention against my bedroom walls for a year until I could get a piece of French hardware to repair them, so don't look askance.

BHV
14 rue du Temple, 4e (Métro: Hôtel de Ville).

See p. 94.

Leroy Merlin Paris Beaubourg
52 rue Rambuteau, 3e (Métro: Rambuteau).

This is the Home Depot of France and if it weren't in a touristy location in Paris, I would not mention it. But since you will be there anyway (the store is next door to the Pompidou Museum) and since the store is often less expensive than BHV, you might want to wander in. It's not as much fun as BHV, but it does carry a lot of the same merchandise, hardware, and armoire screws.

Now, just so you don't make a total fool of yourself, this isn't Leroy as in "Bad Bad Leroy Brown" but in the French style as if Merlin were king—*"le roi Merlan."*

There are stores all over France, mostly in the burbs. The Paris store is open Monday to Saturday 9am to 10pm.

WEB TIPS 🖱 You can actually shop online and have delivery sent to your hotel. Of course, the website is in French so you'd better have a handy vocabulary for tools.

Local phone ☎ **01-44-54-66-66.** www.leroymerlin.fr.

Internet Cafes

Note that more and more of Paris is being wired for Wi-Fi, so if your laptop has a wireless card, you don't need an Internet cafe. In fact, I know many a visitor who dresses to the hilt and marches into one of the palace hotels (all wired for Wi-Fi) to enjoy the gilt and do a little e-mail.

If you have no computer with you, you'll do better price-wise by using a cybercafe instead of your hotel's business center. New cafes arrive every week, so ask your hotel concierge for the one closest to you. My personal best is the one located inside **Häagen-Dazs** on the Champs-Elysées.

The ones listed below are the best known, in easy locations for tourists.

EasyEverything
31 bd Sebastopol, 3e (Métro: Châtelet); 6 rue de la Harpe, 5e (Métro: St-Michel).

Open *24Hsur24*, as they say in France, this fabulous resource has cyberstations all over Europe, with more to open in Paris. Clean, neat, bright, easy to use; cafe.

Gate 104
104 bd St-Germain, 6e (Métro: Odéon or St-Michel).

This is the largest Internet cafe in Paris and the newest in terms of equipment, decor, and scene. Hours are Monday through Friday from 8am to 2am, Saturday from 8am to 7am, and Sunday from noon to 2am. The cost is 3€ ($4.50) per hour.

Le Web Bar
32 rue de Picardie, 3e (Métro: République).

One of the oldest and most established in Paris, with a young crowd and a cafe with DJ.

Jewelry (Costume)

The essence of French fashion, aside from couture, is simplicity—consider the basic black skirt and white silk blouse, a staple of every stylish Frenchwoman's wardrobe. Of course, the way to spruce up these basics has always been accessories. Hence the importance of the Hermès silk scarf.

Should you care to go for something glitzier, these sources offer some of Paris's boldest statements. Their specialty is either copies of more serious jewelry or originals that will have value in the marketplace for years to come. The originals reach beyond the basic definition of "costume jewelry." Coco Chanel invented costume jewelry, and designer costume jewelry, whether new or vintage, remains a solid investment—although it can be pricey.

The major designer brands now make their own costume jewelry, so they are not listed below. The sources here give you a range from fabulous fakes to the boldest bangles.

Anemone
7 rue de Castiglione, 1er (Métro: Tuileries or Concorde).

Year after year, Anemone is a reliable resource for costume jewelry and earrings. It's across from the Hôtel Meurice. Earrings start around 40€ ($60)—this is Paris, you know. Prices are not giveaway, but sometimes you can find good pieces; I bought a YSL gold-tone collar here that I still live in, and it was worth every bit of its 350€ ($525) price tag. It's fun to look in the window even if you don't buy.

Gas
44 rue Etienne Marcel, 2e (Métro: Etienne Marcel).

This is a small store with very inventive pieces, often made from odds and ends. More fun than couture in terms of a look; possibly a good investment as a collectible. It uses faux gemstones in copper settings; I collect the bees. The earrings don't pinch!

Konplott
57 rue Pierre Charron, 8e (Métro: Franklin D. Roosevelt).

Greek designer, German-owned firm, Parisian kindness—costume jewelry begins at 100€ ($150), but many splashier pieces are in the 300€-plus ($450) range. © **01-40-75-02-94.**

Michaela Frey
9 rue Castiglione, 1er (Métro: Concorde); 167 rue St-Honoré, 1er (Métro: Tuileries).

This Viennese design firm has stores in most European capital cities, but none in the U.S., so you may not know the brand. If you are familiar with the enamel bracelets from Hermès, you are unwittingly familiar with Frey's work. Frey did this enamel work long before Hermès put its distinctive twist on it. Most of the Frey designs are inspired by famous artists or historical finds. The classic bracelet costs 667€ ($1,000).

BEST BETS I am wild for the work of Frederich Huntervasser and also Gustav Klimt—this firm does a homage to each that is stunning. A pair of cuffs worn together would make even Diana Vreeland turn dizzy.

Swarovski
7 rue Royale, 8e (Métro: Concorde).

Over the years, this crystal maker has provided much of the glitter to Lesage and Chanel. Now, its own brand has an international reputation and a line of jewelry and handbags. Everything is made from top-of-the-line crystals.

Jewelry (Important)

Traditionally, all of the important Parisian jewelers are on the place Vendôme, with a few moving away from the obelisk and stretching toward Opéra.

Two couture houses, both of which made costume jewelry for decades, have launched stores selling the real thing, and I don't mean Coca-Cola. **Chanel** started a few years ago, and **Christian Dior** has come on board. **Cartier** has just opened a large new showroom right on the Champs-Elysées, at no. 154, near the Arc de Triomphe (Métro: Charles de Gaulle–Etoile).

If you want name-brand real jewelry and don't care if it's used, go to the string of specialty boutiques just outside the place Vendôme on the rue St-Honoré. Family heirlooms cram their windows; prices in cash may be juggled slightly.

Lingerie & Bathing Suits

Most French specialty stores that sell underwear also sell bathing suits. The department stores have enormous "festivals," selling masses of bathing suits in a designated area (the same space will sell coats in late summer). For the largest selection of bathing suits in Paris, try Galeries Lafayette from May to August. You can even buy some suits a la carte—top and bottom in different sizes, as needed.

There are also a number of multiples (chain stores) that sell underwear and bathing suits (in season). These shops sell either one brand (such as Etam) or many, and aim to serve the midmarket; they are much more expensive than similar stores in the U.S.

Not only was the brassiere invented in Paris, but France has always made the latest in industrial equipment for manufacturing modern underwear. Prices are high, but the technology is unsurpassed. I buy most of my lingerie at **Monoprix.**

Eres

2 rue Tronchet, 8e (Métro: Madeleine); 40 av. Montaigne, 8e (Métro: Franklin D. Roosevelt).

Eres is perhaps the most famous name in bathing suits in France—we're talking high-end, almost couture bathing suits. We're also talking owned by Chanel. As with most bathing suit lines, Eres also sells lingerie and is responsible for the tulle craze that's still going strong. Some department stores also sell the line; it is extremely chic and expensive, and wonderful. There are boutiques around town, but this is the main shop. It's next door to Fauchon on the place de la Madeleine.

Made to Measure

Albani

3 rue du Duras, 8e (Métro: Champs-Elysées Clemenceau).

One of the few remaining affordable couturiers, M. Albani is an Italian gentleman who works from his atelier right off the rue du Faubourg St-Honoré. You walk into the door, through the courtyard, and spy his door slightly to your right on the far side of the courtyard. M. Albani does not speak English (he's okay in French or Italian), but he has warm eyes, incredible taste, and gifted hands. His cut, especially in suits, has been known throughout the couture world for years.

All clothes made by M. Albani are made to measure, and you can bring a photo, work with him to create a sketch, or look at other things he has made. His specialty is women's suits; bolts and bolts of fabric are leaning against the walls, so you pick the fabric, work out the design, and have your first fitting. You'll need one more fitting later, and he needs a total of 8 working days to make the garment. Make appointments before arrival by phone or fax; no e-mail. This is old-world tailoring, remember? Prices range from 1,500€ to 2,000€ ($2,250–$3,000). The local phone number is ✆ **01-40-07-12-72** (fax 01-40-07-13-63).

Malls & Shopping Centers

Slowly, Paris has been going mall mad. The shopping center of your teen years does not exist in great abundance in Europe, but Paris is trying out every kind of mall you can imagine. The larger mall structures are often called "commercial centers."

Small malls are springing up in the various train stations, obviously to catch travelers as they move to and fro. Some of the offerings are very enticing—there's a new branch of **Monoprix** in the Gare du Nord and a mall still being built at the **Gare St-Lazare.**

Don't forget that the French had the original versions of the mall, 150 years ago, with their *passages* and *galeries*. For outlet malls, see p. 207.

Forum des Halles
11 bis rue de l'Arc-en-Ciel, 1er (Métro: Les Halles or Châtelet).

The Forum des Halles, built to rejuvenate a slum, serves as an exciting monument to youth, style, and shopping. The atmosphere is rather sterile and American—even Tupperware has a store here. The mall is a huge square with a courtyard; it's easy to get lost once inside, though master maps throughout the place will help you find your way. The Forum was built in stages—be sure to see the newest part, which stretches underground. There are fast-food joints in the Métro part of the complex, and real restaurants among the shops in the regular complex.

Although a number of designers and bridge lines have outposts here, the stores are often not as charming as the boutiques on the street can be. If you ran out of here screaming, I wouldn't blame you at all.

BEST BETS This mall attracts many teens and not many tourists, but it now houses the first of the U.K. chain's **New Look** stores, which is the reason to visit here. It's the poor man's H&M.

Most of the stores here open Tuesday through Saturday between 10 and 10:30am and close between 7 and 7:30pm. All stores are closed Sunday and reopen noon Monday. © **01-44-76-96-56.**

Le Carrousel du Louvre
99 rue de Rivoli, 1er (Métro: Palais-Royal).

This is an American-style shopping mall; but it's not too big and it's open on Sundays, so it has many redeeming features.

The mall is attached to the Louvre and has many entrances and exits. In fact, while it doesn't give you that much of a taste of the real Paris, in a pinch you can do all your shopping here and feel quite good about it. Most major chains have stores here.

For the easiest access, enter from the rue de Rivoli, where a small banner announces the space. This entrance is not particularly prominent, so you may have trouble finding it. The mall is on two subterranean levels; enter and take the escalator down one flight to the food court.

Go down another level and you're in a mall like any other in your neighborhood, except this one has **Lalique, Sephora, La Maison du Chocolat,** and **Virgin Megastore.** There are 45 stores, as well as some excellent museum shops. www.carrouseldulouvre.com.

Men's Shops

Every major shopping area, every major designer, and every department store carries things for men. But when I met a man on an airplane who asked me for a quick and easy list, I scribbled the following names on a napkin for him. I also gave him **Mouton à Cinq Pattes,** a discounter (p. 206).

I warn men to have an honest look in the mirror before they shop in Paris. For the most part, the average American male body is much larger than its French counterpart.

BHV Homme
36 rue de la Verrerie, 4e (Métro: Hôtel de Ville).

This is not a home store but the men's store—sort of a spiffy version of Lafayette Homme for the Marais sportif. It's so cool there's even registration for gay couples. The website is excellent. Local phone ✆ 01-42-74-90-00. www.bhv.fr.

Brummell (Printemps Homme)

Rue Provence and rue Havre-Caumartin, behind Printemps de la Maison, 9e (Métro: Havre-Caumartin).

This is a large, very complete men's department store directly behind Printemps de la Maison. See p. 96.

Dunhill

15 rue de la Paix, 2e (Métro: Opéra).

Hugo Boss

115 av. des Champs-Elysées, 8e (Métro: George V).

Kiton

29 rue Marbeuf, 8e (Métro: Franklin D. Roosevelt).

Lafayette Homme

38 bd Haussmann, 9e (Métro: Chaussée-d'Antin).

Ground floor and up are devoted to men's clothing, then a grocery store.

Loft

12 rue du Faubourg St-Honoré, 8e (Métro: Concorde).

Extremely hip boutique makes a great T-shirt. ✆ 01-42-65-59-65.

Madelois

23 bd de la Madeleine, 1er (Métro: Madeleine).

Department store just for men. ✆ 01-53-45-00-28.

Nickel

48 rue des Francs-Bourgeois, 3e (Métro: Hôtel de Ville).

Men's spa; it has its own line of products. ✆ 01-42-77-41-10.

Zegna

10 rue de la Paix, 2e (Métro: Opéra).

Museum Shops

Almost all Paris museums have gift shops, and there are about 50 museums in Paris. That's a lot of museum gift shops. Some even have their own chains, with branches in various museums. Some just sell slides, prints, and high-minded books or postcards—but several are really with it.

Centre Georges Pompidou

Centre Georges Pompidou, 4e (Métro: Châtelet).

The main gift shop at the entry level is mostly a bookstore, so don't get confused. There are more gifts on the mezzanine, and in sales areas after certain exhibits. The department store Au Printemps runs the shops.

Musee Carnavalet

29 rue de Sévigné, 3e (Métro: St-Paul).

This museum in the heart of the Marais documents the history of the city of Paris; the gift shop sells reproductions of antique items, many owned by famous people. I have the Georges Sand stemware. Closed Monday.

Musee des Arts Decoratifs

107 rue de Rivoli, 1er (Métro: Musée-du-Louvre).

The store sells a mix of books and gift items, all with a wonderful eye toward design. Prices aren't low, but you'll find unique gifts—even a copy of the very first scarf Hermès ever created. There are books on design in several languages. Closed Monday and Tuesday; open Sunday from noon to 5pm.

Musee d'Orsay

Gare d'Orsay, 7e (Métro: Orsay-Ville).

The Musée d'Orsay's gift shop isn't as wonderful as the architecture, but it's damn good; you can buy prints and some reproductions, as well as a scarf or two. Good selection of postcards and gifts (including wonderful art books) for kids.

Musee du Louvre
Palais du Louvre, 1er (Métro: Musée-du-Louvre).

There's a gift shop under that glass pyramid, and it is a beauty, with two levels of shopping space for books, postcards, and repro gifts. *Beaucoup* fun! You do not have to pay admission to the museum to gain entrance. After walking into the pyramid, take the escalator down, and you will be in a lobby reminiscent of a train station. The gift shop is straight ahead.

Music

I've gone nuts for Johnny Hallyday and have bought a number of his CDs. There are zillions of them (the man's career spans decades), but they can be pricey. In fact, CDs in France are much more expensive than in the U.S., so buy only must-have items you can't get elsewhere. Large electronic palaces like **FNAC** and **Virgin Megastore**—which sell CDs, DVDs, videos, books, tickets, and more—have branches in all major shopping areas.

Plus Sizes

Galeries Lafayette has one of the best selections of large sizes in Paris; there are also specialty stores for *les rondes*. Note that **H&M** has a line called BIB (big is beautiful). I shop at **C&A**, which has inexpensive clothes and tends to go up to size 50, which is a size 20 in the U.S.

Cazak
4 rue Marignan, 8e (Métro: Franklin D. Roosevelt).

A one-off boutique with mostly fancy clothes and many designer names for work or dress-up. This street is between avenue Montaigne and the Champs-Elysées. ℰ **01-47-20-31-00.**

Difference
53 rue St-Placide, 6e (Métro: Sèvres-Babylone).

The clothes and accessories here are for all sizes—up to 56.

Elena Miro
14 av. Victor Hugo, 16e (Métro: Victor-Hugo); Angle rue St-Honoré and rue St-Roch, 1er (Métro: Tuileries).

This Italian brand is neither as expensive nor as hip as Marina Rinaldi, but is good for fashion basics, weekend clothes, and some dress-up; from sizes 42 to 56. ℰ **01-45-00-77-62** or 01-42-60-03-90.

Marina Rinaldi
7 av. Victor Hugo, 16e (Métro: Etoile or Victor-Hugo); and many others.

The large-size division of the Italian brand Max Mara, this is one of the best made of the plus-size garment brands. Styles tend to be classics, with a selection of dress-up, weekend, and office clothing.

Olivier Jung
Les Boutiques du Marché St-Germain, 14 rue de Lobineau, 6e (Métro: Mabillon).

Pronounce the *J* as a *Y* and stop by while you're exploring the 6e. The clothes tend to be simple, with clean lines, good fabrics, and easy-to-wear styles . . . nothing too *trop*. Size range is from 38 to 56. ℰ **01-46-33-55-30.**

Shoes (French Fashion)

Shoe freaks will find the Little Dragons neighborhood on the Left Bank (p. 58) a treasure-trove of little stores belonging to famous designers and hoping-to-be-famous designers. Weave along these streets and you can't go wrong. Be sure to stop at the many shops on the rue des Sts-Pères, then make your way onto rue du Four, with more shops for teens. Don't forget to shop rue de Grenelle, too.

The department stores all have enormous shoe departments; Au Printemps is trying to make a reputation for its selection.

Christian Louboutin

19 rue Jean-Jacques Rousseau, 1er (Métro: Les Halles).

How's this for genius: I am watching a late-night chat show in the glories of my own bedroom when some hot-chickie starlet, big-maned girly girl comes on the show (I have no idea who it is), crosses her legs, and lets loose with her chat. I have no idea what she says or even who the host is. I am lost in the soles of her shoes, which are bright red, and I know instantly that she is wearing Christian Louboutin shoes from Paris. Is there anything more chic? ℡ 01-42-36-05-31.

Pierre Hardy

156 Galerie de Valois, Palais Royal, 1er (Métro: Palais-Royal).

Small shop; big name. Hardy (say *Har Dee*) has created shoes for Hermès, among others, and is beginning international expansion. Don't look now, but he's just done a line in the U.S. for Gap. If you don't shop at Gap, you could be looking at over 667€ ($1,000) for shoes ℡ 01-42-60-59-75.

Rene Caovilla

23 rue du Faubourg St-Honoré, 8e (Métro: Concorde).

Italian master of jewel-encrusted shoes, often made in three different heel heights. Shoes start around 467€ ($700) per pair, but *ooh-la-la!* ℡ 01-42-68-19-55. www.caovilla.com.

Rodolphe Menudier
14 rue Castiglione, 1er (Métro: Concorde).

I don't care if you buy here; I don't really even care if you enter. The windows are enough to knock you out. ✆ **01-42-60-86-27.**

Roger Vivier
29 rue du Faubourg St-Honoré, 8e (Métro: Concorde).

Roger does not design the shoes anymore, but don't let that stop you. Here are three rooms filled with enough high heels to make *Sex and the City* come back on air—in a Paris version.

BEST BETS There is a relatively flat, Pilgrim-style shoe that is considered a status item. ✆ **01-53-43-00-00.**

Shoes (Sensible)

Mephisto
78 rue des Sts-Pères, 6e (Métro: Sèvres-Babylone).

Sensible-shoe folks consider this brand of walking shoe for men and women one of the best in the world. You'll pay about half the U.S. price. They're sold in department stores.

Repetto
22 rue de la Paix, 2e (Métro: Opéra).

This is basically a supply house for ballerinas, but it offers much in terms of fashion, including dresses that would be great for black-tie events. This is the firm that introduced *le ballet* into fashion as a shoe, rather than a dance item. Now they have fashion ballet flats, around 133€ ($200) a pair. ✆ **01-44-71-83-00.**

Shop Talk

It was Brigitte Bardot who started the trend to ballerina flats for streetwear. She began with red slippers and then asked Repetto to make her street shoes.

BEST BETS The stock shop is located at 24 rue de Chateau-dun, 9e; this is not far from Galeries Lafayette.

Souvenirs

Paris abounds with souvenir shops. I often call them TTs (tourist traps). They cluster around the obvious tourist haunts (Nôtre-Dame, the Champs-Elysées) and line the rue de Rivoli from the Hôtel Meurice to the front gate of the Louvre.

They all sell more or less the same junk at exactly the same nonnegotiable prices. The only way you can get a break is to make a deal on the amount you buy. If you buy a few T-shirts, you may get a discount. The price of T-shirts fluctuates with the dollar: The price varies in euros (note the handwritten signs).

Some of my favorite things to buy at souvenir stands include a toothbrush with your (or a similar) name in French; a break-fast bowl sponged in blue and white, also with your name in French; boxer shorts with Parisian motifs; T-shirts from French universities; key chains with miniature Eiffel Towers, street signs, Napoleon, and more; and scarves with kitschy tourist-haunt designs that are so bad they're fabulous.

Specialty Looks

Anne Fontaine

81 rue des Sts-Pères, 6e (Métro: St-Germain-des-Prés), and others.

This is a chain of stores with about a dozen shops in Paris alone—I simply chose the first location on the business card. You can go to www.annefontaine.com for more addresses for this firm, which sells only white and black shirts for women. Most cost about 100€ ($150). (Also see p. 117 for Rayure, a copycat brand that costs a little less.) © 01-45-48-89-10.

A.P.C.

112 rue Vieille du Temple, 3e (Métro: St-Paul); rue 20 Charles Nodier, 18e.

This store shows off a look—perfect for those who like minimalist chic and Euro-Japanese drape—as well as an area adjacent to the Marais. Prices are more or less reasonable—around 110€ ($165) for just about anything—and you get a lot of bang.

Compagnie Française de l'Orient et de la Chine

163 and 167 bd St-Germain, 6e (Métro: St-Germain-des-Prés).

This is a chain with stores all over, even in Brussels. Some branches carry the entire line, while some just have clothes or home style. Ignore the boutique in Galeries Lafayette; it doesn't do justice to the line or the look.

As you can guess from the name, the clothes are inspired by the Orient. I have a jacket made of Scottish tweed in a Chinese style—such a brilliant combination of ideas that I wear it all the time. While the clothes are somewhat ethnic, they are not costumey.

Eskandar

7 rue Princesse, 6e (Métro: St-Sulpice).

This is my new favorite line, with droopy-drapey Euro-Chinese chic in easy-to-wear clothes created by a Persian designer. There is also a boutique in London. However, this location has gift and tabletop items, as well as the stunning clothes. And did I mention the elastic waists?

WEB TIPS Eskandar is carried at Neiman Marcus in the U.S. At one of the outlet stores, I found a linen big shirt for 100€ ($150) and some pull-on capris for 133€ ($200)—these were bargains I am proud to claim as my own.

Favourbrook

Le Village Royal, 25 rue Royale, 1er (Métro: Madeleine).

This is an English firm that has moved into the French fabric trend and gone wild for Regency. The wares include men's vests, accessories for men and women, and all sorts of sumptuous creations. With a business suit, one of these ties would make a powerful statement.

L'Escalier d'Argent

42 Galerie de Montpensier, Jardin du Palais Royal, 1er (Métro: Palais-Royal).

I found this shop because it's close to the vintage clothing store Didier Ludot. It's also close spiritually—it specializes in 18th-century textiles. It mostly makes ties and vests; ties cost about 60€ ($90). The location only reinforces the magic of the goods; this is Paris at its best.

Little Black Dress

125 Galerie de Valois, Jardin du Palais Royal, 1er (Métro: Palais-Royal).

Vintage king Didier Ludot has created a line of new dresses—black only, my dear—inspired by famous vintage choices. Prices average around 200€ ($300).

Shanghai Tang

La Maison de la Chine, 76 rue Bonaparte, 6e (Métro: St-Sulpice).

From Hong Kong with love—the Chinese chic created by David Tang has finally come to Paris, where clothing, tabletop, and gift items are sold.

Spices & Flavors

With the influences of French regional cooking as well as some basic ethnic groups—North African and Middle Eastern—you can find a number of different spices for sale in grocery stores, spice markets, and street markets. They often make great gifts. Edible lavender is my number-one choice as an easy-to-bring-home gift; it's usually less than 3.35€ ($5) for a tube or packet.

Amorino

4 rue Buci, 6e (Métro: St-Germain-des-Prés); 47 rue St-Louis en l'Isle, 4e (Métro: Pont Neuf); and 10 others in Paris.

This may, at first glance, appear to be an ice-cream shop or tearoom—some people even blog about it as a place to take your kids.

I'm sending you here for their desserts or coffee and for a glimpse at a bonbon shop that makes Gigi seem unsophisticated. For the most perfect gift in the world, race over here.

WEB TIPS The website lists all the addresses and many of the flavors, but doesn't even mention the bonbons.

Goumanyat et Fils

3 rue Charles-Francois Dupuis, 3e (Métro: Temple).

The space is for the spice and the chefs know where it's at, and you will too if your Paris travels take you off the beaten path into the real neighborhoods, slightly east of the main fray of TTs. In business since Napoleon's time, this spice store sells everything from real saffron (fake is much easier to find—usually dried marigold leaves) to the spices of faraway lands. ℂ 01-44-78-96-74. www.goumanyat.com.

> **Shopping Adventure**
> The Goumanyat et Fils owner speaks English and will be happy to give you a free lesson on real and fake saffron.

Sneakers

They're called *les baskets* in French, so forget references to trainers (Brit-speak), sneakers, or running shoes.

Citadium

50 rue de Caumartin, 9e (Métro: St-Lazare).

This large store, right behind Printemps and standing over a branch of Monoprix, specializes in all things sport—with a wide range of many brands of sneakers and gear. ✆ 01-55-31-74-00.

Le Shop

3 rue d'Argout, 2e (Métro: Etienne Marcel).

This store is for young people with a need to grab the latest looks—see the full listing below. ✆ 01-40-26-07-75.

Shinzo

39 rue Etienne Marcel, 1er (Métro: Etienne Marcel).

Located on a street of cutting-edge fashion, this shop specializes in custom-made and collectible *baskets*, but at affordable prices. ✆ 01-42-36-40-57.

Teens & Tweens

Teens will have no trouble spending their allowances, and all future allowances, in Paris. Many will like the tourist traps along the rue de Rivoli, with sweatshirts and boxer shorts; others will go for the *fripes* and vintage clothing. Any young woman will be mad for **Monoprix,** the big chain of dime stores—all have tons of fashion at pretty fair prices, but they are best for accessories, grooming items, and small items.

Most of the Left Bank is awash with stores that cater to students, some more fashionable than others. American-style clothes are in vogue with the French, so be careful—those Levi's could cost twice what you'd pay at home. For hot, body-revealing looks, check out **Kookaï,** 1 rue St-Denis, 1er (Métro: Châtelet), and 15 rue St-Placide, 7e (Métro: Sèvres-Babylone); and **Morgan,** 165 rue de Rennes, 6e (Métro: St-Sulpice), on the Left Bank, and 81 rue de Passy, 16e (Métro: La Muette), on the Right Bank. **H&M** (p. 6) is my best suggestion—it's one of my favorite stores in the world. But the **New Look** store at Forum Les Halles is the new kid.

Major global chains that cater to young people, such as the Swedish giant **H&M,** the Spanish firm **Mango,** and the French chain **Pimkie,** have stores all over town. Many mothers prefer to take their teenagers to the major department stores, as the *grands magasins* carry so many different lines in one place.

Au Vrai Chic Parisien

8–10 rue Montmartre, 1er (Métro: Etienne Marcel); 47 rue du Four, 6e (Métro: St-Germain-des-Prés).

The Left Bank shop is tiny, but exactly what you want in a Left Bank store: cozy, with great stuff at moderate prices. When it's on sale, you'll want to buy armloads of these quasi-teen/quasi-adult fashions.

Etam, Cite de la Femme

73 rue de Rivoli, 1er (Métro: Pont Neuf).

Etam is a gigantic chain—do not confuse this flagship store with the zillions of little Etams all over Paris, France, and the rest of the E.U. There is only one City of Women, and this is it.

Etam bought one of the landmark buildings from the late department store Samaritaine and turned it into a five-floor department store with an entire lifestyle worth of design, including a cafe, hair stylist, spa, and beauty department. The Tammy clothing line was created specifically for hip 9- to 15-year-olds. Prices are low to moderate; high-fashion looks are everywhere.

The cafe is quite good and offers a wonderful view of Paris rooftops, as well as a chance to sip "perfumed" (flavored) iced tea—try rose, the hottest (coolest) taste in town. ℂ 01-44-76-73-73.

Kiliwatch

84 rue Tiquetonne, 2e (Métro: Etienne Marcel or Les Halles).

Near the hottest shops on rue Etienne Marcel and not far from the Forum Les Halles mall, this store is very deep and stocked with an amazing combination of new and vintage clothing. The whole look is pulled together for you under one roof, and you finally understand what being a teen is all about, at least fashionwise. A marvelous mix that includes jeans, shoes, outerwear—everything you need to be trendy.

Le Shop

3 rue d'Argout, 2e (Métro: Etienne Marcel).

Don't let the address frighten you—this is easy to find and worth doing, possibly right after you check into your hotel. The store is huge, has loud music blaring at all hours, and hosts quite the teen scene. The clothes are cutting edge; this is where you'll find what's coming up next, as well as the crowd that wears it. Plenty of giveaways for clubs and concerts as well. This is one of the most important stores in French fashion. ✆ 01-40-26-07-75.

New Look

Forum les Halles (Métro: Les Halles).

British import of really low-cost clothing. Good for trend busters. I prefer Target in the U.S. for similar things, but the area is fun for teens and tweens.

Pro Mod

67 rue de Sèvres, 6e (Métro: Sèvres-Babylone); and many others.

This French chain is somewhere between Gap and Ann Taylor. It is not that teen-oriented unless your look is BCBG; it's for all female members of the family. In summer, the clothes are perfect for any beach destination. In fall, they're more serious and businesslike, copies of current styles. Everything is priced so you can wear it one season and forget about it the next year. ✆ 01-42-22-33-90.

Wine

Auge

116 bd Haussmann, 8e (Métro: Madeleine).

It's not hard to find a great wine shop in Paris; but this one is special, so try to pop in. This immediate neighborhood has enough of interest to be worth a trip; see the Boulangerie St-Ouen listing on p. 102. ✆ **01-45-22-16-97.**

Autour du Vin

1 rue Scribe, 9e (Métro: Opéra).

Conveniently located next to a famous restaurant, this wine shop sells it all, including accessories, and it has tastings. The store is owned by EuroCave, the wine-cooling people. ✆ **01-55-27-10-90.**

Dernier Goutte

6 rue de Bourbon le Château, 6e (Métro: St-Germain-des-Prés).

There is only one Juan in Paris, and he is half of the team that owns this small wine shop—an American in Paris by way of Puerto Rico. He is the mentor to just about everyone with good taste on the Left Bank. You can buy by the region, by the price, or by trust. ✆ **01-46-29-11-62.**

La Cave de Robuchon

5 rue Montalembert, 7e (Métro: Rue du Bac); and (around the corner) 3 rue Paul-Louis Courier.

Once the most famous chef in France (now several chefs hold this title), Joel Robuchon changed the direction of eating in Paris with the opening of his atelier in the 7e. Now he has opened a wine shop nearby with more than 600 different labels. There are three sommeliers on staff to guide you toward the right choice for the meal or the budget. Monday to Saturday 10am to 8pm. ✆ **01-42-22-11-02.** www.joel-robuchon.com.

Lavinia

3–5 bd de la Madeleine, 8e (Métro: Madeleine).

Another of the handful of new wine shops, this one specializes in wines from outside of France. There's also a wine bar inside the store. ℭ 01-42 -97-20-20. www.lavinia.fr.

Lovin'

40 rue St-Honoré, 1er (Métro: Pont Neuf).

Read this address carefully and pay attention to the Métro stop—this is not where you think it is, but thankfully it is convenient to many places you must visit. The large wine shop has tastings, information services, and a cave that you can use to store your treasures. Monday through Friday, it's open only in afternoons, beginning at 2:30pm; on Saturday, it's open from 10am to 8pm. ℭ 01-42-33-34-58. www.lovin.fr.

Tchin-Tchin

9 rue Montorgueil, 1er (Métro: Les Halles).

I've included this special shop because I adore it, but also because I love the entire block, which is in a convenient part of Paris where you will undoubtedly be prowling. This is a wine and champagne shop that specializes in small and unknown labels and specialty champagne. ℭ 01-42-33-07-77.

Shopping Adventure

For more on buying champagne in the Champagne region, see p. 230.

Chapter 6

Paris Beauty

Perfume and makeup can still be good buys in Paris, often depending on the brand. You also must take into account French style. Don't underestimate the power of novelty, new launches, or experience as a souvenir. (Look at the **Biguine** line for some newfangled eye shadow tricks.)

You may want to invest in some wild new products that aren't available in the U.S., if only to amuse your friends . . . or you may vote to spend money on spa time, to get a piece of the famed French *bien-être* (well-being).

Because money does matter, remember that you have two big choices for savings—through department stores with their discount schemes or through duty-free shops in town (not at the airport).

Note that the department store **Au Printemps** has redone, expanded, renovated, re-created, and gone nuts with its beauty department—it now takes up three levels of the Printemps Maison store and is the largest beauty hall in the world. In other news, the professional brand **Make Up For Ever** has launched a low-cost line, sold in Monoprix and *hypermarchés*.

Because French stores, like those all over the world, are stuck within the war of the brands, the latest way to bring novelty to French shoppers is to launch American brands. They just keep coming!

Vive la Difference

Makeup in France is different from French makeup in the U.S. This is because makeup (even French brands) sold in the United States must be made according to FDA regulations, regardless of where it's manufactured. When you get to France, the names of your favorite products may be the same or different, and even makeup with the same name may not be identical in shade.

In addition, some products available in France are not sold in the U.S. at all, either because they haven't been launched yet or because the FDA has not approved them.

Many American brands that you see in France, such as Estée Lauder and Elizabeth Arden, are made in France (or Europe) for the European market. You may save on these items after the détaxe refund, but generally you do not save on American brands in Europe.

French perfumes are always introduced in France before they come out internationally. This lead time may be as much as a year. If you want to keep up with the newest fragrances, go to your favorite duty-free store and ask specifically for the newest. If you're stumped for a gift for the person who has everything, consider one of these new fragrances. The biggest spring launch comes in time for Mother's Day in France, which is usually a different day than in the U.S., but always in spring (May or early June).

The converse of this rule also applies. Some older scents are taken off the market in the U.S. and U.K. because sales aren't strong enough. These fragrances are still for sale in France. Just ask anyone looking for Je Reviens.

Some scents never come to the U.S. at all. Guerlain is big on this, as are many other design houses when it comes to their ephemeral scents—the ones that come and go for a season or a promotion. If novelty is your goal, start spritzing.

Beauty for Men

I told you to watch out for novelty. But in Paris, makeup and skin care for men are past the novelty stage and even beyond the trendy stage. It's happening, man. There are day spas just for men, treatments at all spas geared specifically toward men (thanks, I needed that), and many, many skin-care products that are packaged for men so they don't think it's sissy stuff.

A study on French spas recently reported that 30% of the clients are men. Firms from Biotherm to Nivea have products just for men; from Sephora to Monoprix there are entire racks of products just for men.

Institut Marc Delacre
17 av. George V, 8e (Métro: George V).

Exclusively for guys, and treatments start at 100€ ($150).

Nickel
48 rue des Francs-Bourgeois, 3e (Métro: Hôtel de Ville).

Men's spa, with its own line of products. ✆ 01-42-77-41-10.

All Beauty, All Day

Nocibe
This is a Sephora wannabe; some of their stores are interesting in that they carry more dime-store and pharmacy brands than Sephora. Size counts in that to compare accurately, you need a large branch store. Otherwise, the same principles apply—it's a beauty and fragrance supermarket. Note that they choose a category of products and offer them up for 20% savings on a rotational or seasonal basis. If it's summer, sunblock is on sale, and so forth.

WEB TIPS ✐ There are e-boutiques, and you can order online. The site is also very easy to understand (even in French) because prices are clearly marked. www.nocibe.fr.

Sephora

70 av. des Champs-Elysées, 8e (Métro: Franklin D. Roosevelt); 21–23 bd Haussmann, 9e (Métro: Chaussée d'Antin); 70 rue de Rivoli, 1er (Métro: Châtelet or Pont Neuf); Forum des Halles, 11 bis, rue de l'Arc-en-Ciel, 1er (Métro: Châtelet or Les Halles); and others.

This is a large chain of cosmetics and beauty-products shops with stores all over France, in most major European cities, and now in the U.S. as well. The flagship Champs-Elysées store, which is open daily, is the best one to visit.

Sephora is not a discounter or duty-free, but it offers instant détaxe and a very, very large selection of brands. You may do better pricewise in a department store (with your discount card), but you'll have more fun at a branch of Sephora.

Those are the facts; the emotions are harder to explain. This is simply a shrine to the beauty industry, and a makeup junkie's best fix. The helpful salespeople wear cute uniforms; if you ask for extra samples, you may get them (samples are not automatically given; you must ask), and this is a great source for inexpensive—and inventive—gifts.

You can buy prepackaged gift boxes of the house brand or build your own box. The animal-shaped bath gels are great for kids. There is also a small bookshop with books and reference materials related to beauty and fragrance.

Shop & Save

Please note the détaxe system here provides one of the best refunds in the country. You will get a refund of slightly over 16%.

Bath & Soap

Since medieval times, the French have been known for their interest in the bathing arts (don't snicker—it's dry cleaning that's expensive in France, not bath water). It was the French who first learned how to mass-produce soap (in Marseille), and they still make some of the best soap and bath products in the world. An inexpensive gift gimmick is to package together a *gant de toilette,* the French version of a washcloth, with a bar of designer soap or a French soap that has a cute story, like one of the new salad soaps (lettuce and tomato with basil, for instance). The total cost will be about 8€ ($12).

Below I have listed some French brands that are known for their bath products and have their own stores; some of them also have U.S. distribution.

Durance
224 rue Vignon, 9e (Métro: Madeleine).

A small but luxe soap brand that uses this store to sell not only soap, body, and bathing products, but also foodstuffs and Provençal-themed merchandise.

BEST BETS Have a test moment with the lavender-scented hand cream. It's very expensive (about 25€/$38) but one of the best products I've ever tried. © 01-47-42-04-10. www.durance.fr.

La Compagnie de Provence
16 rue Vignon, 9e (Métro: Madeleine).

This famous brand from Marseille (sometimes written as LCDP) has finally come to Paris in the form of its own store—the brand has been sold in boutiques and department stores for years. You will recognize the line from its distinctive package, but will also note that it has recently expanded into new scents—I just bought cherry-scented liquid soap. Also note that there are several other soap stores on this street. When I was in the store last, it was mobbed with Japanese tourists who consider this an important status brand to bring home for gifts. I do, too. ☎ 01-42-68-01-60. www.lcdpmarseille.com.

International Beauty Brands

Armani

Armani stores, including 25 place Vendôme, 1er (Métro: Tuileries), and department stores.

Armani makeup is also available in the U.S.; yes, it's made by L'Oréal, but it's still good stuff.

Menard

21 rue de la Paix, 2e (Métro: Opéra).

This is a Japanese line and most of the customers are Japanese; but for those who want to know what's new in Paris— *voilà*. There are color cosmetics and skin care; the Embellir Night Cream is said to have benefits from reishi, which helps regenerate new cells. Also sold in department stores and Sephora. ☎ 01-42-65-58-08.

Shiseido

3 bd Malesherbes, 8e (Métro: Madeleine).

Don't confuse this listing with the Shiseido-owned perfume shop in the Jardin du Palais Royal. This is a brand-new building in a brand-new location, part of a stretch of new installations that have turned this into one of the city's most interesting retail corners. Shiseido is known for pricey but well-made beauty treatments and many innovations in beauty and anti-aging products.

BEST BETS The liquid foundation in the tube is very light and smooth and worth the money.

Shu Uemura

176 bd St-Germain, 6e (Métro: St-Germain-des-Prés).

If you consider yourself an aficionado of cosmetics, to be in Paris and not go here is a sin. Yes, it's even better than Bourjois—more expensive, too. Shu Uemura was one of the most famous makeup artists in the world and a cult hero in his native Japan. You can buy his makeup and skin-care products in every world capital.

Samples, mirrors, and brushes fill this high-tech shop, just encouraging you to come in and do your face. In makeup, color is the name of the game here: The hues are spectacular. A single square of color costs about 17€ ($25), which is actually less than many big-name French brands.

Most department stores also carry the brand; there is a Shu Uemura Nail Bar in Bon Marché. Le Drugstore, on Champs-Elysées, also has Shu Uemura makeup.

Face & Body

Darphin
97 rue du Bac, 7e (Métro: Rue du Bac).

This is a chic, almost secret salon that does facials and treatments (French skin salons never do hair). It sells its own line of natural bath and beauty products, which have made it to America in limited doses—only the rich and with-it know about this line. The salon is big on body shaping and has many hydro-plus (water-added) products to moisturize and balance. Its products are sold in department stores and *parapharmacies* and are known as "the poor man's Sisley." **Note:** Darphin has been purchased by Estée Lauder; I had a note from one reader who says the line is not as good as it used to be, as a result of the takeover.

Decleor
Department stores and parapharmacies.

Decléor is a large line of treatments created around the concept of therapeutic oils, addressing everything from dry skin to aging. I'm not sure if I'm addicted to the benefits or just the scents, but I keep buying. Decléor has teamed with Carita to open its first spa; it's at the Hilton Arc de Triomphe. Non-hotel guests may sign up for treatments.

Exyste

26 Galerie de Montpensier, Palais Royal, 1er (Métro: Palais-Royal).

This is a small line in a small, new shop in the Palais Royal and is considered a cult brand by Japanese beauty mavens who flock here. The line is made up of natural ingredients, such as wild yams. © 01-42-96-00-18.

LeClerc

Department stores and parapharmacies.

This brand, known for its makeup for years, has closed its shop and is concentrating on department-store distribution and research and development. The latest launch is a complete line of face and beauty treatments.

Phytomer

Parapharmacies.

There is a Phytologie hair treatment center at 33 rue des Arcades, 8e (Métro: St-Augustin or Madeleine), but no free-standing shop for the spa or beauty products. There is also a Phytomer spa in Lafayette Homme, at Galeries Lafayette. *Parapharmacies* carry the firm's beauty products.

Sisley

Department stores and duty-free shops.

Perhaps the most famous name in French skin care, this line added makeup a few years ago and is a favorite for Americans who adore the fact that the line is about 30% less in France.

Parapharmacies

These stores specialize in French pharmaceutical brands of makeup and beauty treatments, usually discounted 20%. These are wonderful places to research new products and things you never see in the U.S. All department stores have a *parapharmacie* section, usually adjacent to the makeup department.

Euro Sante Beaute
37 rue de la Boétie, 8e (Métro: St-Augustin), and others.

I love Euro Santé Beauté—I visit one in every French city that has one. More than 200 brands are on sale here, at what I consider one of the better *parapharmacies* in town. Most of the branches are relatively large by French standards. Ask for a price list, which you can pocket and use to comparison shop. This is a large chain; there is also a branch next door to the Hôtel Concorde St-Lazare (Métro: St-Lazare).

French Makeup Secrets

By Terry
21 Galerie Vérot-Dodat, 1er (Métro: Palais-Royal); 6 rue Jacob, 6e (Métro: St-Germain-des-Prés); 30 rue de la Trémoille, 8e (Métro: Franklin D. Roosevelt).

Makeup addicts, search no more: This is the "in" place to visit and test and swoon over. More and more shops are popping up in Paris, as well as other French cities.

Terry de Gunzberg gained fame when she created all the colors and makeup for Yves Saint Laurent's beauty line, for which she still consults. After years in the big-time beauty biz, Terry created her own line that is known for the density of the pigment. Because she uses so much pigment, the color is said to last longer than normal makeup.

About Bourjois

You've heard of Chanel, sure, but Bourjois? Bourjois is the name of the company that owns the Chanel line of makeup and perfume; it makes a lower-priced line of makeup under the Bourjois name—at the same factories where Chanel is manufactured! This doesn't mean that the lines are identical, but if you can't afford Chanel and want to give this line a whirl, you may be pleased with the investment (about 50% less expensive than Chanel). With the weak dollar, this line is not cheap—it just costs much less than Chanel.

Bourjois is hard to find in the U.S., but it's not hard to find in Paris—if you know where to look. You can buy it at any branch of **Monoprix** or **Sephora,** or at any big French department store. What makes the line so special? For starters: many, many shades of eye shadow sold in big containers, which last forever. The nail polishes and lipsticks are also good.

You can get "made over" in the salon and then pick the choices for your palette (a small plastic container that is fitted to hold assorted color pots). The palette is free if you fill it, but you can also buy a la carte. The shops can create custom colors as well; this is pricey, but makes a status statement.

Stephane Marais
217 rue St-Honoré, 1er (Métro: Tuileries).

This makeup artist, the latest Shiseido protégé, works with a line of 188 products. He also does fashion shows in Paris, as well as private faces for civilians.

Perfume & Scent

Annick Goutal
14 rue de Castiglione, 1er (Métro: Tuileries or Concorde); and others.

The tiny shop on the rue de Castiglione is a Paris landmark, but Annick Goutal has a number of other outlets in Paris and elsewhere in the world.

Just step into the Belle Epoque–style salon and sniff the house brands, which include perfumes, lotions, and house scents. Be sure to look at the firm's logo, in a mosaic on the sidewalk in front of the store.

I'm addicted to the soap called L'Hadrien, the house soap for hotels in the Concorde chain. I like it so much, I've been known to pay cash for it. Despite the fact that Mme Goutal died several years ago, her family carries on the business; new scents are continually launched.

Artisan Parfumeur

2 rue de l'Amiral de Coligny, 1er (Métro: Louvre-Rivoli); 24 bd Raspail, 7e (Métro: Rue du Bac); 22 rue Vignon, 9e (Métro: Madeleine).

This source makes its name selling hard-to-find brands in Paris, but beware: Many are American or British.

Creed

38 rue Pierre 1er de Serbie, 8e (Métro: Alma-Marceau).

This was a British perfume house when it was founded in 1760; during Victorian times, the firm moved to France. It is now a cult brand that makes scents for royalty and rich people. Prince Rainier asked the house to create a little something for Grace Kelly to wear on their wedding day. Now you, too, can buy it—or any of the other scents worn by celebs, kings, and queens. You can either commission a custom-made scent or choose from the ready-made fragrances.

Frederic Malle

140 av. Victor Hugo, 16e (Métro: Victor-Hugo).

This jewel-box tiny shop sells specialty brews of Malle's own fragrances—there's much emphasis on consultation in choosing the right scent.

Guerlain

68 av. des Champs-Elysées, 8e (Métro: Franklin D.
Roosevelt); 2 place Vendôme, 1er (Métro: Opéra); 93 rue de
Passy, 16e (Métro: La Muette); 29 rue de Sèvres, 6e (Métro:
Sèvres-Babylone); 35 rue Tronchet, 8e (Métro: Madeleine).

Guerlain Instituts de Beaute

68 av. des Champs-Elysées, 8e (Métro: Franklin D.
Roosevelt).

Perhaps the most famous name in fragrance in France, Guerlain has two types of boutiques in Paris. Some sell products only, while others have salons on the premises. The flagship store on the Champs-Elysées has just been renovated.

Insider's Tip

The maison will create your own fragrance for a mere
30,000€ ($45,000).

Perfumes are sold only through Guerlain stores and are not discounted; the brand is rarely found at duty-free stores. If you see it at a duty-free, chances are there is no discount. Some Guerlain fragrances that you'll see in France are not sold in the U.S.

BEST BETS In the year 2000, I bought a limited-edition fragrance from Guerlain (they do a new one every year) that I flipped for. By the time I wanted more, it was out of production. I spent 8 years tracking it down to discover it was renamed and repackaged and is now sold as *Atrape Coeur*. It's heavy and sweet (just like me).

Jean Patou

5 rue de Castiglione, 1er (Métro: Concorde).

Patou's most famous fragrance is Joy, but the house has numerous scents and now a newish store that happens to be a few doors from my favorite duty-free shop for perfume: Catherine. Patou will custom-blend a scent for you. ✆ 01-42-92-07-22.

Patricia de Nicolai
80 rue de Grenelle, 7e (Métro: Rue du Bac).

A nose is a nose is a nose; this is the granddaughter of the Guerlain family. Fragrance, candles, potpourri, and more. Note the odd hours: It's closed from 2 to 2:30pm daily.

Salon Shiseido
142 Galerie de Valois, Jardin du Palais Royal, 1er (Métro: Palais-Royal).

If you think this store caters to Japanese tourists, you can forget it right now. This happens to be one of Paris's best-kept secrets, and also one of the must-do addresses that any serious shopper (I mean, sociologist) should seek out, merely from an academic standpoint.

First, a quick history lesson: Shiseido is a Japanese makeup firm. A million years ago, it hired the most famous makeup artist in Paris, Serge Lutens, and let him explore his creativity. This tiny shop, with the most glorious decor in Paris, sells his private inventions and designs. It is best known for his custom-made perfumes. Note that everything is a perfume—there are no derivatives. A bottle of scent costs about 90€ ($135). Beware the stopper; it's not set in too well, so you must pack your fragrance carefully or hand-carry it onto the plane.

To find the shop, walk behind the Comédie-Française (next to the Palais-Royal Métro) into the gardens of the Palais Royal. Go past the creative modern sculptures to the centuries-old gardens. Along each side, you'll see an arcade crammed with shops. The Shiseido salon is in the far arcade across the gardens.

Discounters

"Discount" is a dirty word in France, and "duty-free" has become confusing. Even a source that discounts, and has done so for years, is suddenly terrified of mix-ups.

Here's the deal: Discount is one thing, détaxe is another, and duty-free is still another.

The big beauty firms do not approve of **discounting**, but they tolerate it up to 15% or 20%. The percentage varies by brand; at an honest store, the staff will explain that the amount of the discount varies.

Détaxe is the tax refund that any non-E.U. passport holder qualifies for after spending 175€ ($263) at any one store in a single day; for a full explanation, see "Détaxe Details" (p. 34).

Duty-free sold at the airport is a flat 13% off—you qualify to buy duty-free only when you are departing the E.U.

A quick overview:

- At Sephora, you get no discount, but you get instant détaxe (if you qualify)—and détaxe is a higher rate than normal.
- At a major specialty *maison,* such as Guerlain, Creed, or Caron, you get no discount, but you do get détaxe (if you qualify).
- At a major department store, you get a 10% discount with the store's tourist-discount card (obtain it free at the store's welcome desk); you also get 12% détaxe (if and when you qualify).
- At the airport, you pay exactly 13% less than the department-store full price.
- At the few so-called duty-free shops in central Paris, you get the maximum discount that they allow, which ranges from 15% to 25%, plus the détaxe refund of 13% (if and when you qualify). If you do not spend enough to get the détaxe refund, you get the flat upfront discount—even if you buy only one mascara. The amount of the flat discount varies with the store and the brand.

Hairstylists

Going to the hairstylist in Paris is fun if you have the time and the patience. While the fanciest salons are expensive, they offer not only a chance to pamper yourself, but also a social history lesson and glimpse at a way of life that you can't be part of, on any level, unless you marry into it. I'd give up a few hours in the Louvre in order to visit Carita.

Alexandre de Paris

3 av. Matignon, 8e (Métro: Matignon); Les Trois Quartiers, place de la Madeleine, 1er (Métro: Madeleine).

Alexandre is legend, perhaps the most famous of the old-school hairdressers. The name is so well known that there's a separate hair-accessories business, with shops all over the world and products sold in major department stores.

For the avenue Matignon shop, call © **01-43-59-40-09.** For the place de la Madeleine shop, call © **01-49-26-04-59.**

Carita

11 rue du Faubourg St-Honoré, 8e (Métro: Concorde).

Perhaps the most famous name in beauty in all of Paris, Carita offers an entire town house devoted to putting madame's best foot forward. The entrance is on the Faubourg, off the street and set in a little bit.

The great thing about this place, aside from the fact that the reception staff speaks English, is that it's so organized, you can be assured you'll be taken care of. Just walk to the appointment clerk (on street level to your left, once you've parted the waves) and make an appointment. You can also call or fax ahead for an appointment. You can, of course, ask for a particular stylist, but if you don't, not to worry—you'll be in good hands, regardless.

The stylists wear white uniforms; the patrons wear expensive clothes and carry the best handbags in Paris. You receive a paper number when you check your belongings and pick up your smock; don't lose it. This is your client number, which stays with you until you pay the bill.

Note: Patrons do not take off their clothes here; the smock goes over what you are wearing.

The cost of this pampering is the going rate for ultrafancy in Paris; you can do better pricewise, but never experience-wise. I consider each trip to Carita a souvenir for myself. I come away with a memory and a good hairdo. A shampoo and blow-dry, which includes service (meaning you do not tip), costs about 100€ ($150), or more if you add hair-care products. In France, you pay for each ingredient they put in your hair when they wash it.

Carita added beauty and skin-care products a few years ago and now offers spa services—a natural extension of what it has always done, and done so well. The back desk at street level sells beauty products and accessories.

Carita has branches in various shopping districts of Paris; there is also a Carita spa in the Hilton Arc de Triomphe. Call ℂ 01-44-94-11-00 or send a fax to 01-47-42-94-98.

Jean-Marc Maniatis

35 rue de Sèvres, 6e (Métro: Sèvres-Babylone); 18 rue Marbeuf, 8e (Métro: Franklin D. Roosevelt); Galeries Lafayette, 40 bd Haussmann, 9e (Métro: Chaussée-d'Antin); Beauty school: Forum des Halles, 2e (Métro: Les Halles).

Still one of the hot shops for models and runway stars, Maniatis has salons in Paris (one is in Galeries Lafayette), as well as a beauty school. The beauty school has a service that offers free haircuts to clients who are willing to let a student practice on them. Men, women, and teens may participate; the stylists make all the choices—you are the guinea pig.

If you want to go for a regular Maniatis session, note that the Right Bank salon is open on Monday; the Left Bank salon is not. You can reach the Rue de Sèvres location at ℂ 01-45-44-16-39, the Rue Marbeuf location at ℂ 01-47-23-30-14, the Galeries Lafayette location at ℂ 01-42-82-07-09, and the beauty school at ℂ 01-47-20-00-05.

SHOP TALK For those trying Systeme D, head to the beauty school.

Hair-Salon Chains

Jacques Dessange (see below) is a chain of salons with locations all over France. The latest trend is toward less expensive and less formal chains. Many of them do not require appointments, and some have salons in the U.S. Check out **Jean Louis David, Camille Albane,** and **Jean-Claude Biguine.** All three have convenient salons; your hotel concierge will tell you which is nearest. They are all relatively inexpensive (by Paris standards), but do not expect the same quality of work or service that you get at a big-name salon. If you're having a number of services performed and price is an issue, go over a price list with someone who speaks English before you begin. Most Paris salons charge a la carte, which means you can be charged for each shampooing. The price includes service; only regulars top off the bill.

Jacques Dessange

37 av. Franklin D. Roosevelt, 8e (Métro: Franklin D. Roosevelt).

Still famous after all these years, Dessange has a number of shops in Paris and other locations, including the U.S. The clientele is younger and not as fancy as that at Carita's, but Dessange has a big-time reputation nonetheless. Hollywood's José Eber started here. The beauty and makeup line is available at

---

The Discount 'Do

Most of the chains have training sessions at which you can get a free or cheap hairdo. The best of the bunch is **Centre Camille Albane,** 114 rue de la Boétie, 8e (Métro: Franklin D. Roosevelt). For reservations and availability, women ages 20 to 50 can call ✆ **01-43-59-31-32.** Another option is **Jacques Dessange** (✆ **01-44-70-08-08**), which also does training sessions and imposes similar age restrictions.

the salon and at pharmacies. There are hundreds of salons in France; call ℂ 01-43-59-31-31 for the one nearest you.

Lucie Saint-Clair

4 av. Pierre 1er de Serbie, 16e (Métro: Alma-Marceau).

This location is the chain's flagship, also called Top International. There's a special that includes a cut, *balayage* (streaks), and blow-dry for about 100€ ($150). The salon offers some spa services. Call ℂ 01-47-20-53-54.

Spa Me

Water, water everywhere and not a drop to drink: Of course not, this is Paris. You drink wine; bathe in water; and celebrate beauty, health, and science in salt water, mud, algae, scented oils, honey, and wine.

Spas have been around France since the Romans marched through, and *maman* trains every French girl to visit the *esthéticienne* (beautician) regularly for *les soins* (the cures). The beauty "cures" are not considered a luxury, but a necessity.

What has changed in France, especially in Paris, is the idea of the day spa—borrowed from New York and translated with French style, as well as French prices. Because *les soins* are part of everyday life in Paris, they are very affordable. Even the fanciest spas and salons in Paris are a bargain compared to U.S. prices for the same or similar treatments.

While French families may still sign up for a 1-week cure at famous spas all over the country (mostly in coastal destinations like La Baule, Biarritz, and Monte Carlo), more and more of the working public is taking advantage of the day spa. The customers are almost equally men and women—in France there is nothing sissy about a guy having a spa treatment, especially when he's traveling.

Spa Thoughts

Whatever spa you choose, remember some basics:

- In France, body treatments are likely to be done on your naked body. No paper panties.
- Although prices include service, you do tip (give a small token, not a percentage).
- Most spas will try to sell you their products; some will be rather aggressive about it. The products may be less expensive at Monoprix or a parapharmacie—and you don't need to buy the products in order to have them respect you in the morning.
- Sometimes a spa will take a walk-in, but it's usually best to book ahead. If you want a jet-lag treatment on arrival, book before you depart for France.
- Smaller spas may not have English-speaking personnel; ask your hotel concierge for help if you do not speak French.

There is a difference between an *Institut de Beauté* and a spa. One is a fancy salon with a few treatments; the other is a full-service place, with many treatments and often a gym. Parisian hotels have the best selection of day spas in Paris; many of them are open to nonguests.

HOTEL SPAS

Anne Semonin

Hôtel Bristol, 112 rue du Faubourg St-Honoré, 8e (Métro: Champs-Elysées Clemenceau).

This luxury hotel has the best of all worlds: the Anne Semonin spa, next door but in the same building; an Anne Semonin treatment room adjoining the pool and health club; and Anne Semonin products in the guest rooms.

Semonin is an international cult figure; she does not advertise, but is known for her all-natural products and treatments. The best is a jet-lag cure, which consists of a wrap that eliminates toxins. Prices begin at 50€ ($75). If I had to pick my favorite spa in Paris, this would be it.

There is a men's spa in Madelois, a men's department store. Barneys and Bergdorf Goodman carry Semonin's products in the U.S. ℰ **01-42-66-63-98.**

Carita Mosaique

Hilton Arc de Triomphe, 51 rue de Courcelles, 8e (Métro: Courcelles).

This is the first full Carita spa in the world—although a test spa exists on a cruise ship, and the real Carita (a hairdresser) is still on the Faubourg St-Honoré, so don't get confused. The spa is named Mosaique in honor of the zillions of glittery tiles inlaid in the enormous spa space with giant treatment rooms and private lockers. Products used are either from the Carita line or by Decléor. You need not be a hotel guest in order to book here. I had a very nice facial (for anti-aging, no less), but the product sales pitch afterward was very aggressive. ℰ **01-58-36-17-17.**

Four Seasons George V

31 av. George V, 8e (Métro: Alma-Marceau or George V).

If you want swanky, nothing in Paris compares to this spa, with its neoclassical decorations and swimming pool. It looks like something out of a decor magazine. Treatments are currently for hotel guests only, but the Four Seasons also offers VIP spa rooms (available by the hour) for small groups, such as a bridal party or family. The hotel also offers a package that includes room, breakfast, and a spa treatment. ℰ **01-49-52-70-00.**

InterContinental Hotel le Grand

2 rue Scribe at place de l'Opera, 9e (Métro: Opéra).

InterConti has been upgrading their spas and calls them I-Spa, not to be confused with the British firm E-Spa. The I-Spa in their Paris hotel is brand-new and coordinated with Algotherm, a marine well-being brand. ℰ **01-40-06-01-17.**

DAY SPAS

Anne Fontaine
370 rue St-Honoré, 1er (Métro: Concorde).

It is totally beyond me why a fashion designer known for her white shirts would (1) open a spa and (2) open the spa beneath her new flagship, causing the clothes to smell like chlorine. On the other hand, this woman does everything with great style and this is one of the new faces of Paris. ✆ **01-42-61-03-70.**

Daniel Jouvance, Espace Mer
91 av. des Champs-Elysées, 8e (Métro: Franklin D. Roosevelt or George V).

You don't need to go to a hotel to enjoy a spa day: Daniel Jouvance, who operates a spa in La Baule, the French Atlantic center for *thalassotherapie,* also has Espace Mer, right on the Champs-Elysées. You can test and choose from his wide range of products on the ground level, or go upstairs for traditional Brittany-style treatments, most of which involve the use of water.

The spa offers cures broken down into types (serenity, kinestherapy, skin, and beauty). The 30-minute treatments cost about 30€ ($45), a 70-minute toning treatment costs about 50€ ($75), and half-day combination packages are available. My idea of heaven? Stroll (and shop, of course) the Champs-Elysées, go to the spa for part of the day, then take in a movie. Call ✆ **01-47-23-48-00.**

Jean-Claude Biguine
10 rue Marbeuf, 8e (Métro: Franklin D. Roosevelt).

The treatment business has become so hot that beauty brands are not the only ones that want a piece of the action. Enter the big-name French hairdressers. Jean-Claude Biguine has expanded his empire from hair to makeup to spas and offers a full program to rehabilitate you. The daylong package costs 250€ ($375) and includes treatments for body and hair, as well as a manicure, pedicure, waxing, haircut, and blow-dry. ✆ **01-53-67-81-90.**

Sothy's

128 rue du Faubourg St-Honoré, 8e (Métro: Champs-Elysées Clemenceau).

Not far from the Hôtel Bristol at the far end of this famous street, the tiny Sothy's shop and spa is an insider's delight. Prices for anti-aging treatments begin at 75€ ($113). Although the product line is not well known in the U.S., the full-service spa is perhaps the best destination for a combination of makeup, beauty, and body treatments. ✆ 01-53-93-91-53.

DEPARTMENT STORE SPAS

The department stores are always at war with one another, seeking out the latest brand names or supporting the classic French lines. Be sure to check for spa news at each store's welcome desk.

Galeries Lafayette has the **Phytomer Spa.** Printemps has **Yves Rocher, Nuxe,** and **Shiseido** minispas as well as a new rooftop spa.

MASS MARKET SPAS

l'Occitane Spa

4 rue de Sevres, 6e (Métro: Sèvres-Babylone).

This maker of oils, soaps, makeup, and body products from Provence is slowly adding spa services to some of its spaces around the world, offering pampering and quick-fix solutions in body care. The first one was in London, and now Paris is getting into the rub. Note that this brand is opening a hotel-cum-spa in Apt in Provence.

There are two dozen free-standing l'Occitane shops in Paris; the line is also sold in department stores and some pharmacies. The spa business is growing slowly and in many cases in conjunction with Hilton Hotels in foreign destinations. ✆ 01-45-44-70-26.

Nuxe Spa

32 rue Montorgueil, 1er (Métro: Les Halles).

Nuxe is a brand sold in *parapharmacies* and popular stores such as Monoprix or even Auchan and Carrefour. It's a terrific brand, made with natural ingredients, and their spa is reasonably priced and sufficiently luxe, with a 2-hour treatment costing about 133€ ($200). ☎ **01-55-80-71-40.** www.nuxe.fr.

Yves Rocher

92 av. des Champs-Elysées, 8e (Métro: Franklin D. Roosevelt).

This makeup, beauty, and hair-care brand has zillions of salons across France. Prices are low; rates for spa services are in keeping with the prices of products and are quite fair. This is the line that many teens begin with; as they gain disposable income, they move on to bigger brands. ☎ **01-45-62-78-27.**

Chapter 7

Ma Maison

Garcia vs. Starck

If I were doing a master dissertation on French hotels or maybe just French style and its evolution in the past 15 years, I'd like to look at the way Jacques Garcia and Philippe Starck have changed, mutated, and influenced most of what we see as the new French look.

The French aristo look with inherited antiques is no longer the mode, so pop into the Hôtel Meurice to see the renovation of the lobby by Philippe Starck and his daughter Asa. This is the new "it" look, which is something like the old Jacques Garcia "it" look for Costes Hotel 10 years ago.

Be prepared to swap gilt for silver spray paint, to mix old-fashioned with new-fashioned, and to raise up the ceilings even higher while you dapple the color and step on the zebra skins. Look out, world.

French Airs

French home scents are so affordable and come in so many formats that they make perfect souvenirs. New methods of scent distribution are invented all the time: You'll find everything from perfumed powder for the vacuum cleaner to devices that sweeten the air.

Diptyque
34 bd St-Germain, 5e (Métro: Maubert-Mutualité).

If you are not seriously into Diptyque, you can buy the candles at Printemps and save yourself a trip. This tiny store is not in the heart of the Left Bank shopping. In fact, it's sort of in the middle of nowhere, and you must make a special trip. So taxi right here and giggle right back to your hotel with a suitcase filled with gifts and goodies. You'll find candles, soaps, and scents; the candles cost 35€ ($53) each, less than the U.S. price. Closed Monday.

Estéban
49 rue de Rennes, 6e (Métro: St-Germain-des-Prés); 20 rue Francs-Bourgeois, 3e (Métro: St-Paul).

One of my favorite scent suppliers is Estéban, which is distributed all over Europe. The store carries diffusers, burners, incense, sprays, scented rocks, and so on. The Marais location is open on Sunday.

Lampes Berger
Department stores.

Lampes Berger makes fashionable oil-burning lanterns, not unlike genie lamps. They come in dozens of styles and cost 40€ to 100€ ($60–$150). You buy the scented liquid oil separately for approximately 15€ ($23); there are more than a dozen scents. The process of using this product is more complicated than lighting an aromatherapy candle—but then, this one works.

If you smoke, look into this product immediately—the scent effectively masks the smell of cigarette smoke.

Shop Talk
Carrying flammable goods on airplanes is illegal (bringing on the lamp itself is not), so you may need to use the toll-free number in the U.S. (provided in the package) to order the liquid. The state of California does not allow these devices.

Mariage Freres

30 rue du Bourg-Tibourg, 4e (Métro: St-Paul); 13 rue des Grands-Augustins, 5e (Métro: St-Michel).

Mariage Frères is one of the most sophisticated and expensive teahouses in Paris. It has its own line of tea-scented candles, which are in demand by those willing to spend about 45€ ($68) for a candle. Also sold in department stores.

Smart Shoppers' Home Style

Let's face it, very few people with any smarts at all go to Paris to buy fine antiques. Okay, maybe you're Lord Rothschild and you go to Paris for a few finishing touches for Spencer House. If you're playing in the big leagues, ignore this paragraph. There's no question that Paris has top-of-the-line resources; but the truth is, if you've ever cast a wary eye at the bottom line, you know that Paris has top-of-the-line prices as well. Even Parisians leave town to buy antiques.

People who have price in mind work the wide network of antiques shows, *brocante* fairs, auctions, flea markets, and weekends in the country, which provide not only wonderful entertainment, but also far better prices than you'll ever find on the Faubourg St-Honoré. Note that there are a number of annual events that charge admission—about 5€ ($7.50), sometimes more.

If you're a serious shopper and plan on some big-time buying, keep the following tips in mind:

- Buy from a dealer with an international reputation.
- Prices are usually quoted in dollars once they top $5,000.
- There is now a value-added tax on some antiques; ask for a détaxe form.
- Make sure you receive the appropriate paperwork so that your purchase can leave the country. The French are not going to let any national treasures slip through their fingers.
- Insure for replacement value, not cost.

Le Look

Paris has its share of home-style shops, similar to Pottery Barn, that sell a Euro look at a fair-to-moderate price. Prices might not be any better than those at home (in fact, they could be higher), but you'll find style galore, not to mention items you can't find elsewhere. I am constantly amazed by this look—it was first mastered by the Englishman Sir Terence Conran and owes its success to many American retailing methods.

The Conran Shop

8 bd Madeleine, 2e (Métro: Madeleine); 117 rue du Bac, 7e (Métro: Sèvres-Babylone).

This is a British shop, but Sir Terence Conran is an expert on French design. The Madeleine store is even more exciting than the Left Bank store; it's newer and has a cafe. Both locations are filled with tons of whimsy and charm. Just browse and breathe the magic: There are books, luggage, foodstuffs, gifts, home style, housewares, pens, paper goods, and more.

Flamant

8 place de Furstenberg, 6e (Métro: St-Germain-des-Prés); 279 rue St-Honoré, 8é (Métro: Concorde).

Long a brand name in French home style, Flamant recently opened stores in all of the major French cities. It makes its own furniture, but also has gift and tabletop items. There's a touch of the English in the look, but it is a dream style for many French families. A new branch will be opening on rue St-Honoré, 8e. ✆ 01-55-04-88-44. www.flamant.fr.

Lafayette Maison

35 bd Haussmann, 9e (Métro: Opéra or Havre Caumartin).

See p. 71 for more details on this newish department store of home style.

Maisons du Monde

Centre Commercial Les Halles, 1er (Métro: Les Halles); 32 rue du Faubourg St-Antoine, 12e (Métro: Ledru Rollin); 57 av. Italie, 13e.

This mass merchant may not interest you—the look isn't that different from Pier 1, and you can do well with this sort of thing (Indian and Asian imports) in the U.S. I have bought candles, picture frames, cutlery, and table accessories here. I happen to love the chain and am pleased to see it expanding in continental Europe. They seem to pick up on trends faster than the U.S. chains, although I promise you everything is made in Asia (and such) to bring in such fair prices. Nonetheless, style is paramount and worth checking out.

BEST BETS I was just on the rue St-Antoine and popped into the branch there . . . where I found a Venetian-style etched and mirrored bathroom glass (plastic) for 2€ ($3), so you never know what novelty items you'll find at fair prices.

The rue du Faubourg St-Antoine is actually an extension of the rue du Rivoli just on the far side of the Bastille, so that's your store. ✆ 01-53-33-83-07. www.maisonsdumonde.com.

Mis en Demeure

27 rue du Cherche-Midi, 6e (Métro: Sèvres-Babylone); 66 av. Victor Hugo, 16e (Métro: Victor-Hugo).

Sort of a hipper, more French Conran's. On my last visit, there were lots of country tabletop looks (items made with twigs) and papier-mâché Christmas ornaments. Some items border on the fabulous; others are ordinary. But when you first step inside and see all the glassware, linens, furniture, and lamps displayed together, you will think it's quite *extraordinaire*.

Specialty Looks

A number of chicer-than-thou shops are so fabulously French that you have to visit them, if only to browse.

Armani Casa

195 bd St-Germain, 6e (Métro: Rue du Bac).

Beyond the superstore in Milan, Armani now has a handful of home-furnishings stores in world capitals. The Paris store is especially well positioned near other designer showrooms, many of them Italian, and not far from the designer shops clustered around St-Germain-des-Prés. It sells tabletop and gift items, as well as furniture. There are no bargains here, but at least it doesn't look like expensive Conran (as it does in Milan).

Astier de Villatte

173 rue St-Honoré, 1er (Métro: Palais-Royal); 23 rue du Bac, 7e (Métro: Rue du Bac).

Blink and you'll miss this small shop. It is deep, but from the front you could pass it and not know that it's one of the most special spaces in France. It sells a look and a way of being and a mishmash of objects displayed to thrill your heart. The business revolves around hand-thrown whiteware (dishes), but there are also sweaters, gloves, socks, gifts, and objets d'art. The dishes are not inexpensive—a large piece can easily cost 120€ ($180)—but this is the chic look of the moment. This is one of those stores that open at 11am, so plan accordingly.

WEB TIPS 🖰 The website has a crystal ball you click on, then some swirling tarot cards and all sorts of fun things, but doesn't show merchandise or give more than store addresses and booth numbers at wholesale shows.

Call ✆ **01-42-60-74-13.** www.astierdevillatte.com.

Caravane

6 rue Pavee, 4e (Métro: St-Paul); 19 and 22 rue St Nicolas, 12e (Métro: Ledru Rollin).

You may not remember this, but early in this new edition I tipped you off that one of the hot new looks in Paris deco is African. Therefore, it stands to reason that this chain of minisouks has nomadic and desert looks from an assortment of third-world countries. ✆ **01-44-61-04-20.** www.caravane.fr.

SHOP TALK The stores are closed on Mondays and do not open until 11am otherwise.

Catherine Memmi

32 and 11 rue St-Sulpice, 6e (Métro: Odéon).

The look is minimalist, which isn't my thing, but the influence is from Kyoto and the designer's motto is "humble but beautiful." There are clean lines, luxury fabrics, and neutral tones galore; even Galeries Lafayette has a Memmi space. The shop at no. 11 sells more of what Memmi calls *les Basiques*.

La Tuile Loup

35 rue Daubenton, 5e (Métro: Monge).

Just trust me on this one. This shop brims with country French charm. It has a slightly out-of-the-way location, but you can easily wander into the 6e from here. If it's a market day—Wednesday or Friday—stop by place Monge, too.

Le Prince Jardinier

117–121 Arcade Vallois, 37 rue de Valois, Jardin du Palais Royal, 1er (Métro: Palais-Royal).

In the far corner of the arcade of shops in the Palais Royal, this store specializes in gardening and country looks. A prince owns it, hence the name. The gardening bags have become the weekend tote of the BCBG chic.

Maison de Famille

29 rue St-Sulpice, 6e (Métro: St-Sulpice or Mabillon); Place Madeleine, 8e (Métro: Madeleine).

This is almost a multiple, since there are now a few in Paris and several in the provinces. And why not? It's a terrific store with a wonderful look. The soothing blend of English, Euro, and chinoiserie will seduce you.

    Note: I love the look and feel here, but a shopper might end up paying high prices for British, American, or other imported goods. I can easily find similar things in the U.S. for less—yet when it's all put together, you have a serious browse along with some drooling.

Rosemarie Schulz

30 rue Boissy d'Anglas, 8e (Métro: Madeleine).

If you check out only one new address this trip, this should be it. It's near Territoire, inside the Galeries de la Madeleine. Be sure to see them both. Emotionally, the two shops are worlds apart. Schultz is a German designer and possibly a florist—her shop sells fabrics, pillows, sachets, and flowers. This is one of the most imaginative stores I've ever been in.

Sia

5 bd Malesherbes, 1er (Métro: Madeleine).

Sia is a mass merchant of style and class; this is its first shop, across from the Madeleine. It is known for fake flowers, and sells all sorts of tabletop items and home style (in department stores, too) at very good prices. I like the plastic container filled with silk rose petals, which you can throw at a bride or scatter on your dinner table.

Simrane

23 and 25 rue Bonaparte, 6e (Métro: St-Germain-des-Prés).

Block prints from India are made into mostly home style, although the smaller boutique of the two stores sells some clothing items. The *boutis* (bed quilts) are to die for, but then, so are the prices. Because the French Provençale fabrics (called *tissus indiennes*) derived from these prints, the look works very well with all things French. © 01-43-54-90-73.

Tabletop & Gifts

Everywhere you look in Paris, there's another adorable shop selling gifts or tabletop items. No one sets a table like the

French. The department stores often have exhibits or even classes in table arts; you can take notes—or pictures.

Diners en Ville
27 rue de Varenne, 7e (Métro: Rue du Bac).

If you take my advice and stroll the rue du Bac, you'll find this store on your own and congratulate yourself for being such a clever bunny. This small, cramped, two-room store is filled with the kind of French tabletop merchandise you and I adore. There's nothing in this store I wouldn't buy.

Muriel Grateau
Galerie de Valois, Jardin du Palais Royal, 1er (Métro: Palais-Royal).

Muriel once designed ready-to-wear for Charles Jourdan; now she has her own place. There are linens in more colors than the rainbow, plus beautiful textiles. Her linen napkins come in 36 colors.

Resonances
3 bd Malesherbes, 1er (Métro: Madeleine).

I find this store very American (part of the New Paris), but because it's easy enough to get to and next door to the Sia store, you may want to pop in. Résonances sells gifts, tabletop design, office design, cards, and novelties. This store has branches in every major French city and another Paris store in the Carrousel du Louvre.

Sabre
13 rue du Marché Saint-Honoré, 1er (Métro: Tuileries); 4 rue des Quatre Vents, 5e (Métro: Odéon).

Although this resource sells dishes and other tabletop items, it is most famous for cutlery. Some pieces boast ceramic handles and come in gingham squares or prints, but the best by far are the marbleized resin bistro sets, made in fashion colors that are so chic you'll lose your mind. I have a set in orange and red shades; I have a friend who did place settings with a rainbow of differing shades. Carried in department stores or in either of its two new Paris boutiques. ℂ **01-42-97-56-88** or 01-44-07-37-64. www.sabre.fr.

Kitchen Style

Paris is rightfully renowned for its table arts; luckily for tourists, there are a number of kitchen-supply houses within a block or two of one another, so you can see a lot without going out of your way. Price is not the object here; selection is everything. Note that most of the kitchen shops open at 9am (sometimes earlier), so you can extend your shopping day by beginning with these resources. The "kitchen neighborhood" is a block and a cross street; you can easily start at one and walk to the others. Remember, rue Montmartre is not in Montmartre; it is near Forum des Halles. And Etienne Marcel is a great shopping street.

A. Simon

48 rue Montmartre, 2e (Métro: Etienne Marcel or Les Halles).

A major supplier of kitchen and cooking supplies for over 100 years, this store is conveniently located down the street from the Forum des Halles mall. You can buy everything from dishes to menus here; I buy white paper doilies by the gross—many sizes and shapes not available in the U.S.—at fair prices. Touch everything in this wonderland of gadgets and goodies. ℂ **01-42-33-71-65**. www.simon-a.com.

Dehillerin

18–20 rue Coquillière, 1er (Métro: Musée-du-Louvre or Les Halles).

Perhaps the most famous cookware shop in Paris, Dehillerin has been selling cookware for over 150 years. It deals mostly with the trade, but you can poke around and touch the copper, cast iron, tools, gadgets, and more. Or someone may even help you. Try out your French—it goes a long way here. The store opens at 8am and closes for lunch. © 01-42-36-53-13. www.dehillerin.com.

Duthilleul & Minart

14 rue de Turbigo, 1er (Métro: Etienne Marcel).

This shop sells professional clothing for chefs, kitchen staff, waiters, and so forth. It's a great resource for creative fashion freaks or teens. You can buy anything from kitchen clogs to aprons. You'll find it around the corner from the other kitchen shops, right at the Métro stop.

Mora

13 rue Montmartre, 1er (Métro: Etienne Marcel or Les Halles).

Similar to A. Simon, but with more utensils (more than 5,000 in stock), Mora has a salon for bakery goods, which sells *fèves* (charms that go into the *gâteau de roi,* or king's cake, for Epiphany) in small and large packages. It has a huge paper-goods section as well.

Candles

One of the first stores in Paris that bowled me over with just how clever the French can be was a candle shop, **Point à la Ligne.** Now that line is available at any French department store and in the U.S. Still, when you wander Paris, you will find extravagance and wit, often at an affordable price, at shops selling candles. I am not talking about scented candles.

Point a la Ligne

67 av. Victor Hugo, 16e (Métro: Victor-Hugo); 25 rue de Varenne, 7e (Métro: Rue du Bac).

Probably the most famous of the contemporary candle makers in Paris, Point à la Ligne has candle sculptures, as well as

ultraskinny, enormously chic, long tapers that make sensational birthday or celebration candles on a cake. In sum, all
sorts of fabulous things. The firm is owned by Lampes Berger
so they can truly light your fire from any end.

WEB TIPS 🖱 They actually show you how the candles are
made on their website. And the site is in English. www.point
alaligne.fr.

China, Crystal & Silver

French crystal and porcelain have been the backbone of
French luxe for centuries. Prices can be fair in France, but the
shipping will kill you. Come with a price list from home—a
sale in the U.S. may wipe out any French savings.

Baccarat
11 place des Etats Unis, 16e (Métro: Iena); 11 place de la
Madeleine, 8e (Métro: Concorde); 10 rue de la Paix, 2e
(Métro: Opéra).

Baccarat's headquarters moved into a palace and began a
chain of new store openings that has turned Paris upside
down. This place not only is swank, but also has a Philippe
Starck restaurant. The location is a bit off the tourist track,
but it's worth seeing if you don't mind being out in public
with your mouth open.

Cristal Lalique
11 rue Royale, 8e (Métro: Concorde).

One glance at Lalique's crystal door and there's no doubt that
you've entered one of the wonders of the world. Get a look at
the Lalique-designed Olympic medals created for the 1992
Winter Games. The headquarters is sort of like a museum: People come to stare more than to shop. This is an excellent case of
a brand name that has expanded like mad—there's everything
from jewelry to handbags to belts to perfumes. There's a smaller
shop in the Carrousel du Louvre; see p. 129.

WEB TIPS 🖰 The site is in three languages and is very slow to load. You need a smattering of French, even in the English version, to see the collections.

Daum
4 rue de la Paix, 2e (Métro: Opéra).

There's a lot more to Daum than large lead-crystal cars, and this two-level shop is a great place to discover just how much more. The extra space allows the display of inventive glass art and colored-glass pieces that will surely become collectors' items one day.

Provençal Fabrics

If you aren't headed for Provence, Paris has a selection of traditional country French prints. Most street markets sell less expensive wares.

Blanc d'Ivoire
50 rue du Bac, 7e (Métro: Rue du Bac).

As the name might suggest, pale is the rule in this shop of reproduction French *boutis* (quilts) and classic antique linens from Provence. There are a few bright pieces, but no hot primary colors. The machine-washable quilts cost a few hundred euros/dollars and have a wonderful old-fashioned feel. This line is also sold in department stores.

Les Olivades
95 rue de Seine, 6e (Métro: St-Sulpice or Odéon).

I have been told that Les Olivades was started in the mid-1970s when someone in the Souleiado hierarchy departed and began a new firm. Indeed, Les Olivades reminds me of the Pierre Deux/ Souleiado look, although the colors (pastels and the like) are more muted. Les Olivades sells much the same merchandise— fabric by the yard, place mats, tablecloths, napkins, umbrellas, travel bags, and so forth. While the goods are not cheap, they are about 30% less expensive than at Souleiado in France.

Souleiado
78 rue de Seine, 6e, and 3 rue Lobineau (Métro: Mabillon).

You have to be a real Pierre Deux freak to know that Pierre Deux is the name of the American franchise for these prints, but is not the name of the company in Europe. So remember the name Souleiado, which will get you happily through France.

The flagship rue de Seine shop is everything it should be; the other address is around the corner. You will be in country French heaven with the look we love—plenty of fabrics, plus clothing and all the tabletop accessories in the world. © 01-43-54-62-25. www.souleiado.fr.

Table Linens

Jean Vier
66 rue de Vaugirard, 6e (Métro: St-Sulpice).

Specializing in Basque country linens, Jean Vier features natural and bleached linen run through with a colored stripe, or several. There are also towels, bath supplies, candles, and more. © 01-45-44-26-74.

SHOP TALK There's a store in St. Helena, California (1219 Main St.), called Jan de Luz which I swear sells this line, although they will not confirm this to me. They also have an embroidery machine and will custom embroider anything you want on the linens or aprons. A great find. www.jandeluz.com.

Le Jacquard Français
12 rue Richepance, 1er (Métro: Madeleine).

Be still, my heart; this is flutter time if you love table style and fabrics and color as much as I do. The brand is well known (it's available at department stores, where you can use your tourist discount card), but this is the first free-standing store. It carries the entire line. There are hanging samples to touch and three video screens to watch. The patterns are all made with a Jacquard loom (as you can guess from the name); they are incredibly sophisticated, very French, and fabulous for gifts.

Bed Linens

Continental bed sizes are metric, but why should that stop you? Just bring your tape measure. Or, if price is truly no object, have Porthault custom-make your sheets.

> **Buyer Beware**
>
> French mattresses are not the same size as those in the U.S., so if you are buying French product, pay attention. An American queen-size bed measures 150 centimeters, so you need sheets marked 160 centimeters, not 140 centimeters.

Descamps

44 rue du Passy, 16e (Métro: La Muette), and others; also department stores.

Descamps no longer has stores in the U.S., but higher-end American department stores sell its products. You may not find prices much better in Paris. Still, every time I visit Paris, I buy a few items (such as oblong terry-cloth bath mittens) that aren't available back home. I also buy Primrose Bordier (that's the designer's name) home scent here. There's a shop in every trading area in Paris.

BEST BETS The outlet shops are named **Texaffaires;** there's one on rue du Temple across the street from BHV (Métro: Hôtel de Ville). © **01-42-88-10-01.** www.descamps.com.

D. Porthault
18 av. Montaigne, 8e (Métro: Alma-Marceau); 370 rue du
Faubourg St-Honoré, 8e (Métro: Concorde); 163 bd St-
Germain-des-Prés (Métro: Rue du Bac).

Porthault was making fancy bed linens long before the real
world was ready for patterned sheets—or the notion that a
person could spend 870€ ($1,305) on bedclothes and still be
able to sleep at night.

Porthault sells two lines in America: One is identical to
what you can buy in France (but costs more in the U.S.);
the other is contracted by the Porthault family and is available only in the U.S. The French laminated products are
not sold in the U.S.; the American wallpaper is not sold in
France. The Montaigne shop has a whopper of a sale in
January, when it unloads everything at half the retail price,
or less.

Shopping Adventure
Chapter 10 has a day trip to the Porthault outlet store, where
discounts are serious. See p. 229.

The shop on the Faubourg St-Honoré is tiny and doesn't
have the selection or the feel of the mother store or the factory shop. If you're headed for Lille, note that discontinued
prints cost a fraction of their regular price at the factory outside Lille. If you're a fan, this is a trip you will never forget.
I'm still drooling; thankfully, I bought a lot of bibs. ✆ 01-47-
20-75-25. www.dporthault.fr.

Olivier Desforges
26 bd Raspail, 7e (Métro: Sèvres-Babylone), and others.

This is Descamps's main competitor, with fewer stores in
France and none (to my knowledge) in the U.S. Sometimes
the line has a country look to it. Don't miss this one if you
adore sophisticated bed linen. There are several Paris shops.

Yves Delorme

Le Louvre des Antiquaires, 2 place du Palais-Royal, 1er
(Métro: Palais-Royal).

Yves Delorme makes linen sold under the Palais-Royal label
in the U.S.; he has a boutique on the street level of the Louvre
des Antiquaires, as well as in Monaco and Lyons. This is
luxury linen that isn't as wildly priced as other premium
French lines (such as Porthault and Descamps), but is still
chic. Bed-linen freaks won't care about the prices; the total
look has a certain French charm that makes it a must-have.

Chapter 8

Bargain Shopping

Systeme D

It was my dear friend Pascale-Agnes who taught me about this, as she has taught me about the most important elements of French life and culture. As mentioned, times are tough for the French too—the inflation and the strong euro are killing locals who strive for alternative methods of saving money or making money go further. They subscribe to a philosophy called *Systeme D* by which they force themselves to find a clever solution to easing lifestyle expenses. This notion is so well established that there are now newspaper columns and radio programs with constant hints and tips.

An example is to suggest to people that they give up their regular hair salons and instead go to the schools where hairdressers train. Born to Shop readers have long known this secret, but the French are now seriously into shopping smarts.

Shoppers' Smarts

Prices in Paris are not low (especially if you're spending U.S. dollars), so to sniff out the bargains, you're going to need some background information and insider tips.

- If you have favorite designers or acquisition targets, shop the major department stores and U.S.-based boutiques for comparison prices. Don't assume you will get a bargain on French brands—or any brands. Many international designers and retailers set prices that are virtually the same around the world; **many are less expensive in the U.S.**

- If you do not live in a city that has a lot of European merchandise, do some research through *Vogue* or *Harper's Bazaar*. In the ads for the designer boutiques, you'll find phone numbers and websites. Check on prices; call boutiques in major U.S. cities for info.

- Read French magazines to get familiar with the French look and the hottest shops. These magazines can cost a fortune (sometimes $15–$20 in the U.S.), but many libraries and hairdressers have them. Most good newsstands sell them; I buy mine at Blockbuster. You can also get a coffee at any Barnes & Noble (with an in-store Starbucks) and leaf through the magazines without buying them. Hey, times are tough.

- Carefully go through the airline magazines that are given away free on the plane. Often they have advertisements and coupons with deals and promotional codes. I just tore an American Express insert from an airline magazine that had such diverse bargains as 10% off on department store purchases or a free dessert from Michel Rostang, the two-star chef. You could also get 10% off and an upgrade on Europcar (www.europcar.com) or a parity deal where dollars and euros are equal at Sofitel Accor Hotels (www.sofitel.com).

- Look for coupons and discounts online. If you book your car through www.bonjourparis.com, you also get a 10% discount. Try hotel websites for upgrades or meal specials.

- Research the goods you are targeting on the trip online before you leave the U.S. With luggage allowances being what they are, it may not pay to stock up and schlep.
- Understand the licensing process. Designers sell the rights to their names, and often their designs, to various makers around the world. Two men's suits may bear a well-known French designer's label, but fit differently because they are manufactured differently. You may be dreaming of merchandise that isn't even made by your favorite designer.
- Don't assume a perfume bargain. Know prices before you leave home.
- Don't be fooled into thinking that merchandise with foreign-sounding names is made in Europe, or is French, or offers a bargain. Because Americans are so taken with European names, many American-made products have foreign—especially French—names. Furthermore, there are a few French clothing designers who didn't make it in France, moved to the U.S. and became famous, and then opened stores in Paris to stick it to the French.
- Don't buy an American brand in France unless you have a very good reason. Clothes from Gap, for instance, may cost more in France than in the U.S., but may also come in colors not available in the U.S.
- French merchandise that might not sell well in the U.S. could be discounted in your hometown or unloaded at an off-pricer. At Marshalls in Los Angeles, I saw scads of French brands at way-low prices. At Loehmann's in Manhattan, I bought French brands at outrageously low prices—esoteric French brands that I'm certain few Americans have ever heard of.
- Yes, the French now have outlet malls, too, and you can save money by shopping at them. See p. 207.

There are specials for times of day, seniors, and so on. The first movie projection of the day is discounted. Some movie theaters have seniors' prices. The train tickets (SNCF) can be discounted 25% to 50% if you are 60 or over.

Alternative markets are part of *Systeme D*. Trade may work (but not in stores). Try to trade for services.

Best Buys

For the most part, you shop in France for selection, not price. There are some items you just can't find in the U.S. or on the Internet. But there are some items that do cost less.

PERFUMES, COSMETICS & HAIR CARE Perfume in France may not involve savings. Know your U.S. prices and understand that new French laws have been passed recently, so what you paid or how discounts were handled during your last visit could be very different now.

But wait, let's talk about my wrinkles and the fact that there are still bargains to be found on some brands and some products. (Also see chapter 6, which is all about beauty products.)

I swear by Sisleya, which costs $350 a pot in the U.S. and can be yours for a mere (!) 165€ ($250) in Paris if you take advantage of all the discounts.

If you are even more flexible on brand-name beauty creams, it may be time to visit a *parapharmacie*. These stores carry drugstore brands—no Chanel or Yves Saint Laurent—at a 20% discount. This is the place to load up on fancy hair-care products, skin creams, bath products, and possibly even face powder. Barneys New York has made T. LeClerc all the rage; now it's everywhere in Paris.

HERMÈS Prices in Paris (with the détaxe refund) are definitely lower than in the U.S. In addition, you can frequently find Hermès bargains at airport duty-free shops and in airline duty-free catalogs, and they're even better than Paris retail prices.

BACCARAT All French glassware can be dramatically less expensive in France, but the cost of shipping it abroad voids the savings. However, have you seen the Baccarat crystal medallions and butterflies that hang from a silk cord? They

Less-Than-Stellar Buys

Some things are simply not a bargain in any sense:

- **Non-French-Made Goods:** Unless you're desperate, avoid buying American-made goods, whether they be designer items (such as a Ralph Lauren jacket) or mass-market items (like a Gap T-shirt or a pair of Levi's). Ditto for British goods (Aquascutum, Hilditch & Key, and so on), men's business attire, electrical goods (wrong voltage), and Coca-Cola at bars, cafes, or hotels.
- **Souvenirs:** Postcards priced at 1€ ($1.50) or more are no bargain; neither are massive numbers of Disneyland Paris souvenirs. Kitschy souvenirs vary in price—shop around or rethink your need for such.
- **Cheapie Fashion:** The French simply don't do cheap very well. Even clothes at H&M, the Swedish firm, are expensive once you switch them into USD; ditto for items at Monoprix, the French dime store.

are drop-dead chic and cost approximately 90€ ($135) in the U.S. Get onto an airplane that has Baccarat in its duty-free catalog, and lo and behold, the same trinket sells for about 40€ ($60).

CANDIES, CHOCOLATES & FOODSTUFFS These make great gifts, especially when wrapped in the distinctive packaging of one of Paris's premier food palaces. I buy Maille's tomato soup–colored Provençale mustard in grocery stores (no fancy wrap for me, thanks) and give it to foodies around the world—it's unique and special. I haven't found it in any U.S. specialty stores yet. Some Maille flavors are available in the U.S. (and the U.K.), but not this one. Maille has a shop at place de la Madeleine (Métro: Madeleine).

ANTIQUE JUNK It's pretty hard to give advice about the ever-changing collectibles market, but things that have caught my eye have all turned out to be bargains when I compared prices at American flea markets (why didn't I buy more?). I bought an empty postcard album—probably from the turn of the 20th century—at the flea market in Vanves, in perfect condition, for 10€ ($15). I saw a similar one at a dealers' show in Greenwich, Connecticut, for $150. Museum-quality antiques offer few bargains, but fun junk is fun—and modestly priced, even now.

Online Answers

If you are the meticulous type, you may want to go online to compare prices on items in France and the U.S. Of course, the biggest issue is that it's often hard to match up apples to apples (the exact same styles), but with some items, this can be done and you can decide if it's wise to pounce or to wait.

Saving Graces

These are tricks that give you more bang for your euro, helping you save on transportation, meals, and more. Combine your luxury hotel room with some down-and-dirty consumer facts, and enjoy the best of both worlds:

- Buy Cokes and mineral water at the grocery store and keep them in your minibar. Every chic Frenchwoman carries a large tote bag with a bottle of mineral water. If you really want to save money, avoid drinking Coke completely—it's expensive everywhere in Europe. One cafe or minibar Coke costs as much as an entire six-pack in the market. If your hotel minibar is electronic and has no room for your extra bottles, keep your beverages on ice.
- Drink tap water. In a restaurant, merely order *un carafe d'eau*—this is also called *eau Sarko*. Tap water in France is perfectly safe to drink.

- Buy food from fresh markets (one of Paris's most beautiful natural resources), supermarkets, and *traiteurs* (stores that sell prepared gourmet meals, hot or cold). You can eat a fabulous French meal for 4€ to 9€ ($6–$14) per person this way. An entire rotisserie chicken, which feeds four, can be a good buy.
- Eat your fancy meals at starred Michelin restaurants that offer fixed-price meals, usually at lunch.
- Get into the hotel dining-room game. Lately, it's become trendy for hotels to bring in a one-star (or more) Michelin chef to attract guests and locals. These hotel restaurants compete so fiercely with each other that they watch their prices carefully.
- Do your gift shopping in duty-free stores (not at the airport; see chapter 6 for examples), *parapharmacies,* flea markets, or *hypermarchés.*

Department-Store Discounts & Deals

The two major department stores in Paris, **Galeries Lafayette** and **Au Printemps,** offer a flat 10% discount to tourists on all nonfood items that are not marked with a red dot. You gain the discount by flashing your special tourist card at the cash register before you pay. Don't get all sweaty in the palms: The big brand names all display a red dot.

In order to get the discount, you need a coupon for the card. These coupons are given away in most hotels and even through U.S. travel agents; they are also available at the Paris Tourist Office on the Champs-Elysées. Or go to the welcome desk of either store and simply ask for the coupon or discount card.

Do not be surprised if you are asked to pay for each purchase at a central cashier rather than the nearest cashier; this has to do with the discount card and the store's accounting process. It's a pain, but nothing in life is free.

Note: This discount card has nothing to do with détaxe.

Mass Market

If you are looking for some French style and some fair prices, don't rule out shopping at the dime store (Monoprix, *mon amour!*) or even the grocery store. In terms of the grocery store, the real fashion finds are in *hypermarchés* that are outside of Paris and in the provinces, so you may not find anything in your average day. (There's an Auchan in La Défense; see below.)

Auchan

Centre Commercial Quat'r Temps, La Défense (RER: La Défense); Centre Commercial Val d'Europe (RER: Val d'Europe).

Should you be staying at a hotel in La Défense, there on business or simply curious, Quat'r Temps is a giant regional mall with every store you can imagine, and it has a *hypermarché*, Auchan. There is another Auchan out near the La Vallée outlet mall.

For the uninitiated, Auchan is a *hypermarché*—a grocery store that sells food, clothes, health and beauty aids, jewelry, office supplies, car supplies, electronics, home appliances, home styles, tabletop items, bed linens, beds, garden supplies, swimming-pool accessories, luggage, pet supplies, and more. You get the drift.

The clerks wear roller skates. Honest.

While the big-brand British grocery stores now have branded clothing lines for sale, at press time, Auchan does not. It soon will, I am sure. I buy all sorts of clothes here—it's particularly great for children's clothing and baby gifts. The quality is what you might expect from Wal-Mart. © 33-1-58-65-08-00.

Monoprix

All arrondissements of Paris.

I have also listed Monoprix under department stores on p. 93. Not all Monoprix were created equal and many are being renovated; so expect changes.

As we go to press, **Monoprix Opéra** (Métro: Pyramides or Palais-Royal) has just been redone and is a smash. Traditionally, **Monoprix Saint Augustin** (Métro: St-Augustin) is one of the flagships, as is **Monoprix Rennes** in the heart of the Left Bank (Métro: St-Germain-des-Prés). **Monoprix Champs-Elysées** (Métro: Franklin D. Roosevelt) is pennies more expensive than other branches and is not that attractive, due to a strange and cramped layout, but it's open late at night.

The Monoprix located directly behind the department store Au Printemps is not worth your time. www.monoprix.fr.

Bargain Basements

There are stores that were created to be low-cost and they offer merchandise that was not made in France but is very affordable. One of my favorites is a chain called **EuroDif,** which sells clothing for all members of the family and home style.

Bouchara Haussmann

1–3 rue Lafayette, 9e (Métro: Chaussée d'Antin).

This store sells fabric upstairs and notions downstairs, but the ground floor is where I am sending you for low-cost home style, including bed linen, tabletop, and bathroom supplies. Granted, you don't need to buy towels in Paris, but the good prices on duvet covers will make you willing to fill your valise with French style. The store is next door to Galeries Lafayette.

BEST BETS I hit the summer sale and struck half-price heaven with a queen-size duvet cover for 35€ ($53).

WEB TIPS Click on "English version" of this excellent website.

Hours are 10am to 7pm Monday through Saturday. ℂ 01-42-80-66-95.

EuroDif

58 rue de la Chaussée d'Antin, 9e (Métro: Chaussée d'Antin).

In Paris this store—located right near Galeries Lafayette—breaks the mold for most branches of this chain by closing out all but its lingerie, sleep, and loungewear lines. I loaded up on sleep shirts as gifts to take home—they were 6.50€ ($10) each—often emblazoned with French slogans on them, such as "Fruits of Summer" with pictures and words. Basic cute stuff in good colors. Best yet, sizes go up and up again, often to 50-52, which is a plus size in the U.S. or a very generous XL.

If you can find one of these stores outside of Paris, don't miss it—it's great for clothes and accessories for all members of the family, as well as home style and gift items.

WEB TIPS The website is in French but you can probably make your way through it to get addresses (click on *magasins*). Note that you can sign up for a fidelity card online which offers a discount after several purchases. © **01-48-78-08-05.** www.Eurodif.com.

Sympa

Multiple shops on rue Steinkerque, 18e (Métro: Anvers); also 18 rue d'Orsel, 18 (around the corner from Steinkerque).

This is only for the strong! This chain offers clothes dumped into bins or straggling from hangers. Prices are low (11€/$17 for a dress) and brand names are big-time—you just have to get lucky in terms of size, condition, and nerves. The area with a cluster of shops is right near the cabel car for Sacré-Coeur and the fabric markets of place St-Pierre.

You'll find all sorts of brands, often big brands but not big-name designers. I often see Kookaï. I have seen Superga shoes from Italy. We're talking battle conditions and low prices. © **01-42-62-22-73.**

Fidelity Cards

Fidelity cards are used all over the world, but seem to be particularly popular in France, especially in midrange designer shops, *parapharmacies*, and even some restaurants. The fidelity card is a small card, like a credit card, that is stamped or punched every time you make a purchase. Make a certain number of purchases or reach a total euro value, and you'll receive a discount or a gift. You get the card simply by asking for *une carte fidélité*. No, department stores do not have them.

Special-Event Retailing

Paris abounds with special shopping events. Ask your concierge for details and the exact dates; events are also advertised in magazines and papers. (I know you read *Madame Figaro* when you're in town, so you probably know it all anyway.)

Hermès has twice-yearly sales that can be described only as world-class sporting events. They take place in March and October (the exact dates are revealed only moments before, in newspaper ads). The sales have become such events that they are no longer held at the store. The average wait in line is 4 hours before admission; items are marked down to just about half-price. Unfortunately, a code is worked into your purchase that tells the world your item was bought on sale. It is not obvious, but look for a teeny-tiny s in a scarf.

The latest trend comes from the New York sample sales. There are several shopping clubs in Paris; some require membership, and others are free but you have to sign up. These are often categorized as *vente privée* (private sales), which I don't find accurate—it's not like these events take place in someone's home or are organized on a personal level. You join up and you get an invite to the event. It's that simple.

My favorite is Catherine Max, who offers up **Espace Catherine Max,** 17 rue Raymond Poincaré, 16e (Métro: Trocadéro), where she unloads designer this and that at unbelievably low prices.

The catch is that in order to know the sale dates, you have to have a membership that costs 25€ ($38) per year; then you get a postcard in the mail. **Born to Shop** readers may gain one-time entrance without membership by showing a copy of this book and paying 10€ ($15) at the door. To get sale dates or current sale information, call ✆ **01-53-70-67-47** or go to www.espacecatherinemax.com.

I have never shopped with anyone except Catherine Max, but I do know she has competition. The one I have heard about from Pascale-Agnes's mother is called **Espace NGR.** This one costs slightly less than Catherine Max and I hear it has good brands. Our reporter Danielle *(maman)* has seen Sonia Rykiel, Ralph Lauren, Guess, and many French brands there. Sales are from 11am to 7pm (some sales on Sun!) at the Espace NGR, 40 bis rue de Boulainvilliers, 16e (Métro: Muette). Check it out at www.espace-ngr.fr. Or call ✆ **01-45-27-32-42.**

Note: Any website ending in an "fr" designation is bound to be in French only.

Special Events: Antiques

For antiques lovers, the event you really want to catch is the **Biennale Internationale des Antiquaires,** the single biggest, most important antiques event in the world. It's held only in even-numbered years, usually in September, at the Grand Palais, roughly halfway between the place de la Concorde and the Rond Point. Check the design trade magazines for the actual dates or ask your concierge. You need not be a designer to attend; it's open to the public.

A number of antiques shows take place at the same time every year and become special events to plan trips around. April or May in Paris means only one thing: time for the

Brocante à la Bastille. Celebrated outside, in stalls planted around the canal at Bastille, it is truly magical. For more information, see "*Brocante* Shows" on p. 216.

For information on big shopping events, look in *Allo Paris, Figaroscope, Zurban,* or antiques journals such as *Antiques, Alladin,* or *Chiner.* The **French Government Tourist Office** in New York (© 212/315-0888) can supply the dates of special events, or you can do some online research at **www.bonjour paris.com.**

Pre-Sale Sales

As discussed, sale dates (Jan and June–July) are set by the government and announced in the papers a few weeks beforehand. What is not announced, or even discussed, is that regular customers can get the sale price a few days before the sale starts or can set aside merchandise to be held for the markdown.

Promotional Sales

If there are only two sale periods during the year, how do you get a break? Well, you wait for the big promotional events. The department stores run them at least twice a year and give them very silly names such as "The Three Days" (which lasts 10 days), "The Days of Gold," or whatever. Note that as with most promotional sales, much of the merchandise is brought in to be sold at the sale price.

Resale & Vintage

The French pride themselves on being practical people. They rarely throw anything away; they buy only the best quality and use it forever; they hate waste of any sort. But if someone in the family dies or if someone falls on hard times, they can sell his fine possessions at a *dépôt-vent*. Or, knowing that good merchandise is being sold, they will frequent a *dépôt-vent*. No one in Paris is ever ashamed to be seen buying used items. They think it's smart. I do, too.

Do note that designer clothing that you may not consider purchasing at regular retail can be sale-priced at the end of a season at virtually the same price you might pay at a *dépôt-vent*. A *dépôt-vent* traditionally sells used clothing of current styles, while a vintage shop sells older clothing. These days, with so many retro looks in vogue, it's hard to tell one from the other. The two big flea markets, St-Ouen and Vanves, each have dealers who sell vintage clothing. The term *fripes* generally refers to nondesigner used clothing from the 1970s—not vintage Chanel or Balenciaga.

Come on Eileen
16 rue des Taillandiers, 11e (Métro: Bastille or Ledru Rollin).

My young friend Ruthie found this source. Ruthie works for Chanel in New York and often buys vintage Chanel when in Paris. She fell in love with a pair of shoes here and warned me that it took the store almost a week to find the second shoe of the pair, so patience can be a virtue. The store doesn't open until 11:30am each day, so don't plan on giving them an early start at finding anything. The store is open on Sunday late afternoons from 4 to 8pm.

Note that this neighborhood is convenient for tourists and shoppers. Call © 01-43-38-12-11.

Depot-Vent Dix-Septieme
109 rue Courcelles, 17e (Métro: Courcelles).

This is the best resale shop in Paris, and the only chic one. It carries men's and women's clothing and a few home items, all in one shop. The prices are sometimes a tad high—I paid about 350€ ($525) for a used Chanel handbag. Some Chanel bags are 500€ to 600€ ($750–$900), or more. You'll see designer costume jewelry, a large selection of Chanel suits, and a little bit of everything else. Sales take place during the regular sale periods. No détaxe. Open Monday at 2pm; otherwise, from 10:30am to 7pm. ✆ **01-40-53-80-82.**

Depot-Vent Passy
14 and 25 rue de la Tour, 16e (Métro: Passy).

Another contender in the used-designer-clothing wars. Catherine Baril has two shops with top-drawer stuff—YSL, Chanel, the works. One shop is for women, the other for men. They are a few yards from each other. Both carry a fair number of samples. On my last visit, I found tons of Chanel straight from the runway. The prices were generally high, but I found a few bargains. A summer-weight Chanel suit for 930€ ($1,395) seemed like a good buy.

The best part about this shop is its location. You can easily combine a stroll along the rue de Passy with a shopping spree here and have a fabulous time. It's open Monday from 2 to 7pm and Tuesday through Saturday from 10am to 7pm. In July, it's open Monday through Saturday from 2 to 7pm. Call ✆ **01-45-20-95-21.**

Didier Ludot
24 passage de la Galerie Montpensier, Jardin du Palais Royal, 1er (Métro: Palais-Royal).

Ludot tries to sell only top-of-the-line used designer goods, specializing in Hermès, Celine, and Chanel. You may find Hermès bags from the 1930s, as well as vintage Vuitton luggage. This store is a standout for old-clothes junkies. Prices are high for quality items, but not unfair. I saw a Pucci in perfect condition and a wool Chanel suit with a matching blouse—both hard-to-find items.

This shop is not easy to find, so have patience and remember that it is on the gallery side of the building, not the street side. Leaving the Métro, zig to the right into the open arcade, then hug the left-hand side of the arcade (where it is covered). Shops line the walkway; Ludot is among them. Do not confuse the vintage clothing with his new Little Black Dress line. Call ✆ **01-42-96-06-56** or 01-40-15-01-04.

Reciproque
89, 92, 95, 97, 101, and 123 rue de la Pompe, 16e (Métro: Pompe).

Réciproque has grown at an alarming rate—there are now more storefronts bearing this store's name along rue de la Pompe than ever before. The main shop, at no. 89, has two floors; don't forget to go downstairs.

There are racks and racks of clothes, all of which are clean. You'll find separates, shoes, evening wear, and complete ensembles. You must look through the racks carefully and know your merchandise, although the labels are always in the clothes. Not everything is used or seriously used—many designers sell samples here. Every big name is represented; this is the best single resource for used couture clothing. Prices are not dirt-cheap—a Chanel suit will cost over 2,000€ ($3,000). There's a shop for men's clothing; there are accessories, furs, and things for the home.

There are sales, too. Danielle says she checks out the merch beforehand and then arrives on the first day of the sales. Call © 01-47-04-30-28 or 01-47-27-93-52.

Scarlett
10 rue Clement-Marot, 8e (Métro: Alma-Marceau).

Scarlett was once a fixture at the flea market at Vanves, but now she has her own shop. Her store carries gently worn clothing and accessories, mostly from Hermès, Chanel, and Vuitton. They aren't funky vintage and may be only a season old. Other items are, of course, older—but are classical enough to be used without implying a retro look. © 01-56-89-03-00.

Brand-Owned Stock Shops

As the word *stock* implies, these stores sell overruns or excess stock. They are located in Paris and are stand-alone stores; the rue d'Alésia has several such stores in a 2-block area.

Most of the stores in this section are in areas that are easy to reach on the Métro; many are in neighborhoods where a tourist would want to go strolling anyway. Alésia is out-of-the-way, but makes up for it with the number of outlets in one place, and it's certainly worth it if you're a Sonia Rykiel freak. Start at Sonia's first store and walk south to the second one; along the way, there are 2 blocks full of stock shops. Explore at will.

Note that later in this chapter, I have listed outlet malls that are just outside Paris—these have a much wider selection of brand-name stores.

Anne Fontaine
22 rue de Passy, 16e (Métro: Passy).

This is a store that sells leftover stock; it's not a true outlet such as the one out in La Vallée. Nonetheless, you may score with a slight discount—since the merchandise is very classical, there's no worry as to what season it is. © 01-42-24-80-20. www.annefontaine.com.

APCG
45 rue Madame, 6e (Métro: St-Germain-des-Prés).

Funky, fabulous line, very trendy and Hollywood—even the discounted prices are not dirt-cheap, but if you like this line, you will find prices moderately better than at regular retail. Expect prices to begin at 95€ ($143). The store is open only in the afternoons, from 1 to 7pm, and is closed on Sundays. © 01-45-48-43-71.

Cacharel Stock
114 rue d'Alésia, 14e (Métro: Alésia).

Men's, women's, and children's clothing in a well-stocked stock shop.

Et Vous Stock
15 rue de Turbigo, 12e (Métro: Etienne Marcel).

Et Vous is a youngish line, a little more hip than Ann Taylor. Career clothes, but no serious bargains.

GR Stock/Georges Rech
100 rue d'Alésia, 14e (Métro: Alésia).

Well-tailored clothing, no matter how old it is. A great brand for women who work and want classic clothes for the office with a twist of fashion but nothing *outre*. ℰ **01-45-40-87-73.**

Kookai
82 rue Réaumur, 2e (Métro: Réaumur-Sébastopol).

Kookai is a young brand, great for teens and tweens. The sizes run small. This location is pretty handy for a tourist. I also often find Kookai at **Sympa** stores in Montmartre (p. 194). ℰ **01-45-08-93-69.**

Lilith/Free
66 rue Parmentier, 10e (Métro: Goncourt).

Lilith is not for everyone—although I have seen short women wear it and look chic. The clothes are often made with lots of fabric that floats or flits, the colors are soft, and the style is droopy. There are many no-waist or elastic-waist styles of which I am fond. This outlet shop is a tad off the beaten track, but well worth a special trip for Lilith fans.

Plein Sud Stock
51 rue Servan, 11e (Métro: St-Maur).

Very trendy line; older clothes are reduced by 50%.

Regina Rubens
88 rue d'Alésia, 14e (Métro: Alésia).

This is a very nice line with a feminine look; clothes here can be older than one season, but are fairly priced.

Scalp
102 rue St-Charles, 15e (Métro: Charles-Michel).

Scalp is the lower-priced line made by Weill, so don't think they're out to scalp you. This line isn't enormously trendy, but it fits larger-size women, with clothes up to size 52. The store is open on Mondays, but not until 11am. On other days, it opens at 10am; closed on Sunday. ℰ **01-45-77-13-09.**

SR/Sonia Rykiel Stock
64 and 112 rue d'Alésia, 14e (Métro: Alésia).

Don't look now, but the best store in the 'hood—and the reason you schlepped over to the 14e in the first place—just got better by adding on another shop. The SR shop at no. 112 is very large and sells all of the Rykiel line, including men's, women's, and kids' things. The best way to attack is to prowl on rue d'Alésia at the first Sonia shop, then survey the other stores in the next 2 blocks and make your way to the shop at no. 64. Then you can decide what's what. ℰ **01-43-95-06-13** or 01-45-43-80-86.

Vidna
9 rue St-Placide, 6e (Métro: Sèvres-Babylone).

This is one of the many discount and stock shops on the rue St-Placide (see "Left Bank Discount Neighborhoods" on p. 64). I specifically point out this one so you don't just walk past it, since nothing about it draws attention to the wonders within.

This is the stock shop for the brand **Nitya,** a chic line with stores all over Europe, including one at 327 rue St-Honoré, 8e. The look is slightly ethnic, but monochromatic and easy for all figures to wear. Don't go by the sizes; try everything on. I'm a 42 here (sometimes) and a 46 in real life. Okay, okay, so sometimes I wear a 48. Clothes are usually 2 years old, but the look is classic enough that it doesn't matter. Call ℰ **01-45-48-95-75.**

Zadig & Voltaire Stock
22 rue du Bourg-Tibourg, 4e (Métro: St-Paul or Hôtel de Ville).

More hip than preppy, but not too weird or too very hip— some house designs and some big-name designer goods. The hours are unusual: The store is closed on Mondays. It is open on Tuesdays from 1 to 7pm, then from 12:30 to 7:30pm the rest of the week. Finally, there are Sunday hours, from 2 to 7:30pm. ✆ 01-44-59-39-62.

Off-Price for Designers

I call stores that sell many brands at lower-than-average prices "bargain basements," and list the best ones in this section.

(For stores that concentrate on one brand, see "Brand-Owned Stock Shops," above. See "Resale & Vintage" on p. 197 for resale shops, which can offer bargains on pre-owned designer clothing. Also see "Left Bank Discount Neighborhoods" on p. 64.)

Paris has seen a lot of stock and so-called discount stores open in the past few years. Some even call themselves outlet stores. Often they are regular mom-and-pop stores that carry name brands, but cut their profit to appeal to shoppers who are disgusted by the high regular retail prices in France.

I don't need to give you the lecture about the nature of bargain shops, but I will say that on my last research trip I noticed two new addresses in popular tourist magazines (no names, please). I eagerly went off to these sources—each in the heart of Paris's best shopping district and convenient for any visitor. Maybe I hit a bad day; maybe I am too big of a snob. I hated both of them so much that I refuse to list them in this book. On the other hand, that doesn't mean that the sources I have listed are going to be super on the day you visit. Bargain hunting in Paris is even harder than in America, so think about how much time you want to invest in this pursuit. Good luck.

Finally, a word about sizes: If you are larger than a size 12 (U.S.), you may not find a fit . . . or should trade yourself over to full-figure sizes, meaning lines made up to size 52. Since I am an American size 14 or 16, the brands I look for are Weill, Elena Miro, Marina Rinaldi, and Weinberg. (When I splurge, I buy Yohji at Galeries Lafayette with my tourist discount card.)

Anna Lowe
104 rue du Faubourg St-Honoré, 8e (Métro: Miromesnil).

If you're looking for me in Paris, step into my parlor. I have a resident's permit on the sofa here at Anna Lowe, where I take a coffee break just about every day I'm in Paris. But enough about me. Let's talk about your fantasies: Want to own this shop? The lease will be up in a year or two and the owner wants to retire. Ask her all about it.

This is a fun store because the owner has an eye for glitz and glamour and has connections with big-name designer shops (yes, Chanel) to get unsold stocks. Her genius is to mix regular retail with designer discount—there is always a sale rack in the rear. The regular stock is especially good on suits, but there are furs, dress-up clothes and gowns, and then the sparkle-plenty kind of clothes that work best on the Riviera. Call © **01-42-66-11-32.**

Annexe des Createurs
19 rue Godot-de-Mauroy, 9e (Métro: Madeleine).

This crowded shop lacks charm, but is crammed with clothes and bolts of fabric. It carries sizes up to 44 (size 12 U.S.). You won't have to make a special trip; it's close to many places in every woman's journey through Paris—halfway between boulevard Madeleine and the big department stores on boulevard Haussmann.

Griffe de Mode
17 rue de la Boétie, 8e (Métro: Miromesnil or St-Augustin).

Before I get into this listing, let me get you here. The street is pronounced "Boh-eh-*see.*" The first Métro stop I have listed is pronounced "Mee-roh-meh-*nee.*" Yeah, I know all about it.

Now then, I am an expert on this store above all others because it is very close to my flat in Paris, and when I go to the grocery store at Monoprix at St-Augustin, I am forced to stop here to see what's new. The store is very junky and may not be for everyone. You really have to wade through the stuff . . . but what stuff! There are shoes, lingerie, hosiery, accessories, bed linens, kids' clothes, and women's fashions. There's a men's clothing store two doors away, at no. 23.

Almost everything sold here is from a major brand. Stock changes quickly. Note that the main store has a few salons, so keep walking toward the rear.

I do especially well when they have Marina Rinaldi, and yes, I pay from 45€ to 100€ ($68–$150) per dress; I am over the moon with delight. Call © **01-49-24-08-81.**

Moda di Andrea

79 rue de la Victoire, 9e (Métro: Chaussée-d'Antin).

Before you don't recognize the address and ignore this listing, let me confess that this is one of my best sources in Paris. You'd be foolish to miss it. The store is also right behind Galeries Lafayette, so it's not hard to find.

Moda sells brand-name shoes for men, women, and children, plus some handbags. By brand name, I mean basics like Prada, Chanel, YSL, Tod's, and Hogan—for about half the regular European price. We are talking about putting down a hunk of money for shoes, and chances are great that you can't stop with just one pair. The selection can make you dizzy, and yes, they do have large sizes in some things.

I recently bought a pair of Hogan's linen trainers for 150€ ($225), which I saw advertised in a U.S. fashion magazine for $365. I thought what I paid was steep, but I got the shoes at almost half-price.

The shop takes credit cards, but does not give détaxe refunds. It's open mornings at 10:30am and closed on Sunday and Monday. Call © **01-48-74-48-89.**

Note: If you're off to Biarritz, there's Moda di Victoria, with two stores.

Mouton á Cinq Pattes

8 and 18 rue St-Placide, 7e (Métro: Sèvres-Babylone); 138 bd St-Germain (Métro: Odéon).

This is a small chain of stock shops; I have always called it "The Lamb Chop Store." Actually the name means "a lamb with five paws." I guess that's the kind of misfits it sells or considers itself to be, because of the unusual savings. You will find big names here.

I shopped at the St-Placide store for about 20 years and was never very impressed; then suddenly I hit pay dirt. In the past 3 years, I've gone nuts with good buys, so you just never know.

So what did I get recently? How about a fully lined, very well-made men's blazer for 50€ ($75)? Or a collection of Japanese fashions to wear en suite: a big twirly skirt, baggy long-sleeved top, and strange pleated white cotton vest. The total for the whole three-piece outfit was 240€ ($360). The Japanese-y outfit was not from a name I knew nor was it low-cost, but I got a great look at decent value—the store offers a lot of that philosophy.

The St-Placide locations are handy to Le Bon Marché department store (℃ **01-45-48-86-26**). The St-Germain location (℃ **01-43-26-49-25**) is not as good as St-Placide, so don't judge the system by this store—stop in only after you've scored on St-Placide.

Vincy
9 bis rue St-Placide, 6e (Métro: Sèvres-Babylone).

Located on the rue St-Placide in the midst of many *dégriffé* (without the label) stores, this is a shoe store that has some name brands for men and women. In fact, I couldn't help but think of O. J. Simpson when I saw what was here. Prices are in the 44€-to-87€ ($66–$130) a pair range, worth a look. Expect classical styles. ℃ **01-42-22-58-96**.

Factory-Outlet Malls

By definition, factory outlets lie outside of major metropolitan areas. As the outlet-mall craze grows in Europe, more and more are opening closer to Paris. A few are within an hour of the city, although only **La Vallée** was created with public transportation in mind. Others may advertise how close they are to transportation, but are really for those with cars.

LA VALLÉE VILLAGE

I have very mixed feelings about this idea—after all, you've come to Paris and the point is to be in Paris. On the other hand, if you want to do a lot of shopping in one big power shopping trip, and if you have a car or a spirit of adventure, this outlet mall is handy to know about. It is also open on Sundays.

La Vallée Village is the fanciest and most chic outlet center in all of France. It's in the American format of a fake village with a pedestrian main street, with each shop along the walkway. *Resident's alert: You cannot bring your dog!* La Vallée was built alongside a regular mall (**Centre Commercial Val d'Europe**), so curious shoppers can have the best of all worlds (although the outlet center has much more liberal hours than the regular mall) and do some discount, as well as regular, shopping. See below for more on **Auchan,** the famed *hypermarché* that is part of the Val d'Europe mall.

La Vallée is excellent on brand-name fashion and so-so on home style. Among the brands with outlet shops here are Armani, Anne Fontaine, Kenzo, Ferragamo, Muriella Burani, Charles Jourdan, Max Mara, Nitya (one of my faves; see p. 203), Camper (Spanish shoe brand for casual shoes), and Ventilo. There's also Bleu Blanc, Burberry, Mandarina Duck, Molton Brown, Ralph Lauren, Zadig & Voltaire, and—get this—Starbucks.

In terms of home, there is a **Bodum** outlet, **Lagostina** (Italian cookware), **Villeroy & Boch,** and an **Anne de Solene** shop that sells bed linen.

I am assuming you know most of these brands or can look them up in the index of this book. There is a fair mix here of French, Italian, and British lines with the odd American brand (Ralph Lauren and Starbucks). There aren't a lot of surprises—but note that **Samsonite** is an Italian brand: It does sell the luggage you expect, but it also has clothes and shoes.

As mentioned, the regular mall has a branch of **Auchan,** which is my favorite *hypermarché* in France. *Note:* Auchan is not open on Sunday and the outlet mall is, so if Auchan is important to you, organize yourself accordingly. As you can imagine, a *hypermarché* is jammed on Saturdays, so the best day to do this is from Monday to Thursday.

If you're staying in a hotel or traveling by train, you may find it too hard to schlep purchases from a *hypermarché.* However, I like their low-cost fashions and home styles and think you'll have fun poking around here while you're in the neighborhood.

Note: If you're driving a rental car, you may want to gas up here—Auchan has the best gas prices in the area. *Further note:* The automatic machines will not take U.S. credit cards.

Hours are Monday through Saturday from 10am to 8pm, Sunday from 11am to 7pm. For information, call © **01-60-42-35-00** or go to www.lavalleevillage.com.

To get there, I would allow an hour of travel time.

- By car, take the autoroute A4 east in the direction of Nancy; look for exit 12, marked val d'europe. Yes, I would consider renting a car for this adventure. The drive is easy and if there are several people along, you can share the rental cost, fill up on gas at the pumps near Auchan (pumps are open Sun), and drive back to Paris.
- By bus, a Cityrama shuttle bus from Paris runs every Tuesday, Thursday, and Sunday (call © **01-44-55-60-00** for reservations).
- By train, take the RER line A4 direct to Val d'Europe in the Disneyland direction. Go out through the mall (Centre Commercial Val d'Europe) to the outlet center on the far side. It is a hike.

USINES CENTER PARIS NORD 2

You will pass this 120-shop center (© **01-48-63-20-72**) as you drive between Paris and CDG Airport in Roissy. It's about

40 minutes from Paris. I wouldn't send anyone here, unless you've lived in Paris for years and are curious or bored with life. However, it is alongside an Ikea and a Castorama, so locals and expats may find it useful.

Open Monday through Friday from 11am to 7pm, Saturday and Sunday from 10am to 8pm. From the A1 autoroute in the direction of Roissy, take exit ZI (Zone Industriel) Paris Nord 2.

TROYES

Troyes is a city, not an outlet center, and is home to two large outlet malls. The one owned by **McArthurGlen** is called Troyes Pont Marie because it's in a suburb of Troyes named, you got it, Pont Marie. This mall offers Saturday bus service (© **08-00-80-92-43;**   www.mcarthurglen.fr/destockage-en/troyes/acces-troie/acces.php). The round-trip fare for the 90-minute trip is 15€ ($23) per person. It departs at 10am from the place de la Bastille in front of the Opéra (Métro: Bastille) and returns back to Paris at 7pm. You can go to www.mcarthurglen.fr for further information, as well as promotions and exceptional opening dates (some Sun).

The mall situation at Troyes has changed enormously. It's much more built up than in past years, there are a lot of choices for young people and young couples, and it's not as chic as La Vallée or even as clean as you'd like it to be. You may get lost if you drive, but that can and will happen all over France.

All that said, the **Armani** at McArthurGlen had so many incredible deals that you could weep. Other tenants at this mall include **Burberry, Georges Rech, Ralph Lauren, Ventilo, Weill,** and **Rodier.** There are stores for men, women, children, home style, and baggage.

Chapter 9

Antiques & Flea Markets

Antiques & Brocante

Paris is one of the world's capitals for antiques. One of the pleasures of shopping here is browsing the wide variety of antiques shops. Whether you're buying real antiques or just some "old stuff," remember that U.S. Customs defines an antique as something that is at least 100 years old. If a piece does not come with provenance papers, you must have a receipt or a bill of lading from the dealer that says what the piece is, its origin, and its age. The French government is rather stringent about what can be taken out of France; it even tries to keep some designer *fripes* (used clothes) in the country.

Expensive museum-quality antiques are generally sold in the tony shops along the rue du Faubourg St-Honoré and in the 16e, although there are plenty of high-end dealers on the Left Bank. Midpriced antiques are predominantly found in antiques shops on the Left Bank, in the antiques *villages*, and at the markets of St-Ouen. *Brocante* (junk) is mostly sold at street markets, fairs, and flea markets (see p. 217 for a list of fairs and flea markets).

If you just want to browse and get the feel of the serious antiques scene, get over to the Left Bank. A grouping of very

211

Worth a Trip

Besides specialty events, there are a few other kinds of antiques events that I recommend, if you have the strength. They are slightly out of town or on the fringes.

- **Chatou** is a fair in the town of Chatou held twice a year—March and September—on dates announced in the antiques magazines. Take the RER A1 train (direction St-Germain-en-Laye) there and walk from the station (it's well marked). The trick, of course, is to be able to carry your purchases back on the train with you—or to move to Paris and have them delivered. There is a shipping office. For event dates, call ⓒ 01-47-70-88-78.
- **Versailles** is known for the palace of the Sun King and even for its hotel, spa, and restaurant, but few people ever talk about the antiques *village* right in the heart of town. See p. 226.
- **Stadium shows** are similar to the Rose Bowl Swap Meet in Pasadena. They take place at stadiums in the outskirts of Paris and are fabulous for their low prices and huge selections. Few are served by public transportation—I hire a car and driver. The shows usually have shipping offices.

important dealers sits between the river and the boulevard St-Germain. They may be a tad more expensive than others in town, but these are the real guys with the real reputations who don't even look up from their newspapers when you walk in. They can tell from your questions just how serious you are, what you know, and, often, whom you know.

If you want to familiarize yourself with the notions and motions of French-style antiques shopping, get to a large news agent and look at the half-dozen magazines devoted to antiques and *brocante*. The most popular is *Aladdin*, but all give the schedules of big shows, fairs, specialty antiques events, and such. You can also check the Friday edition of any of the Paris newspapers for the *brocante* schedule.

ANTIQUES *VILLAGES*

A *village* in Paris is not a subdivision of an arrondissement, but a place for good antiques. *Villages* are buildings that house many antiques dealers under one roof. If you need a rainy-day occupation, a trip to any *village* probably will do it; some are even open Sunday.

Le Louvre des Antiquaires

2 place du Palais-Royal, 1er (Métro: Palais-Royal).

At this virtual antiques department store of some 250 dealers, you may have more fun than at the museum! At least you can shop here. Many mavens claim this is the single best one-stop source in Paris—quality is high and dealers have reputations to protect. You can even bargain a little. There are enough affordable small pieces that you're bound to find something you like without having to pound the pavement. A restaurant and a shipping agent are indoors. Sophisticated, civilized, nothing junky at all. Closed Sundays in August; otherwise, the Sunday scene is from a movie—the other shoppers alone make it worth a visit. Clean bathrooms, too.

Le Village Suisse

54 av. de la Motte-Picquet, 15e (Métro: Motte-Picquet).

You won't find any gnomes making watches here, or handing out chocolate bars, just a lot of dealers in the mid- to high-price range, with some very respectable offerings. Le Village Suisse is near the Hilton Suffren, the Eiffel Tower, the foodie street rue Cler, and l'Ecole Militaire, so don't be baffled by the address. There are 150 shops in an area 1 block long and 2 blocks wide—it's sort of like a mall that rambles from building to building. Prices are not outrageous, but they aren't low, either; most stores offer shipping. There are no cute or funky shops here, but several are theme-oriented, selling nautical items or antique jewelry, for instance. Sunday is a big day here.

Village St-Paul

Rue St-Paul, 4e (Métro: St-Paul).

This *village,* near a block or more of street stalls selling antiques, can be a little hard to find. It's hidden in a medieval warren of streets between the Seine and the church of St-Paul, close to Marais and Bastille. The *village* is between the rues St-Paul, Charles V, des Jardins St-Paul, and Ave-Maria.

Get off the Métro at St-Paul and walk toward the river. Or walk along the quai going toward the Bastille and take a left when you spy the first antiques shop on the corner of the rue St-Paul. If you're coming from the river, you have the advantage of being able to see the village st-paul sign that spans the street across the rooftops.

Hours are generally Thursday through Monday from 11am to 7pm. Prices can be steep, but the variety of the merchandise, combined with the charm of the neighborhood, makes this a delightful way to pass the time. It makes a good stop to piggyback with your visit to the Marais. Yes, there's life on Sunday afternoons.

AUCTION HOUSES

For years, the big name in Paris's auction world was the **Hôtel Drouot.** But ever since Sotheby's gave up its Monaco offices and moved to Paris, and the government allowed others to play in the big leagues, the scene has become much more competitive. **Christie's** and **Sotheby's** are now fairly substantial players; **Tajan** isn't quite as big a name, but has some popular auctions (I went to its Barbie auction; what a scene!).

When an entire estate is being auctioned—usually due to death or bankruptcy—and there is usually nothing "important" (as the dealers tend to say) for sale, you can find bargains. This tip will be most useful for those trying to furnish a home here in France, not for those shopping for shipping.

Hotel Drouot

9 rue Drouot, 9e (Métro: Le Peletier); 15 av. Montaigne, 8e (Métro: Alma-Marceau).

Drouot is a weird and fascinating place. At the entrance, an information counter has catalogs and notices of future sales; three TVs on the ground floor show different parts of the building. There is an appraiser who will tell you, free of charge, if an item you bring in is worthy of auction; he will appraise it for you on the spot in a small private room. If you agree with the estimate, you can set a date for your auction. The seller pays an 8% to 10% commission to the house.

Auctions take place on weekdays in summer and daily the rest of the year. They always begin at 2pm and usually end around 6:30pm. Previews are held on Wednesday until 11am. When you read auction catalogs in Paris, note that Hôtel Drouot listings with an r after them (for Richelieu) refer to the old location; an m refers to the avenue Montaigne location. You can buy Drouot's magazine at newsstands and get an instant look at the auction of the month.

The auction rooms are various sizes; all are carpeted and have art, tapestries, or both hanging on the walls. The clients sit on chairs to watch the bidding. Most of the clients are dealers; I've never noticed a very jazzy crowd here, even at a Goya auction. All business is in French. If you are not fluent, bring your own translator or expert, or book a translator (© 01-42-46-17-11) ahead of time.

You needn't register to bid; anyone can walk in, sit down, and bid. Paddles are not used. Some dealers occasionally use shills to drive up the price. The auctioneers are familiar with all of the dealers and could possibly choose to throw a piece their way; dealers may even pool in on items. All auctions have catalogs, in which the lots are numbered and defined. You do not need a catalog to enter a preview or an auction, as you do in New York. The conditions of the sale are plainly printed (in French) inside the first page of the catalog. You can pay in cash up to 1,500€ ($2,250). French people may write local checks; Americans cannot write checks on U.S. banks. If you have only American dollars on hand, there's an exchange bureau in the house. If you pay cash, you can leave with your item.

BROCANTE SHOWS

Brocante is the French word for junk; it does not include antiques. Those who sell *brocante* are not antiques dealers—this is very strict in the French sense of things. An American might not notice the difference.

Brocante is sold wherever you go in France, from local markets to fancy shoe stores. **Sadema,** 86 rue de Lille, 7e (© **01-40-62-95-95;** fax 01-40-62-95-96; Métro: Solférino), is an organization that hosts *brocante* shows. These shows are annual or semiannual, most frequently held at the same time (more or less) and place each year. They are announced in the papers (check *Figaroscope*) and in weekly guides such as *Pariscope*. You can call, write, or fax for the schedule. Some shows are weekend events; others last up to 2 weeks.

Sadema is not the only game in town; other organizations also sponsor shows. One such agency is Joel Garcia (© **01-56-53-93-93**). Some are fancier and charge more. In fact, the cost of admission mirrors how tony the dealers are: the higher the fee, the more expensive the dealers and their wares. Annual shows include the following:

- **Ferraille de Paris:** Held in the Parc Floral de Paris (Bois de Vincennes), this good-size indoor fair takes place toward the end of February. It includes a lot of affordable merchandise and approachable merchants. There's everything from empty perfume bottles to the kitchen sink—the French country kitchen sink. Métro: Porte Dorée.
- **Brocante de Printemps:** This March event usually lasts 10 days; it heralds the coming of spring, of course. Métro: Edgar Quinet.
- **Brocante à la Bastille:** This event does not take itself or its merchants too seriously. This fair is usually held on both sides of the canal. Pay near the place de la Bastille; there are bridges to the other side. Usually held for 10 days in April or May, and particularly fabulous in fine weather. I'd fly in just for this one. Métro: Bastille.

- **Brocante de Paris:** This huge event is the talk of the town for those who hope to get a designer bargain. It runs for 10 days in May. Métro: Brochant.

Flea Markets

Paris is famous for its flea markets, although I think only two of them are worth getting hot and bothered over. Many people think of the markets in St-Ouen as the only game in town; I think Vanves is better. I give you the information about Montreuil in order to be complete—I don't suggest it.

Puces de Montreuil

Av. André Lemierre and av. Gallieni, 20e (Métro: Porte de Montreuil).

I have included this market because I want you to know that I know it exists and that I've been there. But it's really only for die-hard flea market shoppers. It's a junk fair of sorts, so there are very few diamonds here—and those are artfully hidden. You could hunt for hours before throwing up your hands in disgust, having found nothing.

This immense market absorbed three other nearby markets with a huge path of illegal vendors that stretched from the nearest Métro station all the way across a bridge to the beginning of the market proper. There's a good selection of *fripes,* Victorian bed linens, old hats, new perfumes (look, Mom, who needs détaxe?), work clothes, cheap clothes, records, dishes, junk, junk, and more junk. Did I mention there is a lot of junk? This is a really low-end market without any charm whatsoever. Dealers work this one very thoroughly—it runs a good 10% to 20% cheaper than St-Ouen, but it's 50% harder to find anything. This is for those with a strong heart and a good eye; princesses and blue bloods need not apply. Open Saturday and Sunday morning through evening.

Puces de Vanves

Av. George Lafenestre, av. Marc Sangnier, and av. Maurice d'Ocagne, 14e (Métro: Porte de Vanves).

When people tell me they are headed to the flea market in Paris, I always ask, "Which one?" They look at me like I'm an idiot, then stammer and finally say it's "the big one" or "the famous one." That means they are headed to St-Ouen, which is a lot of fun.

However, I think the number-one flea market in Paris is Puces des Vanves. This market is not like any other; it's more like a bunch of neighbors who've gone in together on a multifamily garage sale stretching for a mile or so. The market is L-shaped: On the main part of the street are the licensed vendors who pay taxes to the city; on the branch part are the illegal tag-sale vendors, who are, of course, the most fun.

The tag-sale goods are of lesser quality, but together with the licensed vendors, they make for wonderful strolling and browsing. If you don't have much time or can't stand the strain of St-Ouen, try this neighborhood affair that's perfect for a weekend. Saturday is the best day to shop Vanves. Early birds get the worms, of course; I'm here at 9:30am.

The main part of the market is on the avenue Georges Lafenestre. With the legal and the illegal guys, there are almost 200 vendors here. A crepe stand is at the bend in the road; the Sunday food market on avenue Marc Sangnier enhances the experience.

Note: The basic part of the market closes at noon, but some dealers stay on. In the afternoon, around 1 or 2pm, a new bunch of dealers moves in to sell new (cheap) ready-to-wear, shoes, socks, towels, and so on. Open Saturday and Sunday from 9am to 1pm.

The Markets of St-Ouen

St-Ouen (Métro: Porte de Clignancourt; Bus: PC1).

Also known as the Marché aux Puces or "the famous flea market," St-Ouen comprises several markets, each with its own dealers and each with its own special feel.

St-Ouen Markets

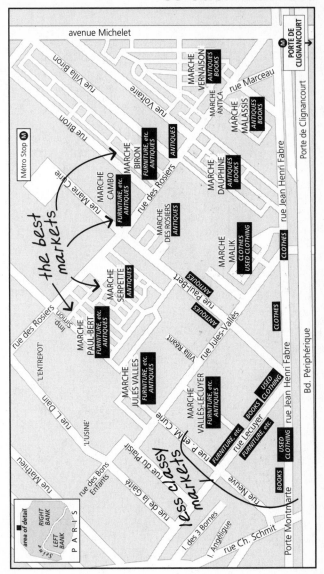

The St-Ouen markets grew from a series of little streets and alleys. Today, more than 30 hectares (75 acres) of flea market sprawl through this suburb. Each market most frequently bears the name of the street on which it rests, even though you may be hard-pressed to find the original street sign. The markets themselves are usually well marked; they often have doors on two different streets.

These are not garage sale–style street vendors: Usually the stalls open onto the street or a walkway, but have some covered parts; even the informal markets are sheltered. You will see limited street action and selling off makeshift tables. However, as you walk from the Métro to the flea market, you will see candy stands and bluejeans dealers. The first market you see is not the flea market you're looking for; ignore these dealers.

Places to eat are numerous, bathrooms are not, and more pickpockets or rowdy boys abound than the French government would like to admit. I was once terrorized with lighted cigarettes and burning matches held by teenage boys who wanted to chase me. While they burned holes in my clothes, I refused to run or surrender my packages. I mention it because it happened to me, so it could happen to you.

If you feel you need a system for working this vast space, try mine: Start with the big guns (Biron, Cambo) and the markets in that area, then walk back so that Malik is one of your last stops. In fact, if you like the Marché Malik as little as I do, you'll be happy to run from there and call it a day.

To do it my way, turn into the market streets on the rue des Rosiers (with your back to the Métro station you came from, turn left). Work this street until the good stuff peters out; then cut to the left by way of the Marché Paul Bert. Then go right on the rue Vallès. At that point, retrace your steps by cutting through Malassis. Note that there are free-standing antiques stores, as well as big (and small) markets. Open Saturday through Monday from 8:30am to 7pm.

Note: Business has been bad with fewer American visitors at St-Ouen, so various promotional deals and events are popping up. The **Mondial de l'Antiquité** lasts for a few days in October, including 1 day when people sell from trucks—it's wild and well priced. To promote business with Americans, often the markets offer parity days, when the U.S. dollar is at parity with the euro in figuring prices.

MARCHE ANTICA (99 rue des Rosiers) Just a little bitty building refinished in the Memphis Milano teal-blue-and-cream look. This market abounds with cute shops selling small collectibles of good quality at pretty good prices. It's on a corner of the Marché Vernaison, at rue des Rosiers and rue Voltaire.

MARCHE BIRON (85 rue des Rosiers) The fanciest market in the place is one of the first markets on rue des Rosiers. Biron should be the first stop for dealers who are looking for serious stuff. If you come here and are looking for fleas, you may be turned off—it's quite hoity-toity.

MARCHE CAMBO (75 rue des Rosiers) Another serious market, but a little less refined—the dealers are usually busy hobnobbing with one another and may ignore you. You'll see furnishings in various states of refinishing and find dealers in various states of mind—some know what they have and are hard-nosed about it; others want to move the merchandise and will deal with you. They are particularly responsive to genuine dealers who know their stuff and speak some French. The selection is less formal and more eclectic than at Biron (next door); there are rows of stalls along lanes or aisles.

MARCHE DAUPHINE (140 rue des Rosiers) A newer *village* of some 300 shops opposite the Marché Vernaison, this is one of the first places to hit when you get to the market area. It's enclosed, with a balcony, industrial lighting, and a factory-like, high-tech atmosphere under a glass rooftop. A shipping agency is on hand. Some dealers are affordable; I found a button dealer and a specialist in vintage designer clothing that flipped me out for *fripes*.

MARCHE DES ROSIERS (3 rue Paul Bert) A very small market specializing in the period between 1900 and 1930. There are about 13 small stalls in an enclosed horseshoe-shaped building.

MARCHE JULES-VALLES (7 rue Jules Vallès) I like this one, although it's small and junky; reproduction brass items for the home mix with real antiques and real repro everything else. Cheap, cheap, cheap.

MARCHE PAUL-BERT (96 rue des Rosiers) Are we having fun yet? If not, send the husband and the kids for pizza and go for it on your own—this is too good to not enjoy. Marché Paul-Bert is more outdoorsy than the rest; it surrounds the Marché Serpette in three alleys forming a U. This market is both outside and inside, with lower-end merchandise, including Art Deco, *moderne,* and country furniture. Most of the items here have not been repaired or refinished. There could be some great buys, but you need to have a good eye and know your stuff. Piles of suitcases, carts, dolls, and buttons in bins. Yummy. If you visit only one market, want to start with the very best, or think the weather may turn on you, start here.

MARCHE SERPETTE (110 rue des Rosiers) This market is in a real building, not a Quonset hut. There is carpeting on the floor, and each vendor has a stall number and a metal door. There are also nice, clean bathrooms on the second floor. Serpette is on the edge of the Marché Paul-Bert, but you can tell the difference because this one is totally indoors and is dark and fancy.

MARCHE VERNAISON (99 rue des Rosiers) I like this market a lot, although the new building puts me off a bit. There isn't that much I want to buy; I just like to prowl the various teeny showrooms. There are a few fabric, textile, trim, and needlework mavens who always have things I covet. You may not realize at first that this sprawling market alone constitutes a *village*, with its own streets and byways. A good first stop, it has a lot of natural charm and many affordable places; it's also first if you follow my walking path.

Helpful Hands

If you're interested in these market sources—and ones that might be open only to the trade—you might want to call a local expert who arranges everything and even does the bargaining for you. My friend **Carole Carlino** has been taking dealers around Paris and the provinces for almost 20 years. Her home phone number is © 01-30-73-06-85; her cellphone is 06-80-63-71-74.

You can latch onto a shopping tour that will take you to the flea markets; these are usually general tours that aren't too expensive and provide someone who may speak French better than you do. You can go to www.chicshopping.biz for some ideas as to what tours are offered.

Need a shipper for items of furniture, not household goods? Hmmm, this one is tricky because you will do better by bulk than by piece. Shipping prices have gone so far up that you do better to buy a house in France than to ship your buys to the U.S. Try art shipper **Alain Franklin** (© 01-40-11-50-11) if you have a single piece. I prefer to send 5m³, or 5 cubic meters, which is the minimum on groupage—you can ship such a selection for about 2,000€ ($3,000) door-to-door. My most recent shipment is mid-Atlantic, maybe even through the Panama Canal as I write. I used Schmid & Kahlert and was thrilled with them (© 03-88-96-59-03). Note that my friend Sally shipped with them and was not as happy due to paperwork snafus. Five cubic meters turned out to be two armoires, a bureau, a coffee table, a wardrobe of clothes, and four boxes of linens and returned goods.

Chapter 10

Day Trips & Weekends Away

The Other Paris

While I have hopefully done a fairly decent job covering the 20 *arrondissements* of Paris within the main body of this book, I want to stress some geopolitical/cultural facts that can allow you to stay within the Peripherique (the ring road that encircles Paris) and think you are out of town by seeing a whole new Paris.

I won't get into a big history lesson—most of us already know that Paris began on the islands in the Seine and then branched out. As the city built up, the money went west. To this day you will find French aristocrats who will only live in the 16e, their stomping ground. The furthermost eastern parts of Paris were basically Indian Territory. Montmartre was its own city until very recently and has its own history, but such *arrondissements* as the 10e, 11e, and 12e were homes to train stations and factories and had a seedy reputation.

Not any more. In his book *Hungry for Paris* (Random House), Alexander Lobrano talks about the most exciting and affordable eating adventures in Paris found in these three districts, which even 10 years ago were considered no man's land.

The more you explore eastern Paris, the greater your chance of finding affordable retail, funky stores, cutting-edge designers, and noteworthy breakthroughs in design and architecture and adventure.

Before you leave Paris for an out-of-town destination, consider if you really even know the New Paris.

The 20% Raison d'Être

If you're still ready to roam, note that areas outside of Paris are at least 20% less expensive than Paris. You may find that you want to take advantage of the excellent French infrastructure and take a day trip to go shopping or get in some extra culture (and shopping).

While you can make a day trip or overnight to London via the Chunnel, I am not including that choice in this chapter. The point is to lower costs and see something new. Brussels? Sure, it's a good idea—especially for the flea markets on Saturdays. But I've got lots of ideas here and none of them refers to the U.K.

LA FRANCE PROFONDE

Paris is Paris, we all know that. And the rest of France is not Paris. It is often called *la France profonde,* and while I find my true France driving in the countryside, just getting into some of the real-people towns (even touristy ones) gives you a totally different sense of what France is.

The train track and infrastructure of France is such that there is a vast system of highways and railways . . . although there are more that go north-south than east-west. Still, we do have the new TGV Est, which will take you from Paris to Strasbourg in 3 hours. With this system of high-speed trains, you can get to just about any place in France for lunch and return to Paris for dinner.

I'm not saying you want to do that, I'm just noting that you can. Please note that Cannes, Nice, and Monte Carlo are not included in that stretch—you will have to fly there and I don't suggest them for a day trip. A weekend? Maybe. But let's face it, Cannes is not *la France profonde!*

Never mind.

Granted, you can get a tour bus or even a car and driver (call Mathieu; see p. 31) to take you to the Normandy beaches, to Mont St-Michel, to the vineyards of Champagne . . . but there's something much more *sympa* about popping on the train or in your own rental car and doing this yourself.

Car rentals, especially for 1 day, can be very, very expensive. Research this and book from the U.S.; in terms of the car-rental prices, it may be more economical to spend a weekend away rather than a day out. Note that drive times are given from the edge of Paris to the destination—it can take you an hour to get through the city if the traffic is rough.

Versailles

DESTINATION Versailles

TRAINS RER C to Rive Gauche; St-Lazare to Versailles Chantiers; from Montparnasse to Rive Droite

TRAVEL TIME 30 minutes

Château is closed on Mondays; the flea market is just on weekends.

The Château (as it is called) has been closed for renovations for several years, so now is your chance to get a good look-see. Then you can buy the movie. This is not a destination you need to drive to; there are numerous trains all day long.

Just a few words of warning: If you want to shop and really enjoy this charming suburb of Paris, spend a night. The Château is totally overwhelming. And there is a nice little flea market on weekends that I don't want you to miss.

Chatou, I Love You

Chatou is a fair in the town of Chatou held twice a year—March and September—on dates announced in the antiques magazines. It takes about a half-hour to get here from Paris, so you can actually do this as a half-day excursion.

Take the RER A1 train (direction St-Germain-en-Laye) there and walk from the station (it's well marked). Getting back to the station to return to Paris is slightly harder, or just longer, since you have to walk an extra 2 blocks in order to get to the other side of the tracks. Why did the shopper cross to the other side of the tracks?

Plan to eat lunch here—there's a corridor of food stalls and everything is glorious.

There are between 800 and 1,000 dealers set up in a little village that is funky and fun—prices are much lower than in Paris. Yes, you can bargain.

The trick, of course, is to be able to carry your purchases back on the train with you—or to move to Paris and have them delivered.

There is a shipping office on site.

For event dates, call © **01-47-70-88-78** or do a Google search.

On approach to the Château, you will be horrified by the motorcoaches and the hordes. You may want to skip the Château and just shop.

The "downtown" part of town is called the *Quartier Notre Dame*; the main shopping streets are rue Hoche and rue Paroisse. The flea market is in the *Quartier des Antiquaires* and is formed by several alleys and passageways and shops all joined together around a courtyard. Find it on the rue du Baillage, not far from the Château.

Insider's Tip

There are two train stations in Versailles, so pay attention. I like to arrive by one and depart by the other because this means I've thoroughly done it. (I use Rive Droite to arrive and Rive Gauche to depart.)

Lille

....

DESTINATION Lille (two different train stations; see below)

TRAIN Thalys from Gare du Nord

TRAVEL TIME 1 hour by train; 2½ to 3 hours by car

There are few Frenchmen who will send you to Lille. What do they know? I am a shopper; I love Lille and I think it's a great day trip or overnight.

On the Thalys fast train, Lille is only 1 hour from Paris and is worth doing for zillions of reasons, many of them related to shopping and some to outlets, factories, and big-time bargains. Since there are two different stations, you need to pay attention. I personally like Lille Flandres, which is the "old" station but it's right in the heart of shopping land. Lille Europe is the newfangled station built for the Eurostar, and while it's not inconvenient, I'd take a taxi from here to Vieux Lille, the old town.

Now then, before I go into the charms of Lille (of which there are many), may I suggest that you think about driving? If you are at CDG (or leaving from CDG), you have half the battle fought and won't even need to tackle Paris traffic. If you do drive, plan to at least spend a night.

You can consider this as an overnight adventure or a week-end away and throw in Brussels, which is only about a half-hour away. The reason to drive is to be able to get to factory outlets without having to run up taxi fares. You can also rent a car in Lille at the train station, although 1-day car rentals can be pricey.

Lille is the industrial north of Paris, home to cotton mills. (Silk mills are south, in and around Lyon.) The main industry in these mills is luxury bed linen, and prices are a fraction of regular retail. Yes, I am talking $1,000 sheets for $100.

There are two outlet malls in Lille; both have numerous shops selling bed linen. The heart of the old town is the cutie-pie shopping district; there are a few free-standing outlet

Lille's French Linen Factory Trail

The most famous brand of French luxury linens is **Porthault** (www.dporthault.fr), made about an hour outside of Lille. They have a factory store on the premises, at 19 rue Robespierre, Rieux en Cambrésis (© **01-27-82-22-33**). If you're driving from Paris, this outlet is midway between Paris and Lille; then, the various villages between the Porthault factory and downtown Lille are dotted with factory stores selling all the major French linen brands at discount prices. Choose **Kenzo,** 52 rue Grande Chaussée (© **01-20-51-78-79;** www.kenzo.com); **Yves Delorme,** 20 rue Nationale (© **03-20-12-90-85;** www.yvesdelorme.com); **Descamps,** 40 rue Grande Chaussée (© **01-28-04-01-91;** www.descamps. com); and more—and you'll find several of these brands at the **McArthurGlen Outlet Center** in the town of Roubaix, 44 Mail de Lannoy (© **01-28-33-36-10;** www.mcarthur glen.fr). This is an American-style outlet store and the stuff of legends; the best linen outlet here is **Sous-Signe.** Visit www. lilletourism.com.

stores here. The main **Porthault** outlet, in the factory, is actually about an hour away (see box above).

Deauville

DESTINATION Deauville-Trouville

TRAIN St-Lazare

TRAVEL TIME 2 hours by train; 2 hours by car

When I lived in Paris and kept my car there in winter, we had a favorite day trip—Deauville and Trouville. You can get to Deauville by train (use Gare St-Lazare); it takes about 2 hours and you can walk just about everywhere you want to go. If you spend a night, or stay the weekend, you'll really get a better taste of life on the French coast.

Sometimes laughingly called the 21st arrondissement, as many Parisians weekend and summer here, Deauville has a twin sister (Trouville) which is also worth visiting, if you have a car. (Good **Monoprix** in Trouville.) Hmmm, there must be a bus.

Of course, only real people go to (or want to go to) Trouville. It's Deauville, where Coco Chanel opened her first shop, that you go for sun, sea, surf, and horses. The summer season is the reason, but I happen to like to go in the winter.

SHOP TALK In his totally yummy book *Bringing Home the Birkin,* Hermès "re-seller" Michael Tonello says he got more Birkin handbags from the Deauville branch of Hermès than from any other store in the world.

Reims

DESTINATION Reims

TRAIN Gare de l'Est

TRAVEL TIME 45 minutes by train; 2 hours by car

This is another destination that gives you more leeway if you drive, but takes more time out of your day. And having a car just makes you more nuts that it's so hard to carry wine bottles back to the U.S. (Bring lots of bubble wrap; buy splits.)

The new TGV Est line that stretches eastward to Germany will get you here in no time at all, and there is enough to see (and buy) for a nice day trip. Reims, after all, is the heart of champagne country. My coupe runneth over.

You can rent a car in Reims if you want to drive to various vineyards, or do a lot by foot. You'll want to head to the famous cathedral (of Joan of Arc fame); surrounding the cathedral are several stores that specialize in local champagnes. This part of town is to one side of the main heart of downtown; a taxi to the cathedral will have you right where you want to be.

If you want to tour a *cave* (wine cellar), there are a few in town (**Pommery** is the most famous); you will need a taxi to get there from the cathedral, or vice versa.

Rouen

DESTINATION Rouen

TRAIN St-Lazare

TRAVEL TIME 2 hours by train; 2 hours by car

This is another Joan of Arc favorite . . . or maybe not.

The cathedral is in the heart of the old town and this is a walk-ably adorable and cutie-pie perfect town, known for its faience. You get a nice dose of Norman architecture, the main shopping street is suitably adorable, and you can even buy a brand of coffee named Jeanne d'Arc, which (don't snicker) is marked "French roast." Everything revolves around the Big Clock—all chains and multiples are represented in terms of shopping. This is more of a real-people town than a deluxe status-symbol kind of town (like Deauville).

Dijon

DESTINATION Dijon Ville

TRAIN From Gare de l'Est

TRAVEL TIME 1 hour, 40 minutes by train; 3 hours by car

Will your horizons be greatly enhanced if you take a day off to go to Dijon? No, not really. But you'll have a nice day out, walk some charming little streets, and come back with heaps of mustard.

Dijon is the heart of the Côte d'Or and a city that is small enough and off the tourist path just enough to be a perfect little side trip. You can walk to town from the train station; but it could exhaust you (although it's only about 10 min.), so consider a taxi to the **Maille** shop (32 rue de la Republique) and start your day with the Grey Poupon.

If you are into French history at all, you'll note that Dijon was part of the Kingdom of Burgundy and is now at the top of the burgundy winegrowing region. So this part of France is very much associated with food—be it the mustard, the wine, the gingerbread, the kir (the drink was invented here), or even the *boeuf*-you-know-what.

The main shopping street is the rue de la Liberte, with the usual multiples (yes, Monoprix) and a handful of mustard shops. Of course, mustard is everywhere—even in Monoprix. The somewhat hidden rue Amiral Roussin hosts the designer shops. There is a strong market and an okay flea market.

If you have a car and stay overnight or for a weekend, you can see nearby vineyards and get to Beaune, one of France's cutest wine towns.

Pardon My French

Useful Terms & Phrases

If you don't speak Bad French as fluently as I do, you may find this glossary helpful. Just remember to not pronounce the "h" at the beginning of the word, to drop most of the letters off the end of the word, and to speak through your nose. Merci.

LE BASICS

English	French	Pronunciation
Yes/No	**Oui/Non**	Wee/Nohn
Okay	**D'accord**	Dah-*core*
Please	**S'il vous plaît**	Seel voo *play*
Thank you	**Merci**	Mair-*see*
You're welcome	**De rien**	Duh ree-*ehn*
Hello (during daylight hours)	**Bonjour**	Bohn-*jhoor*
Good evening	**Bonsoir**	bohn-*swahr*
Good-bye	**Au revoir**	O ruh-*vwahr*
What's your name?	**Comment vous appellez-vous?**	Ko-mahn voo za-pell-ay-*voo?*
My name is . . .	**Je m'appelle . . .**	Jhuh ma-*pell* . . .
Happy to meet you	**Enchanté(e)**	Ohn-shahn-tay
Miss	**Mademoiselle**	Mad-mwa-*zel*

English	French	Pronunciation
Mr.	**Monsieur**	Muh-*syuh*
Mrs.	**Madame**	Ma-*dam*
How are you?	**Comment allez-vous?**	Kuh-mahn tahl-ay-*voo?*
Fine, thank you, and you?	**Très bien, merci, et vous?**	Tray bee-ehn, mare-ci, ay *voo?*
Very well, thank you	**Très bien, merci**	Tray bee-ehn, mair-*see*
So-so	**Comme ci, comme ça**	Kum-*see*, kum-*sah*
I'm sorry/excuse me	**Pardon**	Pahr-*dohn*
I'm so very sorry	**Désolé(e)**	Day-zoh-*lay*
That's all right	**Il n'y a pas de quoi**	Eel nee ah pah duh kwah

GETTING AROUND/STREET SMARTS

English	French	Pronunciation
Do you speak English?	**Parlez-vous anglais?**	Par-lay-voo ahn-*glay?*
I don't speak French	**Je ne parle pas français**	Jhuh ne parl pah frahn-*say*
I don't understand	**Je ne comprends pas**	Jhuh ne kohm-*prahn* pas
Could you speak more loudly/ more slowly?	**Pouvez-vous parler un peu plus fort/ plus lentement?**	Poo-vay-voo par-lay un puh ploo for/ ploo lan-te-*ment?*
Could you repeat that?	**Répetez, s'il vous plaît?**	Ray-pay-*tay*, seel voo *play*
What is it?	**Qu'est-ce que c'est?**	Kess kuh *say?*
What time is it?	**Qu'elle heure est-il?**	Kel uhr eh-*teel?*
What?	**Quoi?**	Kwah?
How? or What did you say?	**Comment?**	Ko-*mahn?*

English	French	Pronunciation
When?	**Quand?**	Kahn?
Where is . . . ?	**Où est . . . ?**	Ooh eh . . . ?
Who?	**Qui?**	Kee?
Why?	**Pourquoi?**	Poor-*kwah*?
Here/there	**ici/là**	ee-*see*/lah
Left/right	**à gauche/à droite**	a goash/a drwaht
Straight ahead	**tout droit**	too drwah
I'm American/ Canadian/British	**Je suis américain(e)/ canadien(e)/ anglais(e)**	Jhe sweez a-may-ree-*kehn*/ can-ah-dee-*en*/ ahn-glay (*glaise*)
Fill the tank (of a car), please	**Le plein, s'il vous plait**	Luh plan, seel voo *play*
I'm going to . . .	**Je vais à . . .**	Jhe vay ah . . .
I want to get off at . . .	**Je voudrais descendre à . . .**	Jhe voo-*dray* day-son-drah ah
I'm sick	**Je suis malade**	Jhuh swee mal-*ahd*
airport	**l'aéroport**	lair-o-*por*
bank	**la banquet**	lah bahnk
bridge	**pont**	pohn
bus station	**la gare routière**	lah gar roo-tee-*air*
bus stop	**l'arrêt de bus**	lah-*ray* duh boohss
by means of a bicycle	**en vélo/ par bicyclette**	uh *vay*-low/ par bee-see-*clet*
by means of a car	**en voiture**	ahn vwa-*toor*
cashier	**la caisse**	lah *kess*
cathedral	**cathédral**	ka-tay-*dral*
church	**église**	ay-*gleez*
dead end	**une impasse**	ewn am-*pass*
driver's license	**permis de conduire**	per-mee duh con-*dweer*

English	French	Pronunciation
elevator	l'ascenseur	lah-sahn-*seuhr*
entrance (to a building or a city)	une porte	ewn port
exit (from a building or a freeway)	une sortie	ewn sor-*tee*
fortified castle or palace	château	sha-*tow*
garden	jardin	jhar-dehn
gasoline	du pétrol/de l'essence	duh pay-*trol*/de lay-*sahns*
ground floor	rez-de-chausée	ray-de-show-*say*
highway to . . .	la route pour	la root por
hospital	l'hôpital	low-pee-*tahl*
insurance	les assurances	lez ah-sur-*ahns*
luggage storage	consigne	kohn-*seen*-yuh
museum	le musée	luh mew-*zay*
no entry	sens interdit	sehns ahn-ter-*dee*
no smoking	défense de fumer	day-*fahns* de fu-may
on foot	à pied	ah pee-*ay*
one-day pass	ticket journalier	tee-kay jhoor-nall-ee-*ay*
one-way ticket	aller simple	ah-*lay* sam-pluh
police	la police	lah po-*lees*
rented car	voiture de location	vwa-*toor* de low-ka-see-on
round-trip ticket	aller-retour	ah-*lay*-re-toor
second floor	premier étage	prem-ee-*ehr* ay-*taj*
slow down	ralentir	rah-lahn-*teer*
store	le magasin	luh ma-ga-*zehn*
street	rue	roo

English	French	Pronunciation
suburb	**banlieu/environs**	bahn-*liew*/ en-veer-*ohns*
subway	**le Métro**	le *May*-tro
telephone	**le téléphone**	luh tay-lay-*phone*
ticket	**un billet**	uh *bee*-yay
ticket office	**vente de billets**	vahnt duh bee-*yay*
toilets	**les toilettes/les WC**	lay twa-*lets*/ les Vay-*Say*
tower	**tour**	toor

NECESSITIES

English	French	Pronunciation
I'd like . . .	**Je voudrais . . .**	Jhe voo-*dray* . . .
a room	**une chambre**	ewn *shahm*-bruh
the key	**la clé (la clef)**	la *clay*
I'd like to buy . . .	**Je voudrais acheter . . .**	Jhe voo-dray ahsh-*tay* . . .
aspirin	**des aspirines/ des aspros**	deyz ahs-peer-*eens*/ deyz ahs-*prohs*
cigarettes	**des cigarettes**	day see-ga-*ret*
condoms	**des préservatifs**	day pray-ser-va-*teefs*
dictionary	**un dictionnaire**	uh deek-see-oh-*nare*
dress	**une robe**	ewn robe
envelopes	**des envelopes**	days ahn-veh-*lope*
gift (for someone)	**un cadeau**	uh kah-*doe*
handbag	**un sac**	uh sahk

continued

English	French	Pronunciation
hat	**un chapeau**	uh shah-*poh*
magazine	**une revue**	ewn reh-*vu*
map of the city	**un plan de ville**	unh plahn de *veel*
matches	**des allumettes**	dayz a-loo-*met*
necktie	**une cravate**	uh cra-*vaht*
newspaper	**un journal**	uh zhoor-*nahl*
phone card	**une carte télé-phonique**	uh cart tay-lay-fone-*eek*
postcard	**une carte postale**	ewn carte pos-*tahl*
road map	**une carte routière**	ewn cart roo-tee-*air*
shirt	**une chemise**	ewn che-*meez*
shoes	**des chaussures**	day show-*suhr*
skirt	**une jupe**	ewn jhoop
soap	**du savon**	dew sah-*vohn*
socks	**des chaussettes**	day show-*set*
stamp	**un timbre**	uh *tam*-bruh
trousers	**un pantaloon**	uh pan-tah-*lohn*
writing paper	**du papier à lettres**	dew pap-pee-*ay* a *let*-ruh
How much does it cost?	**C'est combien?/ Ça coûte combien?**	Say comb-bee-*ehn*?/Sah coot comb-bee-*ehn*?
That's expensive	**C'est cher/chère**	Say share
That's inexpensive	**C'est raisonnable/ C'est bon marché**	Say ray-son-*ahb*-bluh/ Say bohn mar-*shay*
Do you take credit cards?	**Est-ce que vous acceptez les cartes de credit?**	Es-kuh voo zaksep-*tay* lay kart duh creh-*dee*?

IN YOUR HOTEL

English	French	Pronunciation
Are taxes included?	**Est-ce que les taxes sont comprises?**	Ess-keh lay taks son com-*preez*?
balcony	**un balcon**	uh bahl-cohn
bathtub	**une baignoire**	ewn bayn-*nwar*
bedroom	**une chambre**	ewn *shawm*-bruh
for two occupants	**pour deux personnes**	poor duh pair-sunn
hot and cold water	**l'eau chaude et froide**	low showed ay fwad
Is breakfast included?	**Petit dé jeuner inclus?**	Peh-*tee* day-jheun-ay ehn-*klu*?
room	**une chambre**	ewn *shawm*-bruh
shower	**une douche**	ewn dooch
sink	**un lavabo**	uh la-va-*bow*
suite	**une suite**	ewn sweet
We're staying for . . . days with	**On reste pour . . . jours avec**	Ohn rest poor . . . jhoor ah-*vek*
with air-conditioning	**avec climatisation**	ah-*vek* clee-mah-tee-zah-sion
without	**sans**	sahn
youth hostel	**une auberge de jeunesse**	oon oh-bayrge-duh-jhe-ness

IN THE RESTAURANT

English	French	Pronunciation
I would like . . .	**Je voudrais**	Jhe voo-*dray*
to eat	**manger**	mahn-*jhay*
to order	**commander**	ko-mahn-*day*

English	French	Pronunciation
Please give me . . .	**Donnez-moi, s'il vous plaît . . .**	Doe-nay-*mwah*, seel voo play . . .
a bottle of . . .	**une bouteille de . . .**	ewn boo-*tay* duh . . .
a cup of . . .	**une tasse de . . .**	ewn tass duh . . .
a glass of . . .	**un verre de . . .**	uh vair duh . . .
an ashtray	**un cendrier**	uh sahn-dree-*ay*
a plate of . . .	**une assiette de . . .**	ewn ass-ee-*et* duh . . .
bread	**du pain**	dew pan
breakfast	**le petit déjeuner**	luh puh-*tee* day-zhuh-*nay*
butter	**du beurre**	dew burr
check/bill	**l'addition/ la note**	la-dee-see-*ohn*/ la noat
Cheers!	**à votre santé**	*ah* vo-truh sahn-*tay*
Can I buy you	**Puis-je vous payer**	*Pwee*-jhe voo pay-ay
a drink?	**un verre?**	uh *vaihr*?
a cocktail?	**un aperitif?**	uh ah-pay-ree-*teef*?
coffee	**du café**	dew ka-*fay*
coffee (black)	**un café noir**	uh ka-*fay* nwahr
coffee (decaf)	**un café décaféiné**	uh ka-*fay* day-kah-fay-*nay*
coffee (espresso)	**un café express**	uh ka-fay ek-*sprehss*
coffee (with cream)	**un café crème**	uh ka-*fay* krem
coffee (with milk)	**un café au lait**	uh ka-*fay* o *lay*

English	French	Pronunciation
dinner	le dîner	luh dee-*nay*
fixed-price menu	un menu	uh may-new
fork	une fourchette	ewn four-*shet*
Is the tip/service included?	Est-ce que le service est compris?	Ess-ke luh ser-vees eh com-*pree?*
knife	un couteau	uh koo-*toe*
napkin	une serviette	ewn sair-vee-*et*
pepper	du poivre	dew *pwah*-vruh
platter of the day	un plat du jour	uh plah dew jhoor
salt	du sel	dew sell
soup	une soupe/ un potage	ewn soop/ uh poh-*tahj*
spoon	une cuillère	ewn kwee-*air*
sugar	du sucre	dew *sook*-ruh
tea	un thé	uh tay
tea (with lemon)	un thé au citron	uh tay o see-*tron*
tea (herbal)	une tisane	ewn tee-*zahn*
Waiter!/ Waitress!	Monsieur!/ Mademoiselle!	Mun-*syuh*!/ Mad-mwa-*zel*!
wine list	une carte des vins	ewn cart day *van*
appetizer	une entrée	ewn en-*tray*
main course	un plat principal	uh plah pran-see-*pahl*
tip included	service compris	sehr-*vees* cohm-*preez*
wide-range sample of the chef's best efforts	menu dégustation	may-new *day*-gus-ta-see-on
drinks not included	boissons non comprises	bwa-*sons* no com-*preez*
cheese tray	plâteau de fromage	plah-*tow* duh fro-*mahj*

SHOPPING

English	French	Pronunciation
antiques store	**un magasin d'antiquités**	uh maga-*zan* don-tee kee-*tay*
bakery	**une boulangerie**	ewn boo-lon-zhur-*ree*
bank	**une banquet**	ewn bonk
bookstore	**une librairie**	ewn lee-brehr-*ree*
butcher	**une boucherie**	ewn boo-shehr-*ree*
cheese shop	**une fromagerie**	ewn fro-mazh-*ree*
dairy shop	**une crémerie**	ewn krem-*ree*
delicatessen	**une charcuterie**	ewn shar-koot-*ree*
department store	**un grand magasin**	uh grah maga-*zan*
drugstore	**une pharmacie**	ewn far-mah-*see*
fishmonger shop	**une poissonerie**	ewn pwas-son-ree
gift shop	**un magasin de cadeaux**	uh maga-*zan* duh ka-*doh*
greengrocer	**un marchand de légumes**	uh mar-*shon* duh lay-*goom*
hairdresser	**un coiffeur**	uh kwa-*fuhr*
market	**un marché**	uh mar-*shay*
pastry shop	**une pâtisserie**	ewn pa-tee-*sree*
supermarket	**un supermarché**	uh soo-pehr-mar-*shay*
tobacconist	**un tabac**	uh ta-*bah*
travel agency	**une agence de voyages**	ewn azh-ahns duh vwa-*yazh*

COLORS, SHAPES, SIZES & ATTRIBUTES

English	French	Pronunciation
black	**noir**	nwahr
blue	**bleu**	bleuh
brown	**marron/brun**	mar-*rohn*/bruhn
green	**vert**	vaihr
orange	**orange**	o-*rahnj*
pink	**rose**	rose
purple	**violet**	vee-o-*lay*
red	**rouge**	rooj
white	**blanc**	blahnk
yellow	**jaune**	jhone
bad	**mauvais(e)**	moh-*veh*
big	**grand(e)**	gron/gronde
closed	**fermé(e)**	fer-*meh*
down	**en bas**	on *bah*
early	**de bonne heure**	duh bon *urr*
enough	**assez**	as-*say*
far	**loin**	lwan
free, unoccupied	**libre**	*lee*-bruh
free, without charge	**gratuit(e)**	grah-*twee*/grah-*tweet*
good	**bon/bonne**	bon/bun
hot	**chaud(e)**	show/shoad
near	**près**	preh
open (as in "museum")	**ouvert(e)**	oo-*ver*/oo-*vert*
small	**petit(e)**	puh-*tee*/puh-*teet*
up	**en haut**	on *oh*
well	**bien**	byehn

NUMBERS & ORDINALS

English	French	Pronunciation
zero	**zéro**	zare-*oh*
one	**un**	uh
two	**deux**	duh
three	**trois**	twah
four	**quatre**	*kaht*-ruh
five	**cinq**	sank
six	**six**	seess
seven	**sept**	set
eight	**huit**	wheat
nine	**neuf**	nuf
ten	**dix**	deess
eleven	**onze**	ohnz
twelve	**douze**	dooz
thirteen	**treize**	trehz
fourteen	**quatorze**	kah-*torz*
fifteen	**quinze**	kanz
sixteen	**seize**	sez
seventeen	**dix-sept**	deez-*set*
eighteen	**dix-huit**	deez-*wheat*
nineteen	**dix-neuf**	deez-*nuf*
twenty	**vingt**	vehn
twenty-one	**vingt-et-un**	vehnt-ay-*uh*
twenty-two	**vingt-deux**	vehnt-*duh*
thirty	**trente**	trahnt
forty	**quarante**	ka-*rahnt*
fifty	**cinquante**	sang-*kahnt*
sixty	**soixante**	swa-*sahnt*

English	French	Pronunciation
sixty-one	**soixante-et-un**	swa-*sahnt*-et-*uh*
seventy	**soixante-dix**	swa-sahnt-*deess*
seventy-one	**soixante-et-onze**	swa-sahnt-et-*ohnze*
eighty	**quatre-vingts**	kaht-ruh-*vehn*
eighty-one	**quatre-vingt-un**	kaht-ruh-vehn-*uh*
ninety	**quatre-vingt-dix**	kaht-ruh-venh-*deess*
ninety-one	**quatre-vingt-onze**	kaht-ruh-venh-*ohnze*
one hundred	**cent**	sahn
one thousand	**mille**	meel
one hundred thousand	**cent mille**	sahn meel
first	**premier**	*preh*-mee-ay
second	**deuxième**	*duhz*-zee-em
third	**troisième**	*twa*-zee-em
fourth	**quatrième**	kaht-ree-em
fifth	**cinquième**	*sank*-ee-em
sixth	**sixième**	*sees*-ee-em
seventh	**septième**	*set*-ee-em
eighth	**huitième**	*wheat*-ee-em
ninth	**neuvième**	*neuv*-ee-em
tenth	**dixième**	*dees*-ee-em

THE CALENDAR

English	French	Pronunciation
January	**janvier**	*jhan*-vee-ay
February	**février**	*feh*-vree-ay
March	**mars**	marce
April	**avril**	a-*vreel*

English	French	Pronunciation
May	**mai**	meh
June	**juin**	jhwehn
July	**juillet**	*jhwee*-ay
August	**août**	oot
September	**septembre**	sep-*tahm*-bruh
October	**octobre**	ok-*toh*-bruh
November	**novembre**	no-*vahm*-bruh
December	**decembre**	day-*sahm*-bruh
Sunday	**dimanche**	dee-*mahnsh*
Monday	**lundi**	*luhn*-dee
Tuesday	**mardi**	*mahr*-dee
Wednesday	**mercredi**	*mair*-kruh-dee
Thursday	**jeudi**	*jheu*-dee
Friday	**vendredi**	*vawn*-druh-dee
Saturday	**samedi**	*sahm*-dee
yesterday	**hier**	ee-*air*
today	**aujourd'hui**	o-jhord-*dwee*
this morning/ this afternoon	**ce matin/cet après-midi**	suh ma-*tan*/set ah-preh-mee-*dee*
tonight	**ce soir**	suh *swahr*
tomorrow	**demain**	de-*man*

Index

Parlez-vous français?

Find the right words fast with a *Frommer's PhraseFinder & Dictionary*. Put one in your pocket or purse for quick access to more than 5,000 words and phrases. Real-world situations and expressions. A two-way dictionary with pronunciation guide. Phrases listed by topic *and* dictionary entry. Basic grammar. Sample dialogues. And much more.

Real language for real travelers—new from the most trusted name in travel guides.

Also available:
Frommer's Italian PhraseFinder & Dictionary
Frommer's Spanish PhraseFinder & Dictionary

Available wherever books are sold.

The best conversations start here.

Frommer's
A Branded Imprint of ⊕WILEY
Now you know.

FROMMER'S® COMPLETE TRAVEL GUIDES

FROMMER'S® DAY BY DAY GUIDES

PAULINE FROMMER'S GUIDES: SEE MORE. SPEND LESS.

FROMMER'S® PORTABLE GUIDES

Acapulco, Ixtapa & Zihuatanejo
Amsterdam
Aruba, Bonaire & Curaçao
Australia's Great Barrier Reef
Bahamas
Big Island of Hawaii
Boston
California Wine Country
Cancún
Cayman Islands
Charleston
Chicago
Dominican Republic

Florence
Las Vegas
Las Vegas for Non-Gamblers
London
Maui
Nantucket & Martha's Vineyard
New Orleans
New York City
Paris
Portland
Puerto Rico
Puerto Vallarta, Manzanillo & Guadalajara

Rio de Janeiro
San Diego
San Francisco
Savannah
St. Martin, Sint Maarten, Anguila & St. Bart's
Turks & Caicos
Vancouver
Venice
Virgin Islands
Washington, D.C.
Whistler

FROMMER'S® CRUISE GUIDES

Alaska Cruises & Ports of Call

Cruises & Ports of Call

European Cruises & Ports of Call

FROMMER'S® NATIONAL PARK GUIDES

Algonquin Provincial Park
Banff & Jasper
Grand Canyon

National Parks of the American West
Rocky Mountain
Yellowstone & Grand Teton

Yosemite and Sequoia & Kings Canyon
Zion & Bryce Canyon

FROMMER'S® WITH KIDS GUIDES

Chicago
Hawaii
Las Vegas
London

National Parks
New York City
San Francisco

Toronto
Walt Disney World® & Orlando
Washington, D.C.

FROMMER'S® PHRASEFINDER DICTIONARY GUIDES

Chinese
French

German
Italian

Japanese
Spanish

SUZY GERSHMAN'S BORN TO SHOP GUIDES

France
Hong Kong, Shanghai & Beijing
Italy

London
New York
Paris

San Francisco
Where to Buy the Best of Everything

FROMMER'S® BEST-LOVED DRIVING TOURS

Britain
California
France
Germany

Ireland
Italy
New England
Northern Italy

Scotland
Spain
Tuscany & Umbria

THE UNOFFICIAL GUIDES®

Adventure Travel in Alaska
Beyond Disney
California with Kids
Central Italy
Chicago
Cruises
Disneyland®
England
Hawaii

Ireland
Las Vegas
London
Maui
Mexico's Best Beach Resorts
Mini Mickey
New Orleans
New York City
Paris

San Francisco
South Florida including Miami & the Keys
Walt Disney World®
Walt Disney World® for Grown-ups
Walt Disney World® with Kids
Washington, D.C.

SPECIAL-INTEREST TITLES

Athens Past & Present
Best Places to Raise Your Family
Cities Ranked & Rated
500 Places to Take Your Kids Before They Grow Up
Frommer's Best Day Trips from London
Frommer's Best RV & Tent Campgrounds in the U.S.A.

Frommer's Exploring America by RV
Frommer's NYC Free & Dirt Cheap
Frommer's Road Atlas Europe
Frommer's Road Atlas Ireland
Retirement Places Rated